TEFAL AIR FRYER

COOKBOOK FOR BEGINNERS

The Delicious and Healthy & Affordable Recipes for Your Tefal Air Fryer

TABLE OF CONTENTS

INTRODUCTION 6

BEEF, PORK & LAMB RECIPES.........................8

Dijon Steak Tips....................................8
Air Fryer Steak Fajitas 8
Air Fryer Mini Swedish Meatballs...........8
Honey-mustard....................................9
Air Fryer Sausage Patties.......................9
Juicy Air Fryer Meatballs 9
Steak Bites With Mushrooms 9
Air Fryer Stuffed Peppers 10
Air-fryer Pork.....................................11
Air Fryer Prime Rib 11
Air Fryer Pork And Apple Sausage Rolls 12
Coffee Rubbed Steak............................12
Breaded Air Fryer Pork Chops..............12
Balsamic Glazed Pork 13
Air-fryer Mini Chimichangas.................13

Reheat Steak In The Air Fryer 14
Air Fryer Cowboy Casserole..................14
Air Fryer Bacon Cheese Crackers...........15
Bbq Air Fryer Ribs 15
Grilled Sriracha Honey Glazed Ribs 15
Air Fryer Pork Tenderloin.....................16
Air Fryer Meatball Subs 17
Air Fryer Breaded Pork Chops...............17
Pork Roulade......................................17
Air Fryer Shake 'n Bake Pork Chops 18
Lightly Fried Lamb Chops 19
Air Fryer Glazed Ham Recipe 19
Air Fryer Stuffed Avocado.....................19
Meatball Sliders 20

BREAKFAST & BRUNCH RECIPES 21

Lentil Patties......................................21
Air Fryer Garlic Bread 21
Air Fryer Pretzel Bites 22
Air Fryer Frozen Pretzels......................22
Air Fryer Bacon And Egg Bites 23
Pumpkin Bread Pudding 23
Air Fryer Rusks, With Buttermilk 23
Air Fryer Stuffed Spaghetti Squash 24
Air Fryer Tacos 25
Deviled Eggs 25
Air Fryer Toad In The Hole 25
Air Fryer Hard Boiled Eggs 25
Air Fryer French Toast Sticks 26

Air-fryer Greek Breadsticks 26
Air Fryer Southwest Egg Rolls 26
Air Fryer Poached Egg Avocado.............27
Air Fryer Sausage Rolls 28
Mother's Day Breakfast Galettes............28
Air Fryer Bread 29
Air-fryer Calzones 29
Air Fryer Quiche Lorraine.....................29
Hash Browns In The Air Fryer...............30
Eggs Benedict.....................................30
Air Fryer Nachos 31
Air Fryer Breakfast Burritos 31

FISH & SEAFOOD RECIPES 32

Blackened Air Fryer Salmon..................32
Air Fryer Tilapia In 7 Minutes 32
Air Fryer Salmon Patties 33
Air Fryer Haddock 33

Air Fryer Crab Legs 34
Air Fryer Smoked Salmon Wontons 34
Air Fryer Cod.....................................34
Healthy Baked Fish Sticks 35

Teriyaki Salmon In The Air Fryer..........35

Air Fryer Garlic Butter Shrimp 36

POULTRY RECIPES 37

Air Fryer Chicken Thighs.......................37
Air Fryer Turkey Breast 37
Crispy Air Fryer Chicken Wings 37
Air Fryer Grilled Chicken Breast 38
Air Fryer Rotisserie Chicken 39
Air Fryer Frozen Chicken Nuggets 39
Chicken Parmesan In The Air Fryer 39
Air-fryer Turkey Croquettes 40
Stuffed Chicken Roulade 40
Air Fryer Chicken Breast 41
Chicken Schnitzels 42
Buffalo Chicken Wings 42
Air Fryer Mall Style Bourbon Chicken .. 42
Cilantro Lime Chicken...........................43
Air Fryer Honey Sesame Chicken..........43

Air Fryer Spinach Chicken Breast..........44
Air Fryer Chicken Nuggets....................45
Air Fryer Chicken Fajitas 45
Air Fryer Chicken Leg Quarters 46
Nashville Hot Chicken Recipe...............46
Cherry Glazed Chicken Wings 47
Gluten-free Air Fryer Fried Chicken 47
Air Fryer Whole Chicken.......................47
Air Fryer Chicken Tenders Recipe 48
Pickle Ham And Swiss Chicken 48
Instant Pot & Vortex Roast Chicken 49
Salt And Pepper Chicken Nuggets 49
Air Fryer Turkey Tenderloin 50
Air-fryer Chicken Legs 50

DESSERTS RECIPES 51

Air Fryer Cranberry White Chip Cookies 51
Chocolate Chip Salted Cookie Skillets 51
Sesame Seed Balls.................................52
Air Fryer Brie En Croûte........................53
Air Fryer Blackberry & Apple Crumble ..53
Air Fryer Cookies 54
Air Fryer Frozen Waffle Cut Fries 54
Air Fryer Cake.......................................54
Air Fryer Cherry Pie Taquitos.................55
Cherry Cheesecake Egg Rolls.................55
Air Fryer Pumpkin Spice Muffins...........56
Fried Banana Smores 56
Zucchini Cakes......................................56

Air Fryer Strawberry Roll-ups 57
Air Fryer Caramelized Bananas 57
Easy 3-ingredient Air Fryer Bagels 58
Air Fryer Banana Blueberry Muffins 58
Air-fryer Cheesecake 59
Baked Apple Chips 59
Air Fryer Oreo Cheesecake....................60
Cheat's Air-fryer Churros.......................60
Vortex Air Fryer Sweet Potato Cups 61
Air Fryer Copycat Red Bay Biscuits 61
Banana Split 61
Air Fryer Snickerdoodle Cookies 62

SALADS & SIDE DISHES RECIPES 63

Air-fryer Nuggets Lunch Boxes 63
Air Fryer Chimichangas.........................63
Buffalo Chicken Salad...........................63
Air Fryer Roasted Garlic 64
Air Fryer Egg Salad............................... 64

Air Fryer Artichoke 65
Teriyaki Root Vegetable Salad 65
Air Fryer Portobello Mushroom 66
Air Fryer Lemon Pepper Wings 66
Fried Eggplant.......................................67

Air Fryer Tempeh 68
Green Goddess Carrot Salad................. 68
Homemade Tortilla Chips & Salsa......... 69
Chestnut Stuffing 69

SANDWICHES & BURGERS RECIPES 70

Beyond Burger In The Air Fryer 70
Air Fryer Hamburgers 70
Air Fryer Falafel With Vegan Sauce........70
Air-fryer Chicken Katsu Sandwiches 71
Air Fryer Mozzarella Burgers 72
6 Ingredient Veggie Burgers..................72
Air Fryer Frozen Impossible™ Burgers . 73
Frozen Burgers In The Air Fryer............ 73
Homestyle Cheeseburgers...................... 73
Air Fryer Burgers 74
Air Fryer Grilled Cheese Sandwiches..... 74
All-american Grilled Burgers 75

FAVORITE AIR FRYER RECIPES 76

Air-fryer Brats With Beer Gravy 76
Air Fryer Taquitos And Charred Salsa....76
Pepperoni Pizza 77
Air Fryer Churros Twists 77
Peanut Sauce Soba With Crispy Tofu 77
Reheat Pizza In Air Fryer.......................78
Carrot Chip Dog Treats..........................78
Curried Parsnip Soup 79
Italian Sausage In Air Fryer...................79
Nana's Macaroni 80
Air Fryer Brats 80
Air Fryer Oven Corn Dogs 80
Air Fryer Hot Dogs 80
Easy Air Fryer Pepperoni Pizza 81
Air Fryer Fig And Camembert Phyllo Parcel.. 82
Air Fryer Mozzarella Sticks 82
Air Fryer Pizza Quesadilla.................... 82
Air Fryer Gnocchi, And Green Beans..... 83
Air Fryer Frozen Jalapeño Poppers 83
Garlic Parmesan Pull-apart Rolls 83
Air Fryer Pizza...................................... 84
Air Fryer Sausage And Peppers 84
Rice Paper Dumplings 84
Sicilian Pizza 85
Air Fryer Toasted Perogies Recipe......... 86
Air-fryer Pizza 86

VEGETABLE & & VEGETARIAN RECIPES..87

Poblano And Black Bean Baked Potato ..87
Mushroom Fajitas.................................87
Air Fryer Buffalo Cauliflower Wings 88
Air-fryer Mushrooms............................. 88
Lamb Chops With Roast Potatoes 89
Air Fryer Garlic Zucchini 89
Air Fryer Cauliflower Recipe 89
Air Fryer Zucchini................................. 90
Air Fryer Stuffed Peppers 90
Air Fryer Tofu 91
Air Fryer Broccoli Recipe...................... 91
Air Fryer Acorn Squash 91
Air Fryer Veggie Dippers....................... 92
Air Fryer Mushrooms............................. 92
Sausage And Cabbage 93
Mini Air Fryer Hasselback Potatoes 93
Loaded Air Fryer Smashed Potatoes...... 93
Air Fryer Blooming Onion Recipe 94
Air Fryer Fingerling Potatoes................. 95
Cauliflower Tots 95
Crispy, Cheesy Cauliflower Balls............ 95
Air Fried Crunchy Onion Rings 96
Air Fryer Pickles................................... 96
Air Fryer Spinach-artichoke Bites 97

Roasted Tomato Bruschetta 97

Air Fryer Tomatoes 98

SNACKS & APPETIZERS RECIPES 99

Tater Tots In The Air Fryer.................... 99

Avocado Fries 99

Air Fryer Green Beans 99

Air Fryer Baked Sweet Potatoes 100

Air Fryer Kale Chips 100

Air-fried Chips 100

Air Fryer Crispy Herbed Chickpeas...... 101

Sesame Air Fryer Green Beans 101

Air Fryer Loaded Tater Tots 101

Air Fryer Tater Tots 102

Air Fryer Potato Chips 102

Fries 102

Yuca Fries Recipe.................................103

Air Fryer Chickpeas 103

Air Fryer Sweet Potato Fries................104

Pumpkin Tortilla Chips........................ 104

Air Fryer Green Bean Casserole........... 105

Air Fryer Pumpkin Seeds Recipe 105

Baked Chipotle Sweet Potato Fries 106

Air Fryer Potato Skins.......................... 106

Air Fryer Tortilla Chips 106

Sweet Potato Wedges 107

Crispy Air Fryer Potato Skins 107

Peri Peri Fries Recipe...........................107

Air Fryer Waffle Fries 107

Spiced Air Fryer Chickpeas.................. 108

Air Fryer Carrot Fries 108

Chunky Chips 108

Roasted Garlic Hummus....................... 109

Air Fryer Cream Cheese Wontons 109

INTRODUCTION

An air fryer is a kitchen appliance that cooks food by using hot air instead of lots of oil. It is considered a healthier alternative to deep-frying. IT also acts as a small and more time-effective oven for baking. Instead of submerging food in oil, an air fryer uses a fan to circulate hot air around the food, creating that familiar crispy, golden-brown exterior. Air fryers come in various sizes and shapes, from small countertop models to larger ones that can cook a whole chicken.

WHY USE AN AIR FRYER?

Healthier cooking: As mentioned earlier, air frying uses little to no oil, making it a healthier alternative to deep-frying. It is a great way to enjoy your favorite fried foods without the guilt.

Time-saving: Air fryers cook food faster than traditional methods, such as baking or frying. They also require less cleanup.

Versatile: Air fryers can cook a wide variety of foods, from vegetables to meats to desserts. They are also great for reheating leftovers, as they can revive the crispiness of fried foods.

WHY AN AIR FRYER SO POPULAR?

The popularity of air fryers can be attributed to several factors:

Health consciousness: As more people become health-conscious, air fryers provide a way to enjoy fried foods without the added calories and fat.

Convenience: Air fryers are easy to use, cook fast and require minimal cleanup.

Social media influence: The rise of social media influencers and their endorsement of air fryers has contributed to its popularity. Many influencers share recipes and cooking tips, showcasing the versatility of air fryers.

MOST POPULAR THINGS TO AIR FRY

Here are some of the most popular things we cook in the air fryer:

French fries: Crispy, golden-brown fries are a classic air fryer recipe.

Chicken wings: Air fryer chicken wings are crispy on the outside and juicy on the inside. Coat the wings with your favorite sauce, and air fry until crispy. Kiddos also love chicken nuggets.

Vegetables: Air fryers are great for roasting vegetables, such as Brussels sprouts, broccoli and cauliflower. Simply spray with a little olive oil and seasoning, and air fry until tender.

Fish: Air fryers can cook fish filets, such as salmon or tilapia, to perfection. Coat the fish with breadcrumbs or a seasoning blend, and air fry until crispy.

Desserts: Air fryers can even be used to make desserts, such as churros, doughnuts and more!

FAQS ABOUT AIR FRYERS

Is air frying healthier than deep frying?
Yes, air frying is generally considered healthier than deep frying, as it uses little to no oil.

Do I need to preheat the air fryer?
Yes, it is recommended to preheat the air fryer for a few minutes before cooking. This ensures that the air fryer is at the optimal temperature for cooking and helps to prevent uneven cooking. My air fryer has a preheat button right on it!

How much can an air fryer hold?
The answer to this really depends on the model you purchase. Some smaller air fryers can hold up to 2 quarts, while larger ones can hold up to 8 quarts. It is important to check the capacity of your air fryer before cooking to ensure that you do not overcrowd the basket. For your air fryer to cook properly, you will want a single layer of food.

Do I need to purchase extras and attachments for my air fryer?
It is not necessary to purchase extras or attachments for your air fryer, but they can be useful. Some popular accessories include baking pans, grilling racks, and skewers.

How do I prevent food from sticking to my air fryer?
To prevent food from sticking to your air fryer, lightly coat it with cooking spray or oil before cooking. You can also coat the food with a thin layer of oil or use a non-stick cooking spray.

HERE ARE SOME EXPERT TIPS FOR GETTING THE BEST RESULTS

1. Preheat the air fryer before adding your food. This will ensure that the temperature is consistent and your food cooks evenly.

2. Don't overcrowd the air fryer basket. Leave some space around each piece of food to allow for proper air circulation and to ensure that everything cooks evenly. You can always cook in batches if necessary.

3. Turn the food. The top portion of the food always crisps more than the underside, so it's super important to rotate everything in the basket part-way through cooking. To air fry small items shake the basket periodically over the cooking time to help ensure even cooking and browning. For larger pieces, like when air frying turkey burgers, flip them halfway through so that the top and bottom both crisp up.

4. It's not oil-free cooking. It's just not as much oil as deep frying. Use a light mist of cooking spray or brush a small amount of oil onto your food to help it crisp up and prevent sticking.

5. Experiment with cooking times and temperatures to find the sweet spot for your favorite foods. Keep notes on what works well for you so you can replicate your successes in the future.

6. Clean your air fryer every time to prevent smoky buildup of grease and food particles. Refer to the manufacturer's instructions for specific cleaning recommendations.

BEEF, PORK & LAMB RECIPES

Dijon Steak Tips

Servings: 4
Cooking Time: 12 Minutes

Ingredients:
- 2 pounds flat iron or flank steak, cut into 1-inch cubes
- 1 yellow onion, thinly sliced
- 2 slices bacon, diced
- 3 tablespoons Worcestershire sauce
- 3 tablespoons Dijon mustard
- 2 tablespoons olive oil
- 2 tablespoon maple syrup
- 1 ½ teaspoon kosher salt
- 1 teaspoon paprika
- 2 tablespoons chopped fresh parsley, for garnish
- Mashed potatoes, for serving

Directions:
1. Select Preheat on the Air Fryer, adjust the temperature to 400°F, then press Start/Pause.
2. Stir together the steak, onion, bacon, Worcestershire, Dijon, oil, maple syrup, salt, and paprika in a medium bowl until evenly combined.
3. Place the meat mixture into the preheated air fryer.
4. Set the temperature to 400°F and time to 12 minutes, then press Start/Pause.
5. Shake the steak tips halfway through cooking.
6. Remove the steak when done, then serve garnished with parsley on a bed of mashed potatoes.

Air Fryer Steak Fajitas

Servings: 4
Cooking Time: 30 Minutes

Ingredients:
- 1 pound beef steaks sirloin or striploin
- 1 red bell pepper sliced
- 1 green bell pepper sliced
- 1 small red onion sliced
- tortillas for serving
- Marinade
- 2 tablespoons olive oil
- 2 tablespoons lime juice
- 1 teaspoon garlic powder
- 1 teaspoon chili powder
- ¼ teaspoon smoked paprika
- ¼ teaspoon cumin

Directions:
1. Mix the marinade ingredients in a small bowl.
2. Slice the onion and bell peppers and toss with 1 tablespoon of the marinade.
3. Slice the beef into ½-inch strips. Toss with the remaining marinade and refrigerate for at least 15 minutes.
4. Preheat the air fryer to 400°F.
5. Place the vegetables in the air fryer basket in a single layer and cook 6-7 minutes or just until tender crisp. Remove from the air fryer and set aside.
6. Place the beef in the air fryer basket in a single layer and cook 4-6 minutes or just until cooked. Add peppers back to the air fryer and cook 1 minute more.
7. Serve in warmed tortillas with toppings.
Notes
Steak does not need to be cooked to well done, it's ok if it's a little bit pink inside.
Check the steak early to ensure it doesn't overcook.

Air Fryer Mini Swedish Meatballs

Servings: 42

Ingredients:
- Deselect All
- 2 slices white bread
- 1/2 cup milk
- 8 ounces ground beef
- 8 ounces ground pork
- 1/4 yellow onion, grated
- 3/4 teaspoon ground allspice
- 1 large egg

- Kosher salt and freshly ground black pepper
- Nonstick cooking spray, for the tray
- Lingonberry jam, for serving

Directions:
1. Soak the bread in the milk in a medium bowl for 5 minutes. Squeeze out excess milk and tear the bread into bite-size pieces. Return the bread to the bowl. Mix the bread with the ground beef, pork, onion, allspice, egg, 1 teaspoon salt and a few grinds of pepper. Form into small balls about the size of a heaping tablespoon.
2. Spray the basket of a 3.5-quart air fryer with cooking spray and preheat to 360 degrees F.
3. Fill the basket with the meatballs and cook, shaking the tray halfway through, until browned, tender and cooked through, about 10 minutes. Serve with lingonberry jam.

Honey-mustard?air Fryer?pork Chops?

Servings: 4
Cooking Time: 15 Minutes

Ingredients:
- 1/3 cup Dijon Mustard
- 1 tablespoon honey
- 4 3/4-inch thick center-cut boneless pork chops, trimmed ((about 5 oz each))
- 1/2 teaspoon kosher salt
- 1 cup seasoned panko (or gluten free panko*)
- olive oil spray

Directions:
1. Season pork chops on both sides with 1/2 teaspoon kosher salt.
2. Combine mustard and honey and marinate the pork chops at least 4 hours or overnight for best results.
3. Place panko in a large shallow bowl.
4. Leaving whatever mustard that clings to the pork, press into the panko crumbs.
5. Discard the rest of the marinade (about 2 tbsp tossed).

6. Lightly spray the basket with oil and transfer the chops, in batches as needed.
7. Spritz the top with oil and air fry 400F 10 to 12 minutes turning half way, spritzing both sides with oil.
8. No Air Fryer, No Problem!
9. Although they come out much crisper in the air fryer, if you don't have one you can bake them 425F 20 to 25 minutes.
Notes
*1/4 cup crumbs get tossed.

Air Fryer Sausage Patties

Servings: 6
Cooking Time: 10 Minutes

Ingredients:
- 1 pound ground pork
- 1 teaspoon salt
- ½ teaspoon black pepper
- ½ teaspoon fennel seeds slightly crushed
- ½ teaspoon garlic powder
- ½ teaspoon sage
- ½ teaspoon onion powder
- ⅛ teaspoon thyme leaves
- ⅛ teaspoon cayenne pepper

Directions:
1. Mix pork and seasonings in a medium bowl until fully combined. Refrigerate for at least 2 hours or overnight.
2. Preheat air fryer to 400°F.
3. Divide meat into 6 patties about ½ inch thick. Place in a single layer in the air fryer basket.
4. Cook for 5 minutes, flip the patties and cook them for another 4-5 minutes or until they reach 160°F internally.

Juicy Air Fryer Meatballs

Steak Bites With Mushrooms

Servings: 4

Ingredients:
- 650g rib eye steak
- 4 tbsp olive oil, divided

- 1 tsp soy sauce
- 2 cloves garlic, crushed, divided
- 1 tsp dried mixed herbs
- 1 tsp salt
- 1/4 tsp pepper
- 400g chestnut mushrooms, whole
- To garnish fresh chopped parsley
- COOKING MODE
- When entering cooking mode - We will enable your screen to stay 'always on' to avoid any unnecessary interruptions whilst you cook!

Directions:
1. Trim fat from steak and cut into 2.5cm cubes. Place in a large bowl. Wipe mushrooms with a damp paper towel and place in a separate bowl. If the mushrooms are large, cut in half
2. In a small bowl, combine olive oil, soy sauce, garlic and herbs. Divide the mixture between the steak and mushrooms
3. Insert crisper plate in both drawers. Add steak to zone 1 drawer and mushrooms to zone 2 drawer and insert both drawers into unit
4. Select zone 1, select AIR FRY, set temperature to 200°C, and set time to 12 minutes. Select zone 2, select AIR FRY, set temperature to 200°C and set time to 9 minutes. Select SYNC. Press the START/STOP button to begin cooking. When zone 1 and 2 reaches 5 minutes, give both drawers a shake. When cook time is finished, use silicone coated tongs to remove food. Garnished with parsley and serve with salad

Air Fryer Stuffed Peppers With Taco Meat
Servings: 4
Cooking Time: 15 Minutes

Ingredients:
- 2 bell peppers
- 1/2 pound (227 g) ground beef, pork, chicken or turkey
- 1/4 cup (60 g) tomato sauce
- 1 cup (113 g) shredded cheddar cheese , divided
- 1 teaspoon (5 ml) chili powder
- 1/2 teaspoon (2.5 ml) garlic powder
- 1/2 teaspoon (2.5 ml) ground cumin
- 1/2 teaspoon (2.5 ml) dried oregano
- 1/2 teaspoon (2.5 ml) salt , or to taste
- 1/4 teaspoon (1.25 ml) black pepper , or to taste
- olive oil or oil spray , for coating
- OPTIONAL TOPPINGS:
- green onions, salsa, guacamole, sour cream
- Oil Sprayer , optional

Directions:
1. In bowl, combine meat, tomato sauce, 1/2 cup cheese, chili powder, garlic powder, ground cumin, dried oregano, salt and pepper.
2. Cut bell peppers lengthwise and remove seeds.
3. Flip the bell peppers over and spray/brush outside of bell peppers with oil.
4. Stuff the pepper halves with the meat mixture. Spray tops of meat and peppers. Lay stuffed peppers inside air fryer basket/tray. If you have a small basket, you may have to cook in 2 batches.
5. Air Fry at 360°F/182°C for 12-16 minutes or until meat is cooked completely. Top the meat with remainder of cheese and cook one more minute to melt cheese.
6. Serve with your favorite toppings.
NOTES
COOKING TIPS:If bell peppers tilt and fall over, place a small crumpled piece of foil under the pepper as a base.
Cutting the peppers lengthwise will help meat cook quicker and all the way through. If. you cut them crosswise, you might need a couple more minutes of cooking time.

Air-fryer Sweet And Smoky Pork Tenderloin With Butternut Squash

Servings: 2
Cooking Time: 1 Hour

Ingredients:
- 1¼ pounds butternut squash, peeled, seeded, and cut into ¾-inch pieces (5 cups)
- 1 tablespoon
- unsalted butter,
- melted
- Salt and pepper
- 3½ teaspoons
- molasses
- 1 teaspoon smoked paprika
- 1 garlic clove, minced
- 1 (1-pound) pork tenderloin, trimmed and halved crosswise
- 1 teaspoon grated lime zest plus 1 teaspoon juice
- 2 tablespoons roasted pepitas
- 1 tablespoon minced fresh chives

Directions:
1. Toss squash with 1½ teaspoons melted butter, 1/8 teaspoon salt, and 1/8 teaspoon pepper in large bowl; transfer to air-fryer basket. Place basket in air fryer and set temperature to 350 degrees. Cook squash for 8 minutes, tossing halfway through cooking.
2. Meanwhile, microwave 3 teaspoons molasses, paprika, garlic, ½ teaspoon salt, and ½ teaspoon pepper in now-empty bowl until fragrant, about 30 seconds, stirring halfway through microwaving. Pat pork dry with paper towels, add to molasses mixture, and toss to coat.
3. Stir squash, then arrange tenderloin pieces on top. (Tuck thinner tail end of tenderloin under itself as needed to create uniform pieces.) Return basket to air fryer and cook until pork registers 140 degrees, 16 to 21 minutes, flipping and rotating tenderloin pieces halfway through cooking. Transfer pork to large plate, tent with aluminum foil, and let rest while finishing squash.
4. Whisk lime zest and juice, remaining ½ teaspoon molasses, and remaining 1½ teaspoons melted butter together in medium bowl. Add squash, pepitas, and chives and toss to coat. Season with salt and pepper to taste. Slice pork ½ inch thick and serve with squash.

Air Fryer Prime Rib

Servings: 5-6
Cooking Time: 1 Hour 15 Minutes

Ingredients:
- 6 pound Prime Rib
- 3 tablespoons olive oil
- 1 ½ teaspoon salt
- 1 ½ teaspoon black pepper
- 1 teaspoon smoked paprika
- 1 teaspoon garlic powder
- ¼ cup minced garlic (about 10 cloves)
- One sprig fresh rosemary, chopped (or 1/2 teaspoon dried rosemary)
- One sprig fresh thyme, chopped (or 1/2 teaspoon dried thyme)

Directions:
1. Preheat your air fryer to 390 degrees.
2. Rub the prime rib with olive oil generously, then sprinkle it with salt, black pepper, paprika, and garlic powder.
3. Cover the prime rib with crushed garlic then the rosemary and thyme. I recommend using fresh rosemary and thyme for the best flavoring, but you can use dried as well.
4. Gently place the prime rib in the air fryer and cook for 20 minutes.
5. Leaving the prime rib steak in the air fryer, turn the temperature down
6. to 315 degrees and continue to cook for about 55 additional minutes until Instant-Read Thermometer reaches desired doneness -- 130 degrees for medium-rare.*
7. Let the prime rib sit for 20 to 30 minutes, then slice and enjoy!
NOTES
*if your thermometer is still reading too low, let prime rib cook in the air fryer for another 5 to 10 minutes, then check the temperature again
HOW TO REHEAT PRIME RIB IN THE AIR FRYER:
TO REHEAT FULL PRIME PRIME RIB:
Preheat your air fryer to 270 degrees.

Lay the prime rib in the air fryer and cook for about 10 to 15 minutes until warmed.
TO REHEAT PRE-COOKED PRIME RIB SLICES:
Preheat your air fryer to 400 degrees.
Place the prime rib slices in the air fryer in a single layer and cook for about 2 minutes. Use a parchment paper or silicone liner if the prime rib is sauced.

Air Fryer Pork And Apple Sausage Rolls
Servings: 18
Cooking Time: 35 Minutes

Ingredients:
- 500g pork mince
- 1 Granny Smith apple, peeled, grated
- 1/2 cup grated vintage cheddar
- 2 green onions, chopped
- 2 garlic cloves, crushed
- 2 tbsp chopped fresh flat-leaf parsley
- 2 tsp fresh thyme leaves
- 2 eggs, lightly beaten
- 3 sheets frozen puff pastry, partially thawed
- 2 tsp fennel seeds
- 2 tsp sesame seeds
- Tomato relish, to serve

- Select all Ingredients:

Directions:
1. Place mince, apple, cheddar, onion, garlic, parsley, thyme and half the egg in a bowl. Season with salt and pepper. Mix well to combine.
2. Place one sheet of pastry on a flat surface. Cut in half to form two large rectangles. Leaving a 1cm edge, spoon 1/3 cup mince mixture along one long side of each piece of pastry. Brush edges with a little of the remaining egg. Roll up pastry to enclose filling. Trim ends. Cut each roll into 3 pieces. Place rolls, seam-side down, on a baking paper-lined tray. Repeat with pastry, mince and egg.
3. Brush tops of rolls with egg. Score lines into the tops of rolls with a small knife.

Sprinkle with fennel and sesame seeds. Season with salt and pepper.
4. Preheat air fryer to 200C. Cook sausage rolls, in batches, for 10 to 12 minutes or until golden and puffed. Serve with tomato relish.

Coffee Rubbed Steak

Ingredients:
- 16 oz rib-eye Steak
- 2 tbsp ground coffee beans
- 2 tbsp ancho chili powder
- 1 tsp cocoa powder
- 1 1/2 tsp coriander
- 1 tsp cumin
- 1 tbsp smoked sweet paprika
- 1 tbsp salt
- 1 1/2 tsp black pepper
- 1 tbsp brown sugar

Directions:
1. Preheat your air fryer oven using the grill setting.
2. In a bowl mix your dry ingredients; ground coffee beans, chili powder, cocoa powder, coriander, cumin, paprika, salt, pepper, and brown sugar. Set aside
3. Lightly coat the steak on both sides with oil. Generously sprinkle the steaks all over with the coffee spice rub and gently massage it in. Let the steaks stand at room temperature for 30 minutes.
4. Grill for 6 minutes, flip and grill 5 minutes (for medium well.)
5. Let the meat rest for 5 minutes for every inch of thickness. Enjoy!

Breaded Air Fryer Pork Chops
Servings: 4
Cooking Time: 10 Minutes

Ingredients:
- 4 (5 ounce) boneless, center-cut pork chops, 1-inch thick
- 1 teaspoon Cajun seasoning
- 1 ½ cups cheese and garlic croutons
- 2 large eggs
- cooking spray

Directions:

1. Preheat an air fryer to 400 degrees F (200 degrees C).
2. Place pork chops on a plate and season both sides with Cajun seasoning.
3. Pulse croutons in a small food processor until fine; transfer to a shallow dish. Lightly beat eggs in a separate shallow dish. Working one at a time, dip pork chops into beaten egg, letting excess drip off; press into crouton breading to coat both sides and place breaded chop, unstacked, onto a plate. Repeat with remaining chops. Mist chops with cooking spray.
4. Spray the air fryer basket with cooking spray and arrange chops in a single layer in the air fryer basket. You may have to do two batches depending on the size of your air fryer.
5. Cook in the preheated air fryer for 5 minutes; flip chops and mist again with cooking spray if there are dry areas. Cook 5 minutes more. An instant-read thermometer inserted into the center of the chops should read 145 degrees F (63 degrees C).
6. Serve hot and enjoy!

NOTES

Play around with different crouton flavors for variety.

Keep chops warm in an oven on the lowest setting while air frying remaining chops.

For thicker chops, add an extra minute to the cook time. For thinner chops, cook 1 minute less.

Balsamic Glazed Pork Tenderloin Skewers

Ingredients:

- 1 lb. pork tenderloin, cubed
- 1 Tbsp. smoked paprika
- 1 tsp salt
- 1 tsp black pepper
- 1 tsp onion powder
- 1/2 tsp garlic powder
- 1/2 tsp white pepper
- 1/4 cayenne pepper
- 1/4 cup balsamic vinegar
- 2 tsp olive oil

- 1 Tbsp. Dijon mustard
- 3 Tbsp. honey
- 10 oz cherry tomatoes
- 1 red onion, largely chopped

Directions:

1. Trim and cube the pork tenderloin and set aside.
2. Make the dry rub for the pork by adding all of the seasonings to a bowl and mix.
3. Add the dry rub to the pork and mix well until all sides of the pork are coated.
4. Next mix the balsamic vinegar, olive oil, Dijon mustard and honey together to make the glaze. Set aside.
5. Spear the pork tenderloin, red onion and tomatoes onto the skewer and repeat. Attach each skewer to the Rotisserie Skewer accessory. See page 16 of the manual for more information on how to use this accessory.
6. Separate half the glaze into another small bowl and reserve for later. Brush the skewers with the glaze.
7. Insert the Rotisserie Skewer accessory into the oven and cook using the Kebab setting (370°F for 12 minutes).
8. Throughout the cooking process, glaze the skewers.
9. Once finished cooking, remove the Rotisserie Skewer accessory using the Rotisserie Tong.
10. Use the reserved glaze for and give the skewers one last glaze. Or, you can use this reserved glaze as a dipping sauce!
11. We sprinkled feta cheese and basil to these to finish them off!

Air-fryer Mini Chimichangas

Servings: 14
Cooking Time: 10 Minutes

Ingredients:

- 1 pound ground beef
- 1 medium onion, chopped
- 1 envelope taco seasoning
- 3/4 cup water
- 3 cups shredded Monterey Jack cheese
- 1 cup sour cream

- 1 can (4 ounces) chopped green chiles, drained
- 14 egg roll wrappers
- 1 large egg white, lightly beaten
- Cooking spray
- Salsa

Directions:
1. In a large skillet, cook beef and onion over medium heat until meat is no longer pink; crumble meat; drain. Stir in taco seasoning and water. Bring to a boil. Reduce heat; simmer, uncovered, for 5 minutes, stirring occasionally. Remove from the heat; cool slightly.

2. Preheat air fryer to 375F. In a large bowl, combine cheese, sour cream and chiles. Stir in beef mixture. Place an egg roll wrapper on work surface with a corner facing you. Place 1/3 cup filling in center. Fold bottom one-third of wrapper over filling; fold in sides.

3. Brush top point with egg white; roll up to seal. Repeat with remaining wrappers and filling. (Keep remaining egg roll wrappers covered with waxed paper to keep them from drying out.)

4. In batches, place chimichangas in a single layer on greased tray in air-fryer basket; spritz with cooking spray. Cook until golden brown, 3-4 minutes on each side. Serve warm with salsa and additional sour cream.

Reheat Steak In The Air Fryer
Servings: 2
Cooking Time: 3 Minutes

Ingredients:
- Leftover steak, any cut

Directions:
1. Preheat the air fryer to 350 degrees F.
2. Place your leftover steak in the air fryer and cook for 3 to 5 minutes, depending on size and thickness. A very thick steak cut may take an additional 1 to 2 minutes.
3. The steak is done cooking when it's warmed thoroughly and checked with a meat thermometer.

4. Remove the reheated steak from the air fryer, let rest for 5 minutes, then enjoy!

Air Fryer Cowboy Casserole
Servings: 4
Cooking Time: 20 Minutes

Ingredients:
- ½ lb lean ground beef 90% lean
- 1 can whole kernel corn drained
- ⅔ cup condensed cream of chicken soup
- ¾ cup shredded cheddar cheese divided into ½ cup and ¼ cup
- ⅓ cup milk
- 3 tbsp sour cream
- ¼ tsp onion powder
- ¼ tsp garlic powder
- ¼ tsp paprika
- ½ tsp ground black pepper
- 2 cups Tater Tots frozen

Directions:
1. In a large skillet, cook and crumble the beef over medium heat until it's no longer pink.
2. Stir in corn, chicken soup, ½ cup cheese, milk, sour cream, onion powder, garlic powder, paprika, and ground black pepper.
3. Preheat the air fryer to 350° Fahrenheit. Place 1 cup of Tater Tots in a greased baking dish that can fit into your air fryer.
4. Layer the tater tots with the seasoned, cooked beef mixture and add the remaining 1 cup Tater Tots.
5. Cook, uncovered, until bubbly, about 15-18 minutes.
6. Add the remaining ½ cup cheese to the top of the casserole and air fryer for an additional 2 minutes at 350 degrees Fahrenheit.
7. Carefully remove from the air fryer and serve.
NOTES
Did you know that this delicious dinner can be frozen? You actually have two options when it comes to freezing it!
The first option is to follow the recipe card and make this simple casserole dish right up to

where you don't bake it. You can then put the entire tater tot casserole recipe into the freezer, covered with an airtight lid. When you're ready to eat it, take it out, and bake it! If you've already cooked this easy weeknight meal, and you want to freeze some for later, just follow the same process of covering it, and then adding it to the freezer.

I make this recipe in my Cosori 5.8 qt. air fryer or 6.8 quart air fryer. Depending on your air fryer, size and wattages, cooking time may need to be adjusted 1-2 minutes.

Air Fryer Bacon Wrapped Cream Cheese Crackers

Servings: 4
Cooking Time: 10 Minutes

Ingredients:
- 12 club crackers
- 4 ounces cream cheese softened
- 1 teaspoon onion powder
- 6 slices bacon halved

Directions:
1. Add the onion powder to the softened cream cheese and mix until combined.
2. Add a teaspoon of the cream cheese mixture to the top of the cracker.
3. Wrap the cracker in a slice of bacon. Continue wrapping the crackers until they are all finished.
4. Place the bacon wrapped crackers in a single layer in the basket of the air fryer.
5. Air fry the crackers at 350 degrees Fahrenheit for 7-9 minutes or until the bacon is brown and reached your desired level of crispiness.
6. Carefully remove from the air fryer and serve immediately.
NOTES
You can use different cheese other than cream cheese. Consider using mascarpone, cottage cheese, or even hummus.
Depending on how crispy you want the bacon, bacon wrapped crackers take between 7-9 minutes at 350 degrees Fahrenheit.

You don't have to use club crackers for this recipe. You can also use whole wheat crackers, Ritz crackers, or even saltine crackers.

Bbq Air Fryer Ribs

Servings: 4
Cooking Time: 35 Minutes

Ingredients:
- 1 3 lb rack of pork baby back ribs cut in half, membrane removed
- 3 Tablespoon bbq rub
- ?-1 cup bbq sauce

Directions:
1. Season the ribs with bbq spice rub, covering both sides of the ribs.
2. Preheat the air fryer to 380 degrees Fahrenheit for a few minutes, then place the ribs in the air fryer basket, meat side down and cook for 20 minutes.
3. Once the 20 minutes is up, grab a pair of tongs and flip the ribs over, and cook for an additional 10 minutes on 380 degrees.
4. Once the timer is up, open the basket and cover with the bbq sauce. Return to Air fryer and cook for 5 minutes on 400 degrees Fahrenheit.
5. Remove and allow the ribs to rest for a few minutes. Feel free to cover with additional bbq sauce if you like saucy ribs.
Notes
The cook times in this recipe are for pork baby back ribs. Beef ribs will likely take longer to cook.
I used my large air fryer (5.3qt) to ensure all my ribs would fit into the basket.

Grilled Sriracha Honey Glazed Ribs

Servings: 2
Cooking Time: 26 Minutes

Ingredients:
- Ribs
- 1 rack pork baby back ribs
- ½ tablespoon kosher salt
- 1 teaspoon freshly ground black pepper

- Sriracha-Honey Glaze
- ½ cup honey
- 2 tablespoons soy sauce
- 2 tablespoons sriracha chili sauce
- 2 tablespoons hoisin sauce
- 1 tablespoon rice wine vinegar
- 1 tablespoon ginger, freshly grated
- 2 tablespoons brown sugar
- 2 tablespoons green onion, thinly sliced, for garnish
- 1 tablespoon sesame seeds, for garnish

Directions:
1. Place the cooking pot into the base of the Smart Indoor Grill, followed by the grill grate.
2. Select the Air Grill function on medium heat, adjust time to 26 minutes, press Shake, then press Start/Pause to preheat.
3. Peel the membrane from the back of the ribs, then cut the ribs crosswise and season on all sides with salt and pepper.
4. Place the ribs meat-side down onto the preheated grill grate, then close the lid.
5. Flip the ribs halfway through cooking. The Shake Reminder will let you know when.
6. Combine the honey, soy sauce, sriracha sauce, hoisin sauce, rice wine vinegar, and ginger in a small saucepan over medium-low heat and stir until the mixture bubbles, rises, and then thickens to coat the back of a spoon, about 4 minutes.
7. Add the brown sugar and cook for 3 more minutes, stirring constantly. Remove from heat and set aside.
8. Open the lid of the grill when the timer goes off and brush the ribs with a thick layer of the glaze.
9. Select the Broil function, adjust time to 2 minutes, and press the Preheat button to bypass preheating. Press Start/Pause to begin cooking.
10. Remove the ribs when done, brush with more glaze, and let cool slightly before cutting between each bone.
11. Garnish with green onions and sesame seeds and serve warm.

Air Fryer Pork Tenderloin
Servings: 4
Cooking Time: 19 Minutes

Ingredients:
- 1 pork tenderloin about 1 ¼ to 1 ½ pounds
- ½ teaspoon kosher salt
- ¼ teaspoon pepper
- Seasoning Mix
- 1 teaspoon dijon mustard
- 1 tablespoon balsamic vinegar
- 1 teaspoon olive oil
- ½ teaspoon Italian seasoning

Directions:
1. Preheat the air fryer to 400°F.
2. Remove the silver skin from the pork tenderloin by slipping a knife under it. Gently pull the silver area off while cutting with the knife.
3. Combine the seasoning mix in a small bowl and brush over the tenderloin on all sides. Season with salt and pepper.
4. Place the pork tenderloin in the air fryer basket (cut it in half to fit if needed) and cook for 16-17 minutes or until pork reaches 145°F. (I remove the pork from the air fryer a few degrees before as it will continue to rise while resting).
5. Let pork rest at least 5 minutes before serving.
Notes
Appliances and cooking times can vary. Check the pork early to ensure it doesn't overcook.
Use an instant read meat thermometer. This is a very lean piece of meat and it will dry out if overcooked.
This recipe is for a 1 1/4 lb tenderloin. If yours is smaller or larger, cooking time will need to be adjusted by a couple of minutes.
If the tenderloin is too large to fit, it can be cut in half. Cooking time will not change.
Rest the tenderloin at least 5 minutes before slicing.
The pork tenderloin can and should be a little bit pink in the middle for the best results.

Air Fryer Meatball Subs

Servings: 4
Cooking Time: 20 Minutes

Ingredients:
- Meatballs
- 1 pound ground beef
- 1 egg
- ¼ cup bread crumbs
- ¼ cup parmesan cheese
- 1 teaspoon garlic powder
- 1 teaspoon salt
- 1 teaspoon pepper
- 1 tablespoon Worcestershire sauce
- Assembly
- 2 cups marinara sauce or pasta sauce
- 4 hot dog buns
- 1 cup mozzarella cheese

Directions:
1. Meatballs
2. Preheat the air fryer to 380°F.
3. Mix all of the meatball ingredients together in a bowl until fully incorporated.
4. Divide the mixture evenly into 16 meatballs.
5. Place them in the air fryer basket and cook for 12-14 minutes or until they reach 165°F internally.
6. Assembly
7. Once meatballs are cooked, toss them with the marinara sauce and place four meatballs into each bun.
8. Place buns in the air fryer basket and top with mozzarella cheese.
9. Cook for 4-5 minutes or until cheese is completely melted.

Air Fryer Breaded Pork Chops

Servings: 3
Cooking Time: 16 Minutes

Ingredients:
- 3 (6oz.) (3 (170g)) pork chops , rinsed & patted dry
- salt , to taste
- black pepper , to taste
- garlic powder , to taste
- smoked paprika , to taste
- 1/2 cup (54 g) breadcrumbs , approximately
- 1 large (1 large) egg
- Cooking spray , for coating the pork chops

Directions:
1. Add seasonings to both sides of the pork chops with salt, pepper, garlic powder, and smoked paprika.
2. Add the breadcrumbs in a medium bowl. In another bowl, beat the egg.
3. Dip each pork chop in egg and then dredge it in the breadcrumbs, coating completely. Lightly spray both sides of coated pork chops with cooking spray right before cooking.
4. Preheat the Air Fryer at 380°F for 4 minutes. This will give the pork chops a nice crunchy crust.
5. Place in the Air Fryer and cook at 380°F (194°C) for 8-12 minutes. After 6 minutes of cooking, flip the pork chops and then continue cooking for the remainder of time or until golden and internal temperature reaches 145-160°F.
6. Serve warm.

NOTES

Recipes were cooked in 3-4 qt air fryers. If using a larger air fryer, the recipe might cook quicker so adjust cooking time.

If cooking in multiple batches & not preheating before first batch, the first batch will take longer to cook.

Preheating the Air Fryer is preferable. If you don't preheat, add more time to the cooking.

Remember to set a timer to shake/flip/toss the food as directed in recipe.

Pork Roulade

Servings: 4

Ingredients:
- 1kg pork
- 150g cooked chestnuts
- 50g dried cranberries
- 50g breadcrumbs
- 3 tbsp softened butter
- 2 rashes of smokey streaky bacon

- 1 tsp thyme
- 2 tbsp parsley
- 14 tsp nutmeg
- Salt and pepper to taste

Directions:

1. Add chestnuts, breadcrumbs, butter, bacon, herbs and seasonings to a small blender and blend until well incorporated. Then add cranberries.

2. Cut pork in half ensuring you leave about 2cm intact at the end. Spread pork out and lightly pound it, then generously season with salt and pepper. Spread stuffing on top of pork evenly.

3. Roll meat up and then secure with cooking twine or toothpicks.

4. Insert pot in unit and close lid. Select ROAST, then PRESET. Using the up and down arrows select PORK and set temperature to MED-WELL. Press START/STOP to begin preheating.

5. While unit is preheating, mix maple syrup, oil, paprika, salt and pepper in a small bowl or a cup. Pour small amount over meat and spread it evenly.

6. When unit beeps to signify it has preheated, insert probe to the middle of the side of the roast. Place meat in the unit, cover with tin foil and close lid to begin cooking.

7. After 45 minutes, open lid, remove tin foil and brush more marinade on top of meat. Close lid to continue.

8. When cooking is complete, carefully remove probe, set roast aside and allow to rest for 10 minutes.

9. Enjoy with side of vegetables.

Air Fryer Shake 'n Bake Pork Chops

Servings: 4
Cooking Time: 8 Minutes

Ingredients:

- 4 pork chops boneless or bone in, ½ inch in thickness
- 2 tablespoons Dijon mustard
- 1 packet Pork Shake and Bake Seasoning
- 1 cup Italian seasoned breadcrumbs
- 1 teaspoon kosher salt
- 1 teaspoon paprika
- 1/2 teaspoon garlic powder
- 1/2 teaspoon black pepper

Directions:

1. Remove pork chops from packaging and place them on a cutting board. Pat them dry with paper towels.

2. Pour store bought packet mixture or homemade version of breading into a storage resealable bag. Lightly coat pork chops with Dijon mustard on both sides, then place them in the storage bag with breadcrumb mixture.

3. Seal the bag and shake them in the mixture, until they are fully coated. Lightly spray olive oil onto the air fryer basket or line with air fryer perforated parchment sheet.

4. Place pork chops in a single layer in basket, without overlapping. Set your air fryer to 400 degrees F and cook for 8-10 minutes, turning chops halfway through the cooking process. Depending on the thickness cooking time will vary 1-3 minutes. Use a meat thermometer to check the internal temperature of meat is 145 degrees F.

NOTES

Place on a baking rack (with olive oil spray) when cooking time is finished if not serving immediately. Because pork will get a soggy crust on the bottom and possibly stick without the olive oil.

Optional flavorings: for an extra kick add hot sauce to the Dijon. Or red pepper flakes, additional teaspoon black pepper or ancho chili powder to either of the breading mixtures.

Optional Ingredients: pour a packet of ranch seasoning into coating mix. A few teaspoons paprika, onion powder

Cooking tips: If you do not have Dijon mustard whisk a couple of eggs to make an egg wash. Place pork chops in a rimmed baking sheet or shallow bowl and pour egg mixture over them and cover both sides before placing them in the bag with seasoning mix. Or use a coating of mayonnaise.

Lightly Fried Lamb Chops With Rosemary And Garlic Recipe

Ingredients:
- 3 lamb rib chops
- 1 tbsp minced garlic
- 1 tbsp fresh rosemary, chopped
- ½ tsp dried crushed red pepper

Directions:
1. In a small bowl, combine the garlic, rosemary, and crushed red pepper, then rub about ¼ tsp of the mixture over both sides of each lamb chop
2. Sprinkle the lamb chops with salt and cover and refrigerate for up to 4 hours
3. Place the lamb chops in a 200°C air fryer and cook for approximately 10 minutes, shaking the basket halfway through

Air Fryer Glazed Ham Recipe
Servings: 8
Cooking Time: 1 Hour

Ingredients:
- 2-4 pound boneless ham fully cooked
- Glaze
- ¼ cup brown sugar
- ¼ cup orange juice
- 2 tablespoons honey

Directions:
1. Preheat air fryer to 320°F.
2. Combine glaze ingredients in a medium saucepan and bring to a simmer until glaze is combined.
3. Place the ham in the foil. Close the foil over the ham, wrap tightly and cook for 20 minutes.
4. Open and brush about ½ of the glaze over the ham. Leave the foil open on top, ensuring the glaze can't leak out. Cook for another 20-30 minutes, brushing with glaze every 10 minutes.
Notes
Wrap leftovers or place them in an airtight container, and refrigerate for up to 4 days.
Air fryer ham freezes well in freezer bags or containers for up to two months. Layer foil or parchment paper between pieces of ham to prevent them from sticking together.

Air Fryer Stuffed Avocado
Servings: 4
Cooking Time: 20 Minutes

Ingredients:
- 1 pound lean ground meat beef chicken, turkey can be used
- ½ medium yellow onion diced
- 2 cloves garlic minced
- 1 packet taco seasoning
- 2 large avocados
- ¼ cup Mexican cheese blend shredded, or more as desired
- Optional Toppings
- ½ cup lettuce shredded
- ½ cup diced tomatoes diced
- ¼ cup red onions diced
- ¼ cup cilantro leaves

Directions:
1. Place ground beef, onion, and garlic in a large skillet and cook until no pink remains. Drain any fat.
2. Add the taco seasonings along with ½ cup of water and allow it to simmer over medium low heat until most of the liquid has evaporated.
3. Cut your avocados in half and remove the pit, use a spoon and scoop out some of the avocado to make a bigger shell. Brush the avocado with olive oil and season with salt & pepper if desired.
4. Generously scoop the taco filling into your avocado halves and sprinkle with cheese.
5. Preheat the air fryer to 370°F. Place the avocado halves in the air fryer and cook 3-4 minutes or until warmed and the cheese is melted.
6. Top as desired and serve.
Notes
Homemade Seasoning Mix
1 tablespoon chili seasoning
½ teaspoon cumin
½ teaspoon smoked paprika
¼ teaspoon dried oregano
salt & pepper to taste

If using homemade seasoning mix, it is recommended to add 1 small chopped tomato with the mix and allow it to simmer.

Depending on the size of your avocados, you may have extra filling. Extras can be stored in the fridge in an air tight container for up to 4 days.

Meatball Sliders

Servings: 9
Cooking Time: 19 Minutes

Ingredients:

- Sliders:
- 3 tablespoons unsalted butter
- 4 cloves garlic, minced
- 9 store-bought pull-apart dinner rolls
- 1 cup prepared tomato sauce
- ½ cup shredded Italian cheese blend
- 2 tablespoons fresh basil, chopped
- Meatballs:
- 2 tablespoons olive oil
- 1 small onion, finely diced
- 3 cloves garlic, minced
- ½ teaspoon red pepper flakes
- 1 pound grass-fed ground beef
- 2 tablespoons fresh parsley, finely chopped
- 1 large egg
- ¼ cup plain breadcrumbs
- 1/4 cup Parmesan cheese, freshly grated
- 1½ teaspoons kosher salt
- 1 teaspoon black pepper
- Olive oil spray

Directions:

1. Place olive oil in a small skillet over medium heat to start the meatballs.
2. Add the diced onion and sauté until translucent and lightly golden, about 3 minutes.
3. Add the minced garlic and red pepper flakes and sauté for another minute.
4. Remove the skillet from the heat and let cool to room temperature.
5. Transfer the cooled onions and garlic to a large bowl.
6. Add the beef, parsley, egg, breadcrumbs, Parmesan cheese, salt, and pepper, and mix with your hands until well combined.
7. Shape all of the mixture into 2-inch balls.
8. Select the Preheat function on the Smart Air Fryer, then press Start/Pause.
9. Place the meatballs into the preheated air fryer and lightly spray the tops with oil spray.
10. Set temperature to 400°F and time to 12 minutes, then press Start/Pause.
11. Remove the meatballs when done and transfer to a plate.
12. Note: Clean the air fryer basket before continuing.Place butter in a small skillet over medium heat to start the sliders.
13. Add the minced garlic once the butter is sizzling, then turn off the heat. Let the garlic infuse the butter for 5 minutes.
14. Cut a 2-inch-diameter circle into the top of each roll without cutting all the way through, creating a well. Discard the removed bread.
15. Brush the garlic butter over the outside and inside of each roll.
16. Line the air fryer basket with foil that goes up the sides of the basket.
17. Place the rolls into the air fryer basket.
18. Set temperature to 400°F and time to 5 minutes, then press Start/Pause.
19. Remove the rolls when golden brown and lightly toasted.
20. Place 1 tablespoon of tomato sauce into the bottom of each well, then place the meatballs on top.
21. Top each meatball with another tablespoon of tomato sauce and sprinkle cheese over the whole roll.
22. Set temperature to 400°F and time to 2 minutes, then press Start/Pause.
23. Remove the sliders when done and the cheese is melted and golden.
24. Serve the sliders warm, topped with fresh basil.

BREAKFAST & BRUNCH RECIPES

Lentil Patties
Servings: 10
Cooking Time: 25 Minutes

Ingredients:
- 3/4 cup (150 g) red lentils dry
- 1 cup (240-300 ml) vegetable broth or water
- 1 small (90 g) red pepper diced
- 1 small/medium (90 g) onion diced
- 2 large cloves of garlic chopped
- 4 tbsp (30 g) chickpea flour more if needed
- 1 tbsp ground chia seeds
- 3 tbsp fresh parsley chopped
- 1 tsp paprika powder
- 3/4 tsp ground cumin
- 1/2 tsp onion powder
- 1/2 tsp salt
- Pepper and red pepper flakes to taste
- Oil for frying

Directions:
1. Watch the video in the post for easy visual instructions.
2. Cook the lentils
3. Rinse the red lentils in a sieve under running water to remove any debris. Transfer them to a pot or pan along with 1 cup of vegetable broth. If using water, add a little salt. Bring to a boil and let the lentils simmer for about 15 minutes, or until they are soft and partially falling apart. There shouldn't be any broth or water left after cooking!
4. Cook the veggies
5. Meanwhile, heat a little oil in a skillet and add the onion, pepper, and garlic. Fry over medium heat for a few minutes, until the onion is translucent (not browned).
6. Shape and cook the patties
7. Once the lentils are cooked, add them to a food processor together with the cooked veggies, spices, parsley, ground chia seeds, and flour. Pulse a couple of times until the mixture is combined. You want to leave some texture, so do not over-process it.

8. The mixture should be shapeable, if it's not, add a little more flour.
9. Form 10 patties (each weighing between 40-50 grams - about 2 1/2 - 3 tablespoons), and fry them with a little oil (I used 2 teaspoons for 4 patties) in a skillet from both sides (about 3 minutes each side) until golden brown and crispy.
10. Serve with a dip of choice, and enjoy! I made a dip from 2 tablespoons of creamy peanut butter mixed with 30 ml dill pickle juice, 10 ml olive brine, a little garlic, and smoked paprika to taste.

Air Fryer Garlic Bread
Servings: 16
Cooking Time: 5 Minutes

Ingredients:
- 1 loaf baguette
- 1/2 cup butter softened
- 1/4 cup garlic minced
- 1 teaspoon dried parsley
- 1/4 cup parmesan cheese optional

Directions:
1. Preheat the air fryer to 180C/350F.
2. Slice the baguette into 2-inch thick slices.
3. In a mixing bowl, add the softened butter, garlic, dried parsley, and parmesan cheese.
4. Spread a very generous amount of garlic butter on slices of the baguette.
5. Generously grease an air fryer basket and air fry the garlic bread for 4-5 minutes, or until golden.
6. Repeat the process until all the bread is cooked.
Notes
TO STORE: You can store the leftovers in the refrigerator in airtight containers for up to 4-5 days.
TO FREEZE: Place leftovers in a ziplock bag and store them in the freezer for up to two months.
TO REHEAT: Reheat the garlic bread in an air fryer or pre-heated oven.

Air Fryer Pretzel Bites

Servings: 8
Cooking Time: 7 Minutes

Ingredients:

- 4 cups all purpose flour
- 2 1/2 tsp active dry yeast
- 1 1/2 cups hot water
- 1 tbsp cinnamon
- 2 tbsp granulated white sugar
- 1 tsp salt
- 4 tbsp unsalted butter melted
- Topping
- 4 tbsp granulated white sugar
- 1 tsp cinnamon
- 2 tbsp brown sugar
- Glaze for dipping (optional)
- 2 cups confectioners sugar
- 1 tsp vanilla
- 3 tbsp whole milk
- 2 tbsp unsalted butter softened

Directions:

1. Add the flour, salt, cinnamon, and sugar to a large bowl and set aside.
2. Add the yeast to the hot water and let it dissolve.
3. Add the water with yeast to the flour mixture and knead with your hands until fully combined.
4. Cover the bowl of dough with a dry cloth and allow to sit covered for 30-45 minutes.
5. Punch down the dough and then set it aside.
6. Dust your work surface with flour and knead the dough lightly.
7. Break the dough into 8 equal pieces. Form a 1" thick rope with each piece. Cut the rope into 1-1 ½" pieces.
8. Preheat the air fryer to 380 degrees Fahrenheit. Prepare the air fryer basket with a nonstick cooking spray or olive oil.
9. Place the pretzels in the prepared air fryer basket in a single layer, careful to leave a little room in between each one. Cook at 380 degrees Fahrenheit for 6-7 minutes or until they are golden brown.
10. Remove the pretzel bites from the air fryer and brush the tops with melted butter.

11. Mix the cinnamon, sugar, and brown sugar together and dip the pretzels in the cinnamon sugar mixture before serving.
12. Serve the glaze as a dipping sauce.
13. How to Make the Glaze Dipping Sauce
14. Add the powdered confectioner's sugar, whole milk, vanilla, and melted butter to a medium bowl. Use a whisk and mix well and serve. (You may need to add a little milk depending on your preferred consistency.

NOTES

HOW DO I STORE LEFTOVER AIR FRYER PRETZEL BITES?

Pretzel bites are really best to be eaten when they are warm and fresh. If you have a lot of leftovers and need to store them, you can store them at room temperature for up to 5 days in an airtight container out of sunlight.

HOW MANY PRETZEL BITES DOES THIS RECIPE MAKE?

This recipe makes 64 pretzel bites. Perfect for a big party, family get-together, or when you're watching the big game.

Air Fryer Frozen Pretzels

Servings: 4
Cooking Time: 3 Minutes

Ingredients:

- 4 Frozen Soft Pretzels
- Salt Topping (if not already added)
- 1 tablespoon water
- 1 teaspoon Coarse Salt

Directions:

1. Place 2-4 frozen pretzels in air fryer basket/rack.
2. Brush tops of pretzels with water and then sprinkle desired amount of pretzel salt from the package of salt in the package, on pretzels.
3. Air fry at 350 degrees F for 3-5 minutes cook time or until cooked through.
4. Carefully remove the pretzels from the basket and serve warm alone or with your favorite dipping sauce, such as a beer cheese dip, honey mustard, marinara sauce, a bit of Dijon mustard, or hot sauce.

Air Fryer Bacon And Egg Bites

Ingredients:
- 6 large eggs
- 2 tablespoons of heavy whipping cream or milk (any is fine)
- Salt and pepper to taste
- ¼ cup chopped green peppers
- ¼ cup chopped red peppers
- ¼ cup chopped onions
- ¼ cup chopped fresh spinach
- ½ cup shredded cheddar cheese
- ¼ cup shredded mozzarella cheese
- 3 slices of cooked and crumbled bacon

Directions:
1. Add the eggs to a large mixing bowl.
2. Add in the cream, salt and pepper to taste. Whisk to combine.
3. Sprinkle in half of the green peppers, red peppers, onions, spinach, cheeses, and bacon. Whisk to combine.
4. Pour the egg mixture into each of the silicone molds. You may want to spray with cooking spray first.
5. Sprinkle in the remaining half of all of the veggies.
6. Cook the egg bites cups for 12-15 minutes on 300 degrees. You can test the center of one with a toothpick. When the toothpick comes out clean, the eggs have set.
7. Enjoy!

Pumpkin Bread Pudding
Servings: 5

Ingredients:
- 1 cup milk
- 1 cup pumpkin puree
- 1 teaspoon vanilla
- ¼ teaspoon kosher salt
- ½ cup brown sugar
- 3 tablespoons granulated sugar
- 1 teaspoon nutmeg
- ½ teaspoon allspice
- ½ teaspoon cinnamon
- ¼ teaspoon ground cloves
- 2 eggs, beaten

- ½ loaf of bread (340 grams), cut into 2-inch cubes
- ½ cup dried cranberries
- ½ cup pecans
- Powdered15 sugar, for garnish (optional)

Directions:
1. Whisk the milk, pumpkin puree, vanilla, salt, both sugars, and all spices together in a large bowl until smooth.
2. Add in the eggs and whisk until fully incorporated.
3. Add the cubed bread to the mixture and let soak for 15 minutes. Then, stir in the dried cranberries and pecans.
4. Line the inner Air Fryer basket with parchment paper, being sure to cover all the sides of the basket.
5. Place the bread pudding into the air fryer basket.
6. Select the Bake function, adjust temperature to 320°F and time to 25 minutes, press Shake, then press Start/Pause.
7. Cover the bread pudding with foil halfway through cooking. The Shake Reminder will let you know when.
8. Remove the air fryer basket and let cool for 5 minutes before removing the bread pudding and transferring it to a serving dish.
9. Serve warm, garnished with powdered sugar if desired.

Air Fryer Rusks, With Buttermilk & Muesli
Servings: 16
Cooking Time: 50 Minutes

Ingredients:
- 500g self-raising flour
- 100g sugar
- Pinch sea salt
- 150g butter, cold & cubed
- 250g buttermilk, room temperature
- 1 large egg
- 140g muesli

Directions:
1. Lightly grease a 20 x 20cm baking tin.

2. In a large bowl whisk together the self-raising flour, sugar and salt.

3. Add the butter and work it into the dry ingredients until the mixture resembles wet sand.

4. Whisk the buttermilk and egg together well.

5. Add the buttermilk mixture and the muesli into the dry ingredients.

6. Mix everything together.

7. Divide the dough into 16 balls and shape them into little logs.

8. Arrange them side by side in the baking tin.

9. Place the tin in the Vortex Plus basket and select Air Fry at 160°C for 40 minutes.

10. Remove the baked rusks from the tin and return them, whole, upside down to the air fryer basket. Air Fry at 160°C again for 5 minutes.

11. Break the rusks apart into individuals and place them in the basket.

12. Dehydrate the rusks at 79°C for 4 hours until hard.

13. Keep rusks in a sealed container and enjoy dunking into your favourite hot beverage!

Air Fryer Stuffed Spaghetti Squash
Servings: 4
Cooking Time: 45 Minutes

Ingredients:
- 1 medium spaghetti squash 3 lbs
- 1 pound lean ground beef
- 1 small onion diced
- 2 cloves garlic minced
- 24 ounces marinara sauce or pasta sauce
- 1 teaspoon Italian seasoning
- 1 cup cheese + extra for topping mozzarella or cheddar, shredded
- ½ cup parmesan cheese shredded
- salt & pepper to taste

Directions:
1. Preheat the air fryer to 370°F. Slice the spaghetti squash in half, scoop out the seeds and discard.

2. Cook Spaghetti Squash

3. Brush the squash with olive oil and place in the air fryer cut side up and cook for 25-30 minutes or until fork tender.

4. Once the squash is cooked, gently scrape the insides into a large bowl and set it aside. Reserve the shells for filling.

5. Prepare Sauce

6. Increase the temperature of the Air Fryer to 380°F.

7. Mix ground beef, diced onion, and minced garlic in a bowl. *see note Place the beef mixture in the air fryer basket and use a spoon to spread it out a little bit. Cook for 5 minutes and use a spoon to break up the meat. Cook for an additional 5 minutes until the beef is browned and no pink remains. Drain any fat.

8. Combine the marinara sauce with the ground beef and Italian seasoning in an air fryer safe pan or bowl. Return to the air fryer and cook for 10 minutes or until bubbly.

9. Assembly

10. While the sauce is cooking combine the cheese with the cooked spaghetti squash and place it back into the squash shell.

11. Top with the ground beef mixture. Top with extra shredded cheese.

12. Place the squash back into the air fryer and cook for 7-9 minutes or until the cheese is melted.

Notes

To make it easy to cut spaghetti squash, poke it with a fork a few times and microwave for 3-4 minutes.

Option: If preferred the ground beef mixture and the sauce can be prepared on the stovetop while the squash is roasting in the air fryer.

Brown the beef, onion and garlic in a pan. Drain fat.

Add sauce ingredients and simmer 5 minutes. Ensure your bowl or container for the sauce is air fryer safe.

Leftover spaghetti sauce or meat sauce can be used in place of the home-made sauce.

Air Fryer Tacos

Servings: 4
Cooking Time: 15 Minutes

Ingredients:
- 1 pound ground beef
- 1 package taco seasoning
- ½ cup water
- 8 tortillas
- 2 cups Mexican cheese blend shredded, divided evenly over tacos
- ½ cup salsa approximately 1 tablespoons per taco

Directions:
1. Preheat Air Fryer to 400°F.
2. Brown ground beef in a frying pan over medium heat until no pink remains and drain any fat (or use air fryer taco meat).
3. Stir in the taco seasoning and water, simmer until water is gone.
4. Place 4-5 tortillas in the air fryer basket and top with ground beef mixture, cheese, and 1 tablespoon salsa. Do not overcrowd the air fryer.
5. Fold in half and place an oven safe trivet over top to hold them in place.
6. Cook for 4-5 minutes or until the cheese is melted and the tortilla is crisp.
7. Top with your favorite taco toppings and serve immediately.
Notes
Store leftover tacos in an air tighter container for up to 3 days in the refrigerator. For best results, reheat in the air fryer.

Deviled Eggs

Servings: 6

Ingredients:
- 6 large eggs, hard boiled
- 2 tbsp. mayonnaise
- 1 tsp. fresh lemon juice
- 1 tsp. Dijon mustard
- 1/2 tsp. hot sauce
- Kosher salt and pepper
- Crumbled bacon, sliced scallions and chives, chopped parsley and dill, for serving

Directions:
1. Halve eggs lengthwise. Transfer yolks to small bowl and mash with mayonnaise, lemon juice, mustard, hot sauce, and 1/8 tsp each salt and pepper. Spoon into egg whites and sprinkle with toppings as desired.

Air Fryer Toad In The Hole

Servings: 2
Cooking Time: 4 Minutes

Ingredients:
- 2 slices bread
- 2 teaspoons butter
- 2 eggs
- 2 tablespoons cheddar cheese shredded
- salt and pepper to taste

Directions:
1. Preheat air fryer to 340°F.
2. Press a 2-inch hole in the middle of the bread using the bottom of a measuring cup. Butter the bread on both sides.
3. Crack the egg into the pressed in circle and cook for 6-7 minutes. You may need a minute or two more or less depending on how runny you like your egg.
4. Add the shredded cheese during the last 2 minutes of cooking time.
Notes
Note: When making toad in a hole in a frying pan, a circle is cut out of the bread. In the air fryer the bread needs to stay in tact to hold the egg so we press and indent instead of cutting hole.
Check your egg early as appliances can vary. The egg will still continue to cook a little bit once removed from the air fryer.

Air Fryer Hard Boiled Eggs

Servings: 4
Cooking Time: 18 Minutes

Ingredients:
- 8 large eggs

Directions:
1. Preheat air fryer to 250°F.

2. Add eggs in a single layer in the air fryer basket.
3. For hard-cooked eggs cook for 16-18 minutes. Once cooked place in an ice bath until cool.
4. Peel under cool running water.
Notes
You can cook as many eggs at one time as you need.
Eggs are cooked directly from the fridge (cold). If your eggs are room temperature, you may need to adjust cooking time.
These were tested in both a Vortex Air Fryer and two different Cosori Air Fryers. Other brands may vary by a minute or two and it may take a couple of batches to learn your machine. Cook just one or two eggs at first to be certain they're cooked how you like them.
Air Fryer Egg Cooking times
Soft: Cook 11-12 minutes
Medium: Cook 13-14 minutes
Hard: Cook 16-18 minutes

Air Fryer French Toast Sticks
Servings: 4
Cooking Time: 8 Minutes

Ingredients:
- 8 slices Italian style bread thickly sliced
- 3 eggs
- 1 cup milk
- 1 tablespoon sugar
- 1 teaspoon vanilla
- ½ teaspoon cinnamon

Directions:
1. Preheat air fryer to 350°F. Spray basket with pan release.
2. Whisk eggs, milk, sugar, vanilla, and cinnamon in a shallow bowl or dish.
3. Cut bread into 1" sticks - roughly 4 sticks per slice of bread.
4. Dip sticks into the egg mixture allowing a few seconds for the egg to soak into the bread.
5. Place the sticks in two rows in the air fryer basket and cook for 4 minutes.
6. After 4 minutes, flip the sticks over and cook for an additional 4 or until they are golden in color.

Air-fryer Greek Breadsticks
Servings: 32
Cooking Time: 15 Minutes

Ingredients:
- 1/4 cup marinated quartered artichoke hearts, drained
- 2 tablespoons pitted Greek olives
- 1 package (17.3 ounces) frozen puff pastry, thawed
- 1 carton (6-1/2 ounces) spreadable spinach and artichoke cream cheese
- 2 tablespoons grated Parmesan cheese
- 1 large egg
- 1 tablespoon water
- 2 teaspoons sesame seeds
- Refrigerated tzatziki sauce, optional

Directions:
1. Preheat air fryer to 325°. Place artichokes and olives in a food processor; cover and pulse until finely chopped. Unfold 1 pastry sheet on a lightly floured surface; spread half the cream cheese over half the pastry. Top with half the artichoke mixture. Sprinkle with half the Parmesan cheese. Fold plain half over filling; press gently to seal.
2. Repeat with remaining pastry, cream cheese, artichoke mixture and Parmesan cheese. Whisk egg and water; brush over tops. Sprinkle with sesame seeds. Cut each rectangle into sixteen 3/4-in.-wide strips. Twist each strip several times.
3. In batches, arrange breadsticks in a single layer on greased tray in air-fryer basket. Cook until golden brown, 12-15 minutes. Serve warm with tzatziki sauce if desired.

Air Fryer Southwest Egg Rolls
Servings: 6
Cooking Time: 10 Minutes

Ingredients:
- Filling
- 1 cup corn kernels frozen or canned (drained)
- 1 cup black beans rinsed and drained
- ½ cup finely diced red bell pepper
- ¼ cup finely diced jalapeno pepper

- ¼ cup chopped green onions
- 2 cups shredded chicken
- 3 cups shredded Monterey jack cheese
- 1 teaspoon paprika
- ½ teaspoon ground cumin
- 1 teaspoon mild chili powder
- ½ teaspoon salt
- Egg Rolls
- 1 egg
- 1 tablespoon water
- 12 egg roll wrappers
- Vegetable oil
- Zesty Dip
- 1 cup sour cream or plain Greek yogurt
- ½ cup buttermilk ranch dressing or light ranch dressing
- 1 tablespoon taco seasoning

Directions:

1. In a large mixing bowl, combine the corn, black beans, bell pepper, jalapenos, green onions, chicken, cheese and seasonings; set aside.
2. In a small bowl, use a fork to whisk together the egg and water.
3. Scoop ½ cup of the chicken mixture onto an egg roll wrapper. Brush the egg wash around the outside of the egg roll. Fold in two sides of the wrapper so the points almost touch. Then fold the top in and tightly roll up the egg roll and place on a sheet pan lined with waxed or parchment paper. Repeat with the remainder of the chicken mixture.
4. Lightly brush each egg roll with vegetable oil. Place egg rolls in an air fryer and cook at 375°F for 5 minutes. Make sure there is space between each egg roll - cook in batches if needed.
5. Use a tongs to flip the egg rolls and continue cooking for 3-5 more minutes or until the exterior is golden brown and crispy. (Cooking times can vary greatly depending on the brand and size of your air fryer. I did four at a time at 375°F and it took between 8-10 minutes total.)
6. While the egg rolls are in the air fryer, combine the sour cream, ranch dressing and taco seasoning to make the zesty dip. Refrigerate until ready to serve.
7. Optional Zesty Dip
8. In a small bowl, combine sour cream, ranch dressing and taco seasoning for the zesty dip. Cover and refrigerate until ready to serve. Serve the egg rolls warm with zesty dip on the side.

Notes

Storage: Allow to cool completely before storing. Store in an airtight container in the refrigerator for up to 3-4 days.

Freezing: Cool completely, then arrange on a baking sheet. Cover with plastic wrap and place in the freezer until firm; about 3-4 hours. Transfer to a freezer bag or freezer safe container and keep frozen for up to 6 months. Thaw completely before reheating.

Air Fryer Reheating: To reheat egg rolls in the air fryer, set the air fryer to 350°F and add 2-4 at a time. Each batch will take around 5 minutes, depending on the size of your air fryer and how many rolls you add to the pan.

Do not reheat in the microwave, or they will become soggy.

Make Ahead: Make a double batch of the recipe, and only air fry what you need. Arrange the rest on a baking sheet and flash freeze for a few hours or until firm. Then transfer to a freezer bag and freeze for up to 3 months.

When you're ready to bake them, place a few in the air fryer and spray with cooking spray. Set the machine to 400 degrees F and cook for 6 minutes on one side, then flip and cook for 4-6 minutes more.

Air Fryer Poached Egg Avocado Smash Toast
Servings: 2

Ingredients:
- 2 thin slices whole wheat bread
- 1 large avocado
- 1 tbsp. fresh lemon juice
- 2 tsp. chopped fresh basil leaves, plus torn leaves for serving
- Kosher salt

- Olive oil cooking spray
- 4 tsp. lukewarm water
- 2 large eggs
- 1/2 c. cherry or grape tomatoes, halved
- Crushed red pepper flakes (optional)

Directions:
1. Working in batches if necessary, in an air-fryer basket, arrange bread in a single layer. Cook at 350°, flipping halfway through, until light golden, 3 to 4 minutes. Transfer toast to plates.
2. Using a spoon, scoop avocado flesh into a medium bowl. Add lemon juice, chopped basil, and a pinch of salt. Mash with a fork until combined yet still chunky; season with salt, if desired.
3. Lightly coat 2 (4-oz.) ramekins with cooking spray. Fill each with 2 teaspoons water. Crack 1 egg into each.
4. Place ramekins in air-fryer basket. Cook at 350° until egg whites are set and yolks are still runny, 6 to 8 minutes.
5. Spread avocado mixture over toasts. Carefully remove ramekins from air-fryer basket one at a time (they will be hot). Run a spatula around edges of eggs, then slide onto avocado mixture, flipping eggs upside down (so bottom of egg in ramekin is face up on plate).
6. Top toast with tomatoes; season with a pinch of salt. Garnish with torn basil and red pepper flakes, if using.

Air Fryer Sausage Rolls
Servings: 3
Cooking Time: 12 Minutes

Ingredients:
- 6 sausage links pre cooked
- 6 puff pastry sheets
- 3 Tablespoons onion chopped, red
- 1 egg beaten

Directions:
1. Remove the puff pastry from the freezer and allow it to thaw at room temperature for 30-40 minutes.
2. In a small bowl, add the egg and whisk.

3. Take a sausage link and add it to a puff pastry sheet with some chopped onion pieces. Roll the puff pastry around the sausage and onion, seal the edges, and then brush with the egg.
4. Repeat the step for the remaining sausage rolls.
5. Place the sausage rolls into the basket of the air fryer in a single layer. Make sure to leave space between the sausage rolls.
6. Air fry the sausage rolls at 370 degrees Fahrenheit for 12-15 minutes, or until the pastry is golden brown. Flip the pastries halfway through the cooking process.
7. Carefully remove the sausage rolls from the air fryer and serve alone or with your favorite dipping sauce if desired.
NOTES
I make this recipe in my Cosori 5.8 qt. air fryer or 6.8 quart air fryer. Depending on your air fryer, size and wattages, cooking time may need to be adjusted 1-2 minutes.
Consider adding additional items to the sausage rolls like scrambled eggs, green onions, or spice things up with diced jalapenos.

Mother's Day Breakfast Galettes

Ingredients:
- 1 Tbsp. olive oil
- 16 oz. bacon, diced
- 1 onion, diced
- 2 sheets puff pastry, defrosted
- 8 eggs, for cracking
- salt and pepper, to taste
- 1 egg + 1 tsp water, for egg wash

Directions:
1. Start by dicing the onion and bacon.
2. In a medium sized pan, add the olive oil, bacon and onion and cook until crispy. Once cooked, set aside to cool.
3. Roll out the puff pastry and cut into 4 equal squares.
4. Add about 2 spoonfuls of the bacon and onion mixture to each puff pastry square.
5. Fold the sides of the puff pastry and pinch corners to secure the edges are sealed. Make a well in the center of each.

6. Working in batches, place galettes in the air fryer basket.
7. Crack an egg into the center of each where you made the well and brush edges with egg wash.
8. Sprinkle the tops with salt and pepper and air fry at 350F for about 7 minutes.
9. Garnish with toppings of choice and enjoy!

Air Fryer Bread
Servings: 1

Ingredients:
- Deselect All
- 2 tablespoons unsalted butter, melted, plus more for the pan
- 1 1/2 teaspoons active dry yeast
- 1 1/2 teaspoons sugar
- 1 1/2 teaspoons kosher salt
- 2 2/3 cups all-purpose flour (see Cook's Note)

Directions:
1. Butter a 6-by-3-inch round pan and set aside.
2. Combine the butter, yeast, sugar, salt and 1 cup warm water in a stand mixer fitted with the dough hook attachment. With the mixer on low speed, add 1/2 cup of the flour at a time, waiting for each addition to be fully incorporated before adding more. Once all of the flour is added, knead on medium speed for 8 minutes.
3. Transfer the dough to the prepared pan, cover and let rise until doubled in size, about 1 hour.
4. Add the pan with the dough to a 3.5-quart air fryer and set to 380 degrees F. Cook until the bread is dark brown and the internal temperature registers 200 degrees F, about 20 minutes. Let cool in the pan 5 minutes, then turn out onto a rack to cool completely.
5. Cook's Note
6. When measuring flour, we spoon it into a dry measuring cup and level off excess. (Scooping directly from the bag compacts the flour, resulting in dry baked goods.)

Air-fryer Calzones
Servings: 2

Ingredients:
- 1 teaspoon olive oil
- ¼ cup finely chopped red onion
- 3 ounce baby spinach leaves (about 3 cups)
- ⅓ cup lower-sodium marinara sauce
- 2 ounce shredded rotisserie chicken breast (about 1/3 cup)
- 6 ounce fresh prepared whole-wheat pizza dough
- 1 ½ ounce pre-shredded part-skim mozzarella cheese (about 6 Tbsp.)
- Nonstick cooking spray

Directions:
1. Heat oil in a medium nonstick skillet over medium-high. Add onion, and cook, stirring occasionally, until tender, 2 minutes. Add spinach; cover and cook until wilted, 1 1/2 minutes. Remove pan from heat; stir in marinara sauce and chicken.
2. Divide dough into 4 equal pieces. Roll each piece on a lightly floured surface into a 6-inch circle. Place one-fourth of the spinach mixture over half of each dough circle. Top each with one-fourth of the cheese. Fold dough over filling to form half-moons, crimping edges to seal. Coat calzones well with cooking spray.
3. Place calzones in air fryer basket, and cook at 325°F until dough is golden brown, 12 minutes, turning calzones over after 8 minutes.

Air Fryer Quiche Lorraine
Servings: 4
Cooking Time: 40 Minutes

Ingredients:
- 1 sheet frozen puff pastry, just thawed
- 2 tsp olive oil
- 175g rindless bacon, cut into batons
- 1 brown onion, finely chopped
- 5 eggs
- 125ml (1/2 cup) thickened cream
- 125ml (1/2 cup) milk

- 100g (1 cup) coarsely grated Swiss-style cheese
- Select all ingredients

Directions:
1. Line a 4cm-high, 18cm (base measurement) round fluted tart tin with removable base with the puff pastry, pushing well into the base and side. Line the pastry with baking paper and fill with pastry weights or rice.
2. Remove the sliding rack from the air fryer. Place the lined tart tin inside the rack. Slide rack back into the air fryer. Cook at 180C for 6 minutes. Remove the pastry weights or rice and the baking paper. Use a fork to prick the base of the pastry. Return to the air fryer and cook for a further 6 minutes or until the pastry feels dry to the touch. Set the pasty aside, in the rack, to cool slightly.
3. Meanwhile, heat the oil in a large frying pan over medium-high heat. Add the bacon and cook, stirring often, for 5 minutes or until starting to turn golden. Add the onion and cook, stirring, for 5 minutes or until bacon is crisp and onion is softened. Set aside to cool slightly.
4. Whisk the eggs, cream and milk together in a medium bowl. Season with pepper. Spoon the bacon mixture into the pastry base. Sprinkle with the cheese. Pour over the egg mixture. Gently slide the rack back into the air fryer. Cook at 160C for 30 minutes or until filling is set. Set aside to cool slightly.
5. Cut into slices to serve warm or cold.

Hash Browns In The Air Fryer
Servings: 4
Cooking Time: 23 Minutes

Ingredients:
- 16 oz frozen shredded hash brown potatoes
- ½ teaspoon garlic powder
- Kosher salt, to taste
- Black pepper, to taste

Directions:
1. Preheat your air fryer to 370 degrees F.
2. Spread the frozen hash browns in a single layer inside, spray the top of the hash brown layer with olive oil spray, then sprinkle with garlic powder, salt, and pepper to taste.
3. Cook for 18 minutes. Use a spatula to divide the hash browns and carefully flip them. Spray with olive oil spray and continue to air fry for about 5 more minutes, or until they're golden brown and crispy to your liking.
4. Remove to a serving plate, season with additional salt and pepper if desired, and serve.
NOTES
HOW TO REHEAT HASH BROWNS IN THE AIR FRYER:
Preheat your air fryer to 370 degrees.
Place the leftover shredded hash browns in the air fryer and cook for 3 to 5 minutes, until warmed and crisped thoroughly.

Eggs Benedict
Servings: 4

Ingredients:
- 4 teaspoons grapeseed oil
- 16 tablespoons water, divided
- 4 large eggs
- 2 tablespoons of whipped salted butter
- 4 English muffins, sliced in half
- 8 slices Canadian bacon
- 1 large egg yolk
- ½ cup clarified butter
- TABASCO® Original Red Sauce, to taste
- 1 teaspoon Worcestershire sauce
- 1 lemon, juiced
- Kosher salt, to taste
- Chives, finely chopped, for garnish
- 1 teaspoon paprika, for garnish
- Items Needed:
- 4 ceramic ramekins
- Heat safe mixing bowl

Directions:
1. Brush each ramekin with 1 teaspoon of grapeseed oil.
2. Place 3½ tablespoons of water into each ramekin.
3. Crack one egg into each ramekin.

4. Select the Preheat function on the Air Fryer, adjust temperature to 310°F, then press Start/Pause.
5. Place the ramekins into the preheated air fryer.
6. Set temperature to 310°F and time to 10 minutes, then press Start/Pause.
7. Remove the ramekins when done.
8. Note: If the egg is not fully cooked, cook for an additional 2 minutes. Drain the water out of each ramekin, being careful of the eggs.
9. Select the Preheat function, adjust temperature to 330°F, and press Start/Pause.
10. Spread whipped salted butter onto the English muffins, then place them into the preheated air fryer buttered side-up.
11. Set temperature to 330°F and time to 5 minutes, then press Start/Pause.
12. Remove the English muffins when done and set aside.
13. Place the Canadian bacon in the air fryer.
14. Set temperature to 330°F and time to 5 minutes, then press Start/Pause.
15. Remove the Canadian bacon when done and set aside.
16. Create a double boiler by filling a small saucepan ⅙ full of water, bringing it to a simmer, and placing a heat safe mixing bowl over the top.
17. Place the egg yolk and 2 tablespoons of water in the mixing bowl to begin the Hollandaise sauce.
18. Whisk vigorously until the egg yolk is fully combined with the water and the mixture is frothy.
19. Stream in the clarified butter slowly while whisking.
20. Continue to whisk until the sauce thickens, about 5 minutes.
21. Remove the mixing bowl from the double boiler and turn off the heat.
22. Whisk the egg and butter mixture vigorously until the sauce thickens further and begins to form soft peaks.

23. Add the Tabasco sauce, Worcestershire sauce, lemon juice, and salt, then whisk until well combined.
24. Taste the Hollandaise sauce and adjust seasonings to taste. Place the Hollandaise sauce in a warm area to prevent separation.
25. Assemble the Eggs Benedict by topping an English muffin half with 2 slices of Canadian bacon, a poached egg, and the Hollandaise sauce.
26. Garnish with chives and paprika.
27. Serve immediately with leftover English muffins on the side.

Air Fryer Nachos
Servings: 4
Cooking Time: 4 Minutes

Ingredients:
- 4 cups tortilla chips
- 2 cups shredded cheese or more as desired
- toppings as desired jalapenos, tomatoes, lettuce, sour cream, salsa

Directions:
1. Place the tortilla chips in a single layer in the air fryer basket making sure there are no gaps in the chips.
2. Sprinkle half of the cheese on top and add another layer of chips on top.
3. Top with remaining cheese and toppings as desired.
4. Place in the air fryer at 320°F and bake for 4-6 minutes or until cheese is melted.
Notes
If using an air fryer with a tray, the tray can be lined with foil before adding the chips if desired.
The chips can be layered, open the air fryer and check them early as cooking time can vary by brand of air fryer and these cook quickly.

Air Fryer Breakfast Burritos

FISH & SEAFOOD RECIPES

Blackened Air Fryer Salmon With Cucumber-avocado Salsa

Servings: 4
Cooking Time: 14 Minutes

Ingredients:
- The salmon:
- 1 tablespoon sweet paprika
- 1/2 teaspoon cayenne pepper
- 1 teaspoon garlic powder
- 1 teaspoon dried oregano
- 1 teaspoon dried thyme
- 3/4 teaspoon kosher salt
- 1/8 teaspoon freshly ground black pepper
- Olive oil spray
- 4 (6 oz each) wild salmon fillets
- The salsa:
- 2 tablespoons chopped red onion
- 1 1/2 tablespoons fresh lemon juice
- 1 teaspoon extra virgin olive oil
- 1/4 + 1/8 teaspoon kosher salt
- Freshly ground black pepper
- 4 Persian (mini) cucumbers* diced
- 6 ounces Hass avocado (1 large) diced

Directions:
1. The salmon:
2. In a small bowl, combine the paprika, cayenne, garlic powder, oregano, thyme, salt and black pepper.
3. Spray both sides fo the fish with oil and rub all over. Coat the fish all over with the spices.
4. Preheat the air fryer to 400 degrees F.
5. Working in batches, arrange the salmon fillets skin side down in the air fryer basket.
6. Cook until the fish flakes easily with a fork, 5 to 7 minutes, depending on the thickness of the fish. (For a toaster oven-style air fryer, the temperature and timing remain the same.)
7. Serve topped with the salsa.
8. The salsa:
9. In a medium bowl, combine the red onion, lemon juice, olive oil, salt and pepper to taste.

Let stand for 5 minutes, then add the cucumbers and avocado.
Notes
Recipe printed with permission from The Skinnytaste Air Fryer Cookbook by Gina Homolka
*If Persian cucumbers are not available, use English cucumbers (unpeeled) instead.
Weight Watchers Points: 3 (Freestyle SmartPoints)

Air Fryer Tilapia In 7 Minutes

Servings: 4
Cooking Time: 7 Minutes

Ingredients:
- 4 tilapia fillets 4-6 ounces each
- 1/2 teaspoon salt
- 1/2 teaspoon pepper
- 1/2 teaspoon garlic
- For the lemon butter sauce
- 1/4 cup butter melted
- 3 cloves garlic minced
- 1 tablespoon lemon juice
- 1 tablespoon parsley

Directions:
1. Preheat the air fryer to 200C/400F. Spray the basket with cooking spray.
2. Pat dry the tilapia fillets. Mix the salt, pepper, smoked paprika, and garlic and using your hands, rub the spices over both sides of the fish.
3. Add the tilapia filets in the air fryer basket and spray the top with cooking spray. Air fry for 7-8 minutes, flipping halfway through.
4. While the fish is cooking, make the sauce. In a small bowl, whisk together the melted butter, garlic, lemon juice and parsley.
5. Brush the lemon butter sauce generously over the top of the fish fillets and serve immediately.
Notes
TO STORE: Leftovers can be stored in the refrigerator, covered, for up to three days.

TO FREEZE: Place cooked and cooled tilapia can in an airtight container and stored in the freezer for up to two months.
TO REHEAT: Either microwave the fish for 20-30 seconds or reheat in the air fryer for 2 minutes, until crispy around the edges.

Air Fryer Salmon Patties
Servings: 3
Cooking Time: 10 Minutes

Ingredients:
- 2 large eggs
- 1/4 cup chopped red onion
- 1/4 cup chopped dill
- 2 tablespoons mayo (I like Sir Kensington)
- 2 teaspoon Dijon mustard
- 1 teaspoon Old Bay seasoning
- 12 ounces cooked or canned wild salmon (flaked (from 1 lb salmon or 2 6-ounce cans))
- 1/2 cup panko (plain or gluten-free)
- olive oil spray
- lemon wedges (for serving)

Directions:
1. Place a piece of air fryer parchment in the air fryer basket, or spray with oil.
2. In a medium bowl combine the egg, onion, dill, mayo, mustard and Old Bay spice and mix. Add the salmon and panko and mix to combine.
3. Freeze for 10 minutes, to help the mixture hold together. (If it's too wet you can add another tablespoon panko)
4. Form into 6 patties, tightly and transfer to the air fryer basket.
5. Air fry them at 400F 8 to 10 minutes, flipping halfway until golden brown.
6. Serve over a bed of greens, on potato buns or in bowls with a squeeze of lemon over the top. Makes 6 patties.
Notes
Optional, to take this over the top make a remoulade sauce: combine mayo,lemon juice and capers and serve over salmon patties.

Air Fryer Haddock
Servings: 4
Cooking Time: 10 Minutes

Ingredients:
- 4 6 oz haddock filets, skinless
- 1 tablespoon olive oil
- 1 teaspoon Italian seasoning
- ½ teaspoon garlic powder
- ½ teaspoon paprika
- ½ teaspoon kosher salt
- ¼ teaspoon black pepper
- Lemon wedges, for serving
- SERVE WITH: greens, rice, pasta, fresh steamed vegetables

Directions:
1. Pat the fish dry with paper towels and place them on a cutting board.
2. Drizzle the fillets with oil, then sprinkle them on the fleshy sides liberally with the seasonings.
3. Place the filets in a single layer in the air fryer without overcrowding.
4. Air fry at 350 degrees F for 8-10 mins, until fully cooked and opaque. Serve as desired.
5. FROM FROZEN:
6. Prepare the fish through step 2, then store the filets in a plastic zipper bag and freeze.
7. When ready to cook, Preheat the air fryer to 350 degrees F for about 5 minutes.
8. Place the filets in a single layer in the air fryer, without overcrowding.
9. Air fry at 350 degrees F for 9-12 mins, until fully cooked and opaque. Serve as desired.

NOTES
HOW TO REHEAT HADDOCK:
Preheat the air fryer to 350 degrees.
Place haddock in air fryer and cook for 3-5 minutes or until hot.

Air Fryer Crab Legs

Servings: 1
Cooking Time: 5 Minutes

Ingredients:

- 1 pound snow crab legs
- 1 tbsp olive oil
- 1 tsp Old Bay Seasoning
- Optional
- 2 tbsp butter melted

Directions:

1. Lightly rinse the crab legs, being sure they don't have any leftover sand, dirt, or store packaging on them.
2. Very lightly coat them with olive oil.
3. Season the shells with Old Bay Seasoning, and then place the legs in the air fryer basket.
4. Cook at 370 degrees F for 5-7 minutes, until the shells are hot to the touch.

Air Fryer Smoked Salmon Wontons

Servings: 48
Cooking Time: 5 Minutes

Ingredients:

- 1 (6 ounce) package cream cheese, softened
- 3 ounces cold-smoked salmon, finely chopped
- 1 ½ tablespoons minced capers
- 1 ½ tablespoons finely minced red onion
- 48 wonton wrappers
- water as needed
- cooking spray

Directions:

1. Combine cream cheese, salmon, capers, and red onion in a bowl. Fill a second small bowl with water.
2. Working with 6 wonton wrappers at a time, separate them out onto a clean work surface. Place 1 teaspoon of salmon mixture in the center of each wonton. Do not overfill, as the mixture may ooze out.
3. Dip your finger in the bowl of water, and lightly wet the 4 edges of each wonton wrapper. Gently fold in half diagonally to make a triangle, and seal the edges. Try not to leave excess air in the wonton, which can cause them to burst. Lightly wet the bottom of the triangle, and fold the right side over the middle, then the left side, pressing all edges to seal. Set wontons aside, covered with a damp paper towel, while you finish making the remaining wontons.
4. Preheat the air fryer to 330 degrees F (166 degrees C). Generously mist both sides of wontons with cooking spray.
5. Place as many wontons in the air fryer basket as will fit, without overcrowding.
6. Air-fry for 5 minutes, flipping halfway through. Remove to a cooling rack and let cool while you cook the remaining wontons in batches. Best served slightly warm or at room temperature.

Cook's Notes:

I have assembled these up to 8 hours ahead of time with great results. Place in a single layer, covered with a damp paper towel, inside a sealed container in the fridge until ready to air fry.

You can also freeze them uncooked. If cooking them from frozen, let sit at room temperature for 15 minutes, and add 1 minute to cook time.

Air Fryer Cod

Servings: 4
Cooking Time: 15 Minutes

Ingredients:

- 1 pound cod filets
- salt and pepper
- 1/2 cup flour
- 2 large eggs
- 1/2 teaspoon salt
- 1 cup Panko
- 1/2 cup grated parmesan
- 2 teaspoons old bay seasoning
- 1/2 teaspoon garlic powder
- olive oil spray if needed

Directions:

1. Salt and pepper the cod filets.
2. Create a breading station for the fish. In one bowl add the flour. In the second bowl

whisk together the eggs and salt. In the last bowl add the Panko, parmesan cheese, old bay seasoning, and garlic powder.

3. First dip the cod in the flour.
4. Then in the egg mixture.
5. And lastly in the Panko.
6. Spray the bottom of your basket with olive oil. Place the fish in the basket of your air fryer. Cook at 400 degrees for 10 minutes. Carefully flip the fish. Continue to cook for 3-5 minutes or until the internal temperature reaches 145 degrees.

Healthy Baked Fish Sticks With Lemon Caper Sauce

Servings: 4
Cooking Time: 15 Minutes

Ingredients:

- Lemon Caper Sauce:
- 1/4 cup fat free plain Greek yogurt
- 3 tablespoons light mayonnaise
- 1 tablespoon drained capers
- 1 tablespoon fresh minced chives
- 1 teaspoon fresh lemon juice
- 1/4 teaspoon kosher salt
- 1/8 teaspoon black pepper
- For the Fish Sticks:
- olive oil spray (I use a mister)
- 1 pound Alaskan skinless cod fillet (about 1-inch thick (thawed if frozen))
- 3 large egg whites (or 2 whole eggs)
- 1 tablespoon Dijon mustard
- 1/2 lemon (squeezed)
- 1/8 teaspoon paprika
- 1/4 teaspoon kosher salt
- 1/8 teaspoon black pepper
- For the crumbs:
- 1 cup plain or gluten-free Panko crumbs
- 1 1/2 teaspoons Old Bay seasoning
- 2 teaspoons dried parsley flakes
- 1/2 teaspoon paprika

Directions:

1. OVEN Directions:
2. Combine all the ingredients for the dipping sauce in a small bowl; set aside.

3. Preheat the oven to 450°F and adjust the rack to the center position. Spray a large rimmed baking sheet with oil.
4. Slice the fish crosswise into 2-inch long strips, about 1-inch wide.
5. Combine egg whites, Dijon mustard, lemon juice, paprika, salt and pepper in a medium bowl.
6. In a second bowl combine the Panko crumbs with Old Bay seasoning, dried parsley and remaining paprika.
7. Pat fish dry with paper towels and dip the fish into the egg mixture, then into crumbs and place on the prepared baking sheet.
8. Spray the top of the fish with oil and bake until the crumbs are golden and the fish is cooked through, about 12 minutes, or until the crumbs are golden and the fish is cooked through.
9. AIR FRYER Directions:
10. Preheat the air fryer to 370F.
11. In batches, transfer to the air fryer basket in a single layer and cook until the crumbs are golden and the fish is cooked through, 7 to 8 minutes, turning halfway.

Teriyaki Salmon In The Air Fryer

Servings: 3-4
Cooking Time: 10 Minutes

Ingredients:

- ½ cup low sodium soy sauce
- ¼ cup light brown sugar
- 2 tablespoons apple cider vinegar
- 2 tablespoons rice vinegar
- 2 teaspoon garlic powder
- ½ teaspoon onion powder
- ½ teaspoon ground ginger
- 1 tablespoon water
- 1 tablespoon cornstarch
- 3 salmon filets

Directions:

1. To make homemade teriyaki sauce, combine soy sauce, brown sugar, vinegars, and seasonings in a bowl.

2. In a separate small bowl, whisk cornstarch and water until the cornstarch is completely dissolved.

3. Pour the soy sauce mixture and cornstarch mixture into a saucepan and heat over medium-low for 3 to 4 minutes, till it begins to thicken. Once it has reached your desired thickness, remove from heat and allow to cool for a few minutes.

4. Preheat your air fryer to 390 degrees F. During this time, season your filets with a little salt and pepper and then, using a basting brush, brush about 2 tablespoons of teriyaki sauce on each filet.

5. Once your air fryer is preheated, lay a parchment sheet down or brush your basket with olive oil. Place your salmon filets in the basket and cook for 10 minutes, or until the internal temperature reaches 145 degrees F. The glaze should be a little sticky and crispy, but the inside nice and juicy.

NOTES
HOW TO REHEAT TERIYAKI SALMON IN THE AIR FRYER
Preheat the air fryer to 350 degrees F.
Place the salmon in the basket on top of the parchment mat.
Cook for 3 to 5 minutes until warmed through.

Air Fryer Garlic Butter Shrimp
Servings: 4
Cooking Time: 8 Minutes

Ingredients:
• 1 pound large shrimp thawed, peeled and deveined
• 1 ½ tablespoon olive oil
• 2 teaspoons lemon juice
• ½ teaspoon parsley
• ¼ teaspoon salt
• ¼ teaspoon pepper
• 2 garlic cloves minced

Directions:
1. Preheat air fryer to 370°F.
2. In a medium bowl toss shrimp with oil and seasonings.
3. Place shrimp in a single layer in an air fryer basket.
4. Cook for 3-4 minutes or until shrimp are cooked through.

Notes
Shrimp should be cooked in a single layer in the basket. To cook in batches, cook shrimp as directed. At the end, add all shrimp to the basket for the last minute of cooking to heat through.

POULTRY RECIPES

Air Fryer Asian-glazed Boneless Chicken Thighs

Servings: 4
Cooking Time: 30 Minutes

Ingredients:
- 8 boneless, skinless chicken thighs, fat trimmed (32 oz total)
- 1/4 cup low sodium soy sauce
- 2 1/2 tablespoons balsamic vinegar
- 1 tablespoon honey
- 3 cloves garlic (crushed)
- 1 teaspoon Sriracha hot sauce
- 1 teaspoon fresh grated ginger
- 1 scallion (green only sliced for garnish)

Directions:
1. In a small bowl combine the balsamic, soy sauce, honey, garlic, sriracha and ginger and mix well.
2. Pour half of the marinade (1/4 cup) into a large bowl with the chicken, covering all the meat and marinate at least 2 hours, or as long as overnight.
3. Reserve the remaining sauce for later.
4. Preheat the air fryer to 400F.
5. Remove the chicken from the marinade and transfer to the air fryer basket.
6. Cook in batches 14 minutes, turning halfway until cooked through in the center.
7. Meanwhile, place the remaining sauce in a small pot and cook over medium-low heat until it reduces slightly and thickens, about 1 to 2 minutes.
8. To serve, drizzle the sauce over the chicken and top with scallions.

Air Fryer Turkey Breast

Servings: 4-5

Ingredients:
- 1 7 lb. bone-in turkey breast, thawed
- 3 tbsp. salted butter, softened
- 1 clove garlic
- 1 tbsp. chopped herbs, like sage, rosemary, and/or thyme
- 2 tsp. olive oil
- 1 tsp. kosher salt
- 1 tsp. ground black pepper
- Turkey gravy, for serving

Directions:
1. Remove the turkey breast from the packaging and pat dry with a paper towel. Cut out the backbone of the turkey with sharp kitchen scissors. Trim the breastbones, so that the turkey can sit breast side up in the basket of an air fryer, and the drawer will slide closed completely. Let rest at room temperature for 30 minutes.
2. Meanwhile, place the butter in a small bowl and mash with a fork. Add the garlic and herbs and mash together. Starting at the top of each breast, near the wishbone, work your fingers between the flesh and the skin to create a pocket. Divide the butter evenly between the two sides and rub all over the breast. Press the skin back down into place.
3. Drizzle the breasts all over with the olive oil, then season with the salt and pepper. Place skin side up in the air fryer basket. Cook for 30 minutes until the skin is golden and crispy. Remove from the air fryer and turn the breast over so that it is skin side down. Cook for another 30 to 40 minutes, until the internal temperature reads at least 160°F.
4. Remove to a cutting board. Tent with foil for 5 minutes. Carve the breasts from the bones. Slice into pieces and serve with turkey gravy, if you like.
Notes
This also works with two, bone-in turkey breast halves. Overlap them slightly in the air fryer basket and cook for about 10 minutes less.

Crispy Air Fryer Chicken Wings

Servings: 4
Cooking Time: 22 Minutes

Ingredients:
- 12 wings whole
- 1 Tablespoon olive oil
- 1 teaspoon baking powder
- 1/2 teaspoon salt
- 1 teaspoon ground black pepper
- 1 teaspoon garlic powder
- 1 cup buffalo hot sauce

Directions:
1. Cut the wings into pieces so that you have 24 wings.
2. Preheat the air fryer to 380 degrees Fahrenheit. Prepare the air fryer basket after preheating.
3. Place the wings in a large bowl and add olive oil, garlic powder, and baking powder. Mix well.
4. Add the seasoned wings in a single layer to the air fryer basket.
5. Air Fry WIngs at 380 degrees Fahrenheit for 20 minutes, flipping the wings every 5 minutes. Increase the temperature to 400 degrees Fahrenheit and cook an additional 2 minutes for extra crispy skin. Use a digital meat thermometer to ensure the internal temperature is 165 degrees F.
6. Carefully remove the air fryer wings from the air fryer, cover with your favorite sauce, and serve with your favorite sides.

NOTES

The best way to make crispy wings in the air fryer is to add a little baking powder to the mixture. Baking powder is what helps make crispy skin.

This recipe was made using the 5.8 qt basket style Cosori Air Fryer. If you're using a different air fryer, you may need to adjust your cooking time accordingly. Smaller wings will cook faster than larger wings.

Place leftover beings in an airtight container in the refrigerator for up to 3 days. To reheat the wings, place them in the preheated air fryer and air fryer at 380 degrees Fahrenheit for 2 minutes, or until heated through. It is best to eat wings fresh on the day you cook them.

Air Fryer Grilled Chicken Breast
Servings: 3
Cooking Time: 20 Minutes

Ingredients:
- 3 chicken breasts boneless, skinless
- 1 Tablespoon olive oil
- 1/2 teaspoon ground black pepper
- 1/2 teaspoon onion powder
- 1/2 teaspoon garlic powder
- 1/4 teaspoon rosemary dried
- 1/4 teaspoon sea salt

Directions:
1. Rinse and use a paper towel to pat dry the chicken breasts.
2. Add the chicken breasts to a large resealable bag.
3. Add the olive oil and seasonings to the bag with the chicken breasts. Seal and gently toss the bag to coat the chicken evenly with the olive oil and seasonings.
4. Coat the basket of the air fryer with cooking spray or parchment paper if needed.
5. Place the seasoned chicken breasts into the air fryer basket in a single layer.
6. Air fry the chicken breasts at 390 degrees Fahrenheit for 20 minutes, flipping the chicken breasts halfway through the cooking time.
7. Use a digital meat thermometer and make sure the chicken has reached an internal temperature of 165 degrees Fahrenheit.
8. Carefully remove the chicken from the air fryer and serve.

NOTES

I love to meal prep with air fryer grilled chicken. I slice the cooked chicken breasts and add them to an airtight container with cooked rice and seasoned and cooked broccoli. You can also consider serving this with sweet potatoes, potato salad, wedge salad, or fries.

The sky is the limit when it comes to seasoning chicken. I love to use rosemary, chili powder, Italian seasoning, brown sugar, lemon pepper with a little lemon juice, and even top the finishe product with BBQ sauce. There are many different options, so you can easily change this recipe up often.

Store leftover grilled chicken breast in an airtight container in the refrigerator for up to 3 days.

Air Fryer Rotisserie Chicken

Servings: 6
Cooking Time: 1 Hrs

Ingredients:

- 1 tablespoon sea salt
- 2 teaspoons ground paprika
- 1 teaspoon onion powder
- 1 teaspoon ground thyme
- 1 teaspoon ground white pepper
- ½ teaspoon ground black pepper
- ½ teaspoon cayenne pepper
- ½ teaspoon garlic powder
- 3 tablespoons vegetable oil, divided
- 1 (4 pound) whole fryer chicken, giblets removed

Directions:

1. Preheat an air fryer to 350 degrees F (175 degrees C) according to manufacturer's instructions.
2. Mix salt, paprika, onion powder, thyme, white pepper, black pepper, cayenne, and garlic powder together in a small bowl.
3. Rub 1/2 of the oil over chicken, then half of the spice mixture.
4. Cook in the preheated air fryer for 30 minutes. Carefully remove chicken from the fryer.
5. Flip chicken over. Oil the other side and sprinkle with remaining spice mixture. Return to the air fryer and continue to cook until no longer pink at the bone and the juices run clear, about 30 minutes more. An instant-read thermometer inserted into the thickest part of the thigh, near the bone, should read 165 degrees F (74 degrees C).
6. Remove from the air fryer, cover with a doubled sheet of aluminum foil, and allow to rest in a warm area for 10 minutes before carving.

Air Fryer Frozen Chicken Nuggets

Servings: 2
Cooking Time: 4 Minutes

Ingredients:

- 10 frozen chicken nuggets

Directions:

1. Preheat your air fryer to 400 degrees.
2. Place the frozen chicken nuggets in the air fryer and cook for 4 to 5 minutes until warmed thoroughly.
3. Remove the chicken nuggets from the air fryer and enjoy!

NOTES
HOW TO REHEAT CHICKEN NUGGETS IN THE AIR FRYER:
Preheat your air fryer to 350 degrees.
Cook the chicken nuggets for 2 to 3 minutes until warmed, remove from the air fryer, and enjoy!

Chicken Parmesan In The Air Fryer

Servings: 4
Cooking Time: 10 Minutes

Ingredients:

- 2 8 ounce boneless skinless chicken breasts (sliced lengthwise to make 4 thinner cutlets)
- 6 tbsp seasoned breadcrumbs (whole wheat or gluten-free)
- 2 tbsp grated Parmesan cheese
- 1 tbsp butter (melted (or olive oil))
- 6 tbsp reduced fat mozzarella cheese (I used Polly-o)
- 1/2 cup marinara
- olive oil spray

Directions:

1. Combine breadcrumbs and parmesan cheese in a bowl. Melt the butter in another bowl.
2. Lightly brush the butter onto the chicken, then dip into breadcrumb mixture.
3. When the air fryer is ready, transfer to the air fryer basket, in batches as needed and spray the top with oil.

4. Air fryer 360F° 5 minutes, turn and top each with 2 tbsp sauce and 1 1/2 tbsp of shredded mozzarella cheese.
5. Cook 3 more minutes or until cheese is melted.

Air-fryer Turkey Croquettes
Servings: 6
Cooking Time: 10 Minutes

Ingredients:
- 2 cups mashed potatoes (with added milk and butter)
- 1/2 cup grated Parmesan cheese
- 1/2 cup shredded Swiss cheese
- 1 shallot, finely chopped
- 2 teaspoons minced fresh rosemary or 1/2 teaspoon dried rosemary, crushed
- 1 teaspoon minced fresh sage or 1/4 teaspoon dried sage leaves
- 1/2 teaspoon salt
- 1/4 teaspoon pepper
- 3 cups finely chopped cooked turkey
- 1 large egg
- 2 tablespoons water
- 1-1/4 cups panko bread crumbs
- Butter-flavored cooking spray
- Sour cream, optional

Directions:
1. Preheat air fryer to 350°. In a large bowl, combine mashed potatoes, cheeses, shallot, rosemary, sage, salt and pepper; stir in turkey. Mix lightly but thoroughly. Shape into twelve 1-in.-thick patties.
2. In a shallow bowl, whisk egg and water. Place bread crumbs in another shallow bowl. Dip croquettes in egg mixture, then in bread crumbs, patting to help coating adhere.
3. Working in batches, place croquettes in a single layer on greased tray in air-fryer basket; spritz with cooking spray. Cook until golden brown, 4-5 minutes. Turn; spritz with cooking spray. Cook until golden brown; 4-5 minutes. If desired, serve with sour cream.

Stuffed Chicken Roulade
Servings: 4-6
Cooking Time: 15-20 Minutes

Ingredients:
- 150-200g Sliced smoked pancetta
- (or replace for 2 packets thin cut streaky bacon)
- 4 Large Skinless Chicken breasts
- Stuffing:
- 1 onion, diced
- 1/4 cup pecans, roughly chopped (can be replaced for almonds, macadamias or pistachios)
- 2 Pork Bangers
- 1/2 tsp each salt and pepper
- 1/8 cup dried cranberries, roughly chopped
- 2 Tbsp Fresh Sage, finely chopped
- 1/8 cup breadcrumbs
- For Serving:
- Gravy

Directions:
1. Butterfly the chicken breasts. Slice evenly through the middle of the chicken breasts, leaving the outer edge intact, so that the breast meat can open up like a book. Repeat with the remaining chicken breasts. Season the breasts on both sides with a little salt.
2. Open the butterflied chicken breasts up and place them on a chopping board. Using a rolling pin, or meat tenderiser, gently beat the butterflied breasts to ensure they are of an even thickness (roughly about 1 cm). Set the chicken aside until needed.
3. To make the stuffing fry the onion on a medium heat, in a little oil, until golden and caramelized (about 10 minutes). Squeeze the sausages from their casings into a bowl. To the sausage mince add the onions, salt, pepper, cranberries, sage, nuts and breadcrumbs. Stir the stuffing together until well combined. Set aside until needed.
4. Fill the Instant Pot with water, then set it to the Sous Vide function on 63 Degrees, for 1 hour.
5. Note that we will be making two small roulades to ensure they fit.

6. While the Instant Pot Sous Vide water comes to temperature, make your pancetta covering for the chicken roulade. On a large, clean surface place about 40cm of eco-friendly "plastic" wrap (or clingwrap), with the long side of the clingwrap rectangle facing towards you. On top of the bio wrap arrange the slices of bacon/pancetta. Lay a slice of pancetta about 5cm from the short edge of the plastic wrap. Place another slice of pancetta next to this, just overlapping the first. Continue until you have used half of your pancetta and formed a large rectangle of overlapping pancetta within the bio wrap.

7. In the centre of the pancetta, arrange two of the butterflied chicken breasts, so that they form a smaller rectangle within the pancetta. Next arrange half the stuffing on top of the chicken, moulding it down the centre of the chicken breasts to form a log.

8. Using the plastic wrap to help you, roll the chicken and pancetta into a cylinder shape, with the stuffing running through the centre. Cover the ends of the roulade with the excess pancetta. Roll the roulade to fully cover it in the plastic wrap (there should be no plastic wrap inside the roulade, only on the outside) and tie the plastic wrap tightly at either end, to ensure the roulade maintains its log shape while cooking.

9. Repeat the process again with the remaining ingredients to make your second roulade.

10. Once the Instant Pot Sous Vide setting has come to temperature, place the roulades into a very large resealable plastic bag, or silicone bag. Lower the bag into the water, making sure the open seal stays above the waterline. As the bag is lowered any air in the bag will be displaced. Once the water is close to the seal, seal the bag. This is called the diffusion method. Roll the seal of the bag over a few times and secure it with a peg or clip to ensure no water accidentally enters into the bag while cooking. Sous Vide the chicken for 1 hour.

11. Once the chicken has cooked, you can place it in the fridge to finish on Christmas day (it can be prepared 2 days in advance). Once ready to crisp the chicken heat the Instant Pot

Vortex to 200C on Air Fry mode. Remove the chicken from the bag and remove the plastic wrap. Place the chicken into the air fryer basket and air fry for 15 minutes, turning half way to ensure even browning.

12. If you do not have a Duo Crisp or Vortex, simply pan fry the roulades until the pancetta on the outside is crisp.

13. Allow to rest for 5 minutes, then slice, and serve immediately with gravy and our delicious sides.

Air Fryer Chicken Breast
Servings: 2
Cooking Time: 12 Minutes

Ingredients:
- 2 boneless skinless chicken breasts
- 1 tablespoon canola oil
- 1/2 teaspoon salt
- 1/2 teaspoon dried parsley
- 1/4 teaspoon black pepper
- 1/4 teaspoon onion powder
- 1/4 teaspoon garlic powder
- 1/4 teaspoon paprika

Directions:
1. Preheat air fryer to 400 degrees according to manufacturer's instructions if your air fryer requires preheating (I simply turn mine to 400 degrees for 8-10 minutes while I prepare the chicken)

2. Pat chicken dry and rub with canola oil.

3. In a small bowl, combine salt, parsley, pepper, onion powder, garlic powder and paprika. Sprinkle over both sides of the chicken.

4. Lightly spray the inside of the air fryer basket with non stick spray and place the chicken breasts in the bottom.

5. Place the basket inside the air fryer and set the cook time for 12 minutes (a couple minutes more or less depending on the size of your chicken breasts -- keeping in mind you can always easily add more time but you can't take it away).

6. At the end of the cook time, check the internet temperature of the thickest part of the chicken with a meat thermometer to

ensure it has reached 165 degrees F. If it has not, return it to the air fryer for 2-3 minutes until cooked through.

7. Allow to rest for 5-10 minutes before slicing and serving.

Chicken Schnitzels

Ingredients:
- 4 Chicken Breasts
- ½ Cup Cake Flour
- ½ Tsp Salt
- ¼ Tsp Black Pepper
- ½ Tsp Garlic Powder
- ¼ Tsp Onion Powder
- 1 Large Egg
- ½ Cup Breadcrumbs
- Zest of 2 LemonGold® Lemons

Directions:
1. Place chicken breasts between plastic wrap and pound using a rolling pin until chicken breast has flattened.
2. In a bowl, combine the cake flour, salt, black pepper, garlic powder and onion powder. Mix until combined then set aside. In a second bowl, add the egg and whisk lightly and set aside. In a third bowl, add the breadcrumbs and LemonGold® Lemon zest, mix and set aside.
3. Coat the chicken in the flour mixture, dust of excess flour. Then coat the floured chicken in the egg. Then coat in the breadcrumbs until fully covered. Then set the chicken aside on a plate.
4. Refrigerate the coated chicken for at least 10 minutes. In the meantime, set your Vortex™ Air Fryer to 200 C for 15 minutes, the air fryer will start to preheat.
5. Add in the coated chicken when the Vortex™ Air Fryer indicates to "Add Food". Turn the coated chicken over when the Vortex™ Air Fryer indicates to "Turn Food".
6. Remove from air fryer when the 15 minutes have elapsed, serve with wedges.

Buffalo Chicken Wings
Servings: 3-4

Ingredients:
- 1 cup Frank's RedHot® Original Cayenne Pepper Hot Sauce
- ¼ cup of melted unsalted butter
- 2 teaspoons kosher salt, divided
- 2 teaspoons lemon juice
- 1 pound chicken wings
- 1 teaspoon grapeseed oil
- 1 teaspoon ground black pepper
- Oil spray
- Ranch or blue cheese dressing, for serving
- Carrot sticks, for serving
- Celery sticks, for serving

Directions:
1. Combine the hot sauce, melted butter, 1 teaspoon of salt, and lemon juice to make the buffalo sauce, then set aside.
2. Toss the chicken wings with grapeseed oil, remaining 1 teaspoon salt, and black pepper.
3. Select the Preheat function on the Air Fryer, adjust temperature to 380°F, then press Start/Pause.
4. Spray the preheated inner basket with oil spray, then place the chicken wings into the preheated air fryer.
5. Select the Chicken function, adjust time to 18 minutes, press Shake, then press Start/Pause.
6. Flip the chicken wings halfway through cooking. The Shake Reminder will let you know when.
7. Remove the wings when done and toss with the buffalo sauce.
8. Serve with ranch or blue cheese dressing, carrot sticks, and celery sticks.

Air Fryer Mall Style Bourbon Chicken
Servings: 4
Cooking Time: 20 Minutes

Ingredients:
- 1 pound chicken leg or thigh meat cut into bite-size pieces
- 4 ounces soy sauce

- ½ cup Jim Beam Bourbon Whiskey
- ½ cup brown sugar
- ½ teaspoon garlic powder
- 1 teaspoon powdered ginger
- 2 tablespoons dried minced onion

Directions:
1. Preheat your air fryer to 350°F.
2. Place chicken in an air fryer safe pan.
3. Mix all remaining ingredients together and pour over top of the chicken.
4. Cover and refrigerate for 1-2 hours. Place the pan in the air fryer basket and cook for 20 minutes or until the chicken reaches 165°F internally.

Notes
1 teaspoon of cornstarch can be mixed with 1 teaspoon of water to create a thicker sauce.

Cilantro Lime Chicken In Your Air Fryer

Ingredients:
- 1 lb. boneless & skinless chicken thighs
- 1 cup cilantro
- 4 Tbsp olive oil
- 2 limes, juiced
- 4 tsp garlic, minced
- 1 tsp onion powder
- 1 tsp chili powder
- 1 tsp cumin
- 1/2 tsp paprika
- 1/2 tsp salt
- 1/2 tsp black pepper
- 1/2 tsp cayenne pepper
- 1/2 tsp sugar

Directions:
1. To make the marinade, add the cilantro, olive oil, lime juice, garlic, sugar and all the spices together in a bowl. Combine using an immersion blender. Add in more olive oil as needed if the consistency is too chunky.
2. Add the chicken thighs and marinade in a Ziploc bag and toss everything around until the chicken in fully coated.
3. Preheat your air fryer to 380F for about 5 minutes.

4. Once preheated, add the chicken thighs to the air fryer basket and cook for 18-20 minutes.
5. Once the chicken has finished cooking and cooling, chop it up.
6. Enjoy this in tacos, on top of a burrito bowl or a romaine salad like we did!
7. Salad toppings: Black beans, corn, Monterey jack cheese, pico de gallo, tortilla strips and served with a spicy ranch!

Air Fryer Honey Sesame Chicken
Servings: 4
Cooking Time: 20 Minutes

Ingredients:
- Chicken
- 3/4 cup cornstarch
- 2 tablespoons garlic powder
- 1.5 teaspoons salt
- ½ teaspoon ground ginger
- 2 tablespoons white sesame seeds separated
- 1.5 lbs. boneless skinless chicken breasts
- 2 large eggs
- Sauce
- 1 tablespoon sesame oil separated
- 7 cloves garlic peeled and minced
- ¼ cup soy sauce
- ½ cup water
- ⅓ cup honey
- 1 teaspoon fish sauce
- 1 tablespoon white vinegar
- 1 tablespoon grated white onion
- 1 tablespoon Gochujang red chili paste works too
- 2 green onions minced

Directions:
1. Preheat the air fryer to 400°F.
2. Begin by adding the cornstarch to a large bowl and remove 1.5 teaspoons of the cornstarch from the bowl and set it aside for later.
3. Add the garlic powder, salt, ginger, and 1 tablespoon sesame seeds to the cornstarch mixture and whisk to combine. Set aside.

4. Add the eggs to a separate large bowl and whisk until combined.

5. Cut the chicken breast into 1-1.5-inch chunks and add the chicken to the bowl with the eggs. Toss the chicken with the egg mixture until the chicken is coated.

6. Remove the chicken pieces from the egg mixture and allow any excess egg to drip from the chicken.

7. Add the chicken pieces to the bowl with the cornstarch. Toss the chicken with the cornstarch mixture until the chicken is coated.

8. Spray the air fryer with cooking spray and then add the coated chicken pieces to the air fryer in one single layer (a few overlaps are ok). Drizzle the chicken with 2 teaspoons of sesame oil.

9. Air fry the chicken for 10 minutes at 400°F. When the chicken has cooked for 10 minutes, flip the chicken over and cook it for an additional 6 minutes until golden brown and crispy.

10. Meanwhile, make the garlic sesame sauce. Add the remaining sesame oil to a small saucepan. When the sesame oil is fragrant add the garlic to the pan.

11. Sauté the garlic for 2-3 minutes and then add the soy sauce, water, honey, fish sauce, white vinegar, grated onion, and Gochuchang to the pan. Whisk the ingredients together.

12. Bring the sauce to a boil over medium/high heat and then turn the heat to low and let the sauce simmer for 5 minutes.

13. Remove ¼ cup of the sauce from the pan and add the remaining 1.5 teaspoons of cornstarch to the ¼ cup of sauce. Whisk the 2 ingredients together. It will thicken. Add it back into the saucepan and whisk the sauce together. Allow the sauce to thicken.

14. When the chicken is golden brown and cooked through, add the chicken to a large bowl and add then add the sauce. Gently toss the chicken in the sauce until coated.

15. Garnish the honey sesame chicken with diced green onion and sesame seeds. Serve over rice and enjoy!

Tips & Notes

We used a 7-qt air fryer for this recipe. We suggest using a larger air fryer.

You can use chicken thighs or chicken breasts for this recipe.

If you don't have sriracha or Gochujang you can use garlic chili sauce.

Air Fryer Spinach And Artichoke Stuffed Chicken Breast

Servings: 4

Ingredients:
- 2 oz. cream cheese, room temperature
- 2 oz. goat cheese, room temperature
- 2 cloves garlic, minced
- 1 tsp. finely grated lemon zest
- Kosher salt
- Freshly ground black pepper
- Olive oil cooking spray
- 5 oz. baby spinach
- 1 (15-oz.) can quartered artichoke hearts, well drained and roughly chopped
- 4 (6-oz.) skinless, boneless chicken breasts
- 1 1/2 tsp. chili powder

Directions:
1. In a medium bowl, mix cream cheese, goat cheese, garlic, lemon zest, 1/4 teaspoon salt, and a few grinds of pepper.

2. Lightly coat an air-fryer basket with cooking spray. Place spinach in basket. Cook at 400°, tossing halfway through, until spinach is wilted, about 4 minutes (some leaves may start to dry out; that's okay). Add spinach and artichokes to cheese mixture and stir to combine.

3. Using a sharp knife, make a pocket in each chicken breast, being careful not to cut all the way through. Stuff pockets with spinach mixture. Season outside of chicken with chili powder, 3/4 teaspoon salt, and 1/4 teaspoon pepper. Arrange chicken in air-fryer basket. Cook at 350°, turning halfway through, until an instant-read thermometer inserted into thickest part registers 165°, 16 to 20 minutes.

Air Fryer Chicken Nuggets

Servings: 20-25
Cooking Time: 15 Minutes

Ingredients:
- 1 large chicken breast, cut into chunks
- Salt and pepper, to taste
- ¾ cup Italian breadcrumbs
- ½ teaspoon garlic powder
- ½ teaspoon Italian seasoning
- ½ cup melted butter

Directions:
1. Trim any visible fat off of the edges of your chicken breast. Then cut it into ½-inch strips and then cut those into desired size chunks. (I would cut it in half if it was a smaller strip and into thirds for the larger ones.)
2. Season the chicken with salt and pepper. Allow your chicken to come to room temperature so that when you dip it in the butter, the butter doesn't solidify.
3. Combine the breadcrumbs, garlic powder, and Italian seasoning and set aside.
4. Melt your butter in a microwave-safe bowl. Dip your chicken nuggets in the butter first and then in your breadcrumbs.
5. Preheat the air fryer to 390 degrees F. Place your nuggets in the basket. There is no need to spray your basket since you have used butter to coat your chicken.
6. Cook for 10 to 12 minutes, flipping halfway through and checking on it the last few minutes since timing will vary on different fryers.

NOTES
HOW TO REHEAT CHICKEN NUGGETS IN THE AIR FRYER:
Preheat your air fryer to 350 degrees.
Place the leftover chicken nuggets in the air fryer and cook for 3 to 5 minutes until warm and crispy.

Air Fryer Chicken Fajitas

Servings: 4
Cooking Time: 15 Minutes

Ingredients:
- 6 boneless chicken thighs (or 4 chicken breasts)
- 1 onion, chopped
- 3 sweet peppers, deseeded and sliced
- 2 tbsp fajita spice mix*
- 1 tbsp olive oil
- 1 tbsp chipotle paste **
- Juice of half a lime

Directions:
1. Slice the chicken into strips.
2. Mix the oil, fajita spice, chipotle paste, and lime juice in a bowl.
3. Add the chicken strips to the bowl and leave to marinate for at least ten minutes.
4. While the chicken is marinating, prepare the onions and peppers by chopping them into equal-sized pieces.
5. Preheat the air fryer to 200C/390F.
6. Transfer the chicken to the air fryer basket and air fry for 10 minutes, shaking halfway through.
7. Add the vegetables and stir through. Close the air fryer and cook for a further 5 minutes.
8. Transfer to a bowl and serve in a tortilla wrap with salsa and guacamole.

Notes
*Fajita Spice Mix
If you don't have a fajita spice mix you can make up your own. Try mixing the following together;
2 tsp ground cumin
2 tsp smoked paprika
2 tsp ground oregano
1 tsp chilli powder
**Chipotle Paste
This is optional but it adds an extra kick to the fajitas flavour

Air Fryer Chicken Leg Quarters

Servings: 2
Cooking Time: 30 Minutes

Ingredients:
- 2 chicken leg quarters
- ½ teaspoon paprika
- ½ teaspoon kosher salt
- ¼ teaspoon black pepper
- ¼ teaspoon garlic powder
- ¼ teaspoon onion powder
- ¼ teaspoon dried mustard
- Pinch crushed red pepper flakes (optional)
- 1 tablespoon olive oil

Directions:
1. Preheat the air fryer to 400 degrees F.
2. In a small bowl, combine the paprika, salt, pepper, garlic powder, onion powder, dried mustard, and red pepper flakes. Rub the chicken on all sides with olive oil, then sprinkle on all sides with the seasoning mix.
3. Place chicken in a single layer, skin-side up, in the air fryer basket. Cook for 15 minutes.
4. Flip the chicken and cook an additional 12-15 minutes, until the internal temperature is 165 degrees F.
5. Remove the chicken and allow it to rest for 10 minutes before serving.
NOTES
HOW TO COOK FROZEN CHICKEN LEG QUARTERS IN THE AIR FRYER:
Preheat the air fryer to 400 degrees F. Spray the inner basket with cooking oil spray.
In a small bowl, combine the paprika, salt, pepper, garlic powder, onion powder, dried mustard, and red pepper flakes. Rub the frozen chicken on all sides with olive oil, then sprinkle on all sides with the seasoning mix.
Place chicken in a single layer, skin-side up, in the air fryer basket. Cook for 20 minutes.
Flip the chicken and cook an additional 15-20 minutes, until the internal temperature is 165 degrees F.
Remove the chicken and allow it to rest for 10 minutes before serving.
HOW TO REHEAT CHICKEN QUARTERS IN THE AIR FRYER:
Preheat your air fryer to 350 degrees.
Place the leftover chicken leg quarters in the air fryer in a single layer. Cook for 5-6 minutes, until warmed through.

Nashville Hot Chicken Recipe

Servings: 4
Cooking Time: 30 Minutes

Ingredients:
- 1-2 pounds bone-in chicken thighs and legs
- salt and pepper, to season chicken
- 2 cups buttermilk
- 2 eggs
- 2 cups flour
- 1 Tablespoon garlic powder
- 1 teaspoon onion powder
- 2 teaspoons paprika
- 1 teaspoon salt
- 1 teaspoon pepper
- olive oil spray
- Nashville hot chicken sauce

Directions:
1. Season the chicken with salt and pepper.
2. In a medium-sized bowl add the buttermilk and eggs and whisk until combined.
3. In another medium-sized bowl add the flour, garlic powder, onion powder, paprika, salt, and pepper.
4. Using tongs, dredge the chicken first in the flour mixture, then the buttermilk mixture, and then lastly again in the flour mixture.
5. Place in the bottom of the air fryer basket.
6. Cook at 360 degrees for 15-20 minutes. Open the basket and spray any flour with the cooking spray. Turn the chicken and cook for another 5-10 minutes until 165 degrees and no longer pink.
7. Prepare the Nashville hot chicken sauce according to the instructions in the link while your chicken is cooking.
8. Immediately baste the hot chicken with the sauce and enjoy!

Cherry Glazed Chicken Wings

Ingredients:

- 12 chicken wings
- 3 tbsp canola oil, divided
- 1 garlic clove, minced
- 1 cup ketchup
- ½ cup apple cider vinegar
- ½ cup cherry preserves
- 2 tbsp Louisiana-style hot sauce
- 1 tbsp Worcestershire sauce
- 3 tsp salt, divided
- 1 tsp ground pepper, divided

Directions:

1. In a small saucepan, heat 1 tablespoon of oil over medium heat. Then, add in the garlic and cook and stir for 1 minute. Stir in ketchup, vinegar, cherry preserves, hot sauce, Worcestershire sauce, 1 teaspoon salt and ½ teaspoon pepper. Cook and stir until heated through.
2. Brush the wings with remaining oil and sprinkle with remaining salt and pepper.
3. Place the wings on the standard rack in the air fryer and air fry them at 350°F for 20 minutes, flipping halfway through. Brush with glaze during the last 5 minutes of air frying.
4. Serve with remaining glaze.

Gluten-free Air Fryer Fried Chicken

Servings: 4
Cooking Time: 25 Minutes

Ingredients:

- 1 1/3 cup buttermilk
- 1kg chicken, breast, legs and thighs, bone in, skin on
- 125g gluten-free plain flour
- 65g cornflour
- 1 tsp smoked paprika
- 1 tsp oregano
- 1/2 tsp chilli powder
- 1/2 tsp black pepper
- 2 tsp salt
- 1 tsp spray oil

Directions:

1. Mix the buttermilk and chicken in a bowl, cover with clingfilm and refrigerate for 1 hour.
2. Place the flour, cornflour, smoked paprika, oregano, chilli powder, black pepper and salt in a bowl and whisk to combine. Spread out on a plate. Take the chicken pieces, shake off excess buttermilk and dip into the coating, covering each side.
3. Place the chicken in the air fryer and cook at 200°C for for 22-25 minutes, turning halfway through, until crisp, golden and cooked through.

Air Fryer Whole Chicken

Servings: 5
Cooking Time: 1 Hour

Ingredients:

- 3 to 5 lb chicken innards removed
- 2 tbsp olive oil I use olive oil spray
- 2 tsp kosher salt
- 1 tsp freshly ground black pepper
- 1 tsp garlic powder
- 1 tsp paprika

Directions:

1. Combine the olive oil and spices and make a paste and rub it all over the chicken.
2. Give the air fryer basket a light spray of oil.
3. Place the chicken breast side down and cook at 350F for 30 minutes and then flip and cook breast side up for another 30 minutes.
4. Using a cooking thermometer check the thickest part of the breast to make sure the chicken has reached 165 F. Let rest for 5 to 10 minutes before serving.

Notes

Be sure to remove innards from the cavity before cooking if they didn't come removed. The giblets are great for making broth or gravy, so freeze them for the next time you make those!

Feel free to tie the legs together with twine and tuck the wings underneath if you're worried about it being overcooked. Some believe that tying the legs together will yield a juicier chicken, but I found it didn't make much of a difference.

Cooking time will vary depending on your air fryer and the size of your chicken. I use a Cosori 5.8 QT air fryer. I recommend you check in on your chicken at the 50-minute mark.

Make sure to pat the chicken dry before adding the seasoning paste to help it stick on better. It will also help the chicken crisp up as moisture will cause steam.

Let air fryer roasted chicken rest, so the juices redistribute. If you cut too early, the juices will end up on your cutting board.

If you have extra time and ingredients, stuff the inside of the chicken with fresh herbs such as rosemary and thyme, lemon wedges, and garlic cloves for additional flavor.

Air Fryer Chicken Tenders Recipe

Servings: 4
Cooking Time: 10 Minutes

Ingredients:
- 1 pound chicken tenderloins (or chicken breasts)
- 2 eggs
- 1/2 cup flour
- 1/2 cup panko breadcrumbs
- 1/2 teaspoon onion powder
- 1/2 teaspoon garlic powder
- 1/2 teaspoon Italian seasoning
- 1/4 teaspoon paprika
- salt and pepper, to taste

Directions:
1. Preheat air fryer to 400 degrees.
2. If using chicken breasts, cut them into thin 1-inch strips.
3. Set up the batter by putting the flour and eggs in separate bowls. Whisk the eggs.
4. Fill a third bowl with panko breadcrumbs, onion powder, garlic powder, Italian seasoning, paprika, and salt and pepper to taste. Mix to combine.
5. Dip chicken tenderloins or breasts into flour, then the eggs, and lastly the breadcrumbs.
6. Place coated chicken in the air fryer. Do not overcrowd. Cook for 7-10 minutes, until 165 degrees F at the thickest part.

7. Enjoy immediately or freeze for up to 3 months.

Pickle Ham And Swiss Chicken Roll Ups

Servings: 4
Cooking Time: 25 Minutes

Ingredients:
- 4 1 lb thin boneless chicken cutlets
- 1 1/4 cups pickle juice (enough to cover chicken)
- 4 teaspoons deli mustard
- 2 oz thin sliced reduced sodium deli ham
- 2 oz shredded Swiss cheese
- 1-2 dill pickles (sliced very thin lengthwise, dried on paper towel (I used a mandolin))
- olive oil spray
- For the breading:
- 1 large egg (beaten)
- 1/3 cup seasoned wheat or gluten-free breadcrumbs*
- 1/3 cup seasoned wheat or gluten-free panko*
- cooking spray

Directions:
1. Oven Directions:
2. Place chicken in a shallow bowl and cover with pickle juice (enough to cover completely). Marinate in the refrigerator 8 hours.
3. After 8 hours, drain and dry the chicken completely on paper towels; discard marinade.
4. Preheat oven to 425F. Spray a baking sheet with oil.
5. Spread 1 teaspoon of mustard over each piece of chicken. Layer the ham on top, then the Swiss cheese and pickles along the center and roll.
6. Place egg in a medium bowl. In a shallow bowl, combine the bread crumbs and panko. Dip chicken in the egg wash, then into the breadcrumb mixture and shake off excess.
7. Transfer to the prepared baking sheet and spray the top generously with oil. Bake 25 minutes, until golden outside and cooked through.
8. Air Fryer Directions:

9. Follow steps 1-5.

10. Preheat the air fryer to 400F. Transfer to the air fryer basket in two batches until golden outside and cooked through in the center, about 12 minutes, turning half way.

Notes

*only 1/4 cup of each gets used in breading, so I subtracted what got thrown out from the macros.

Instant Pot & Vortex Roast Chicken

Servings: 4
Cooking Time: 33 Minutes

Ingredients:

- 1 chicken
- 1 Tbsp olive oil
- 2 Tbsp chicken spice
- 1 lemon
- Thyme
- 3 cloves garlic

Directions:

1. Rub the chicken with olive oil, salt, pepper & chicken spice.
2. Set the Instant Pot to Sauté and brown the chicken all around.
3. Remove from the pot.
4. Place the trivet into the Instant Pot.
5. Pour the white wine & stock into the base of the pot.
6. Cut the lemon in half and place in the cavity of the chicken with the garlic and fresh thyme.
7. Close the lid and set to High Pressure for 18 mins.
8. Allow a Natural Pressure Release.
9. Use the Saute function to thicken the sauce to make the gravy.
10. Serve with crushed potatoes or salad.

Salt And Pepper Chicken Nuggets

Servings: 6
Cooking Time: 30 Minutes

Ingredients:

- 3 large skinless chicken breasts cut into 3 - 4cm chunks
- 150 g wholemeal bread blitzed into breadcrumbs
- 2 medium eggs lightly beaten
- 1 tbsp sea salt
- 1 tbsp granulated sweetener
- 1/2 tbsp Chinese five spice powder
- 1 good pinch of dried chilli flakes
- 1 tsp ground white pepper
- 1/2 green pepper finely diced
- 1/2 red pepper finely diced
- 2 spring onions finely chopped
- 1 small red chilli finely chopped (deseeded if wished)
- low calorie cooking spray

Directions:

1. Pre-heat the oven to 180°C. Line a large baking tray with greaseproof paper and spray with low calorie cooking spray.
2. For the salt and pepper mix: Place a small frying pan over a low heat and add the sea salt. Toast the sea salt in the frying pan for 1 - 2 minutes, stirring, until lightly golden in colour.
3. Place the toasted sea salt in a small bowl and stir in the sweetener, Chinese five spice powder, chilli flakes and white pepper.
4. Place the lightly beaten egg on a plate and the breadcrumbs on another plate.
5. Dip the chunks of chicken in the egg, turning to coat all over, then dip in the breadcrumbs and coat well.
6. Place the breaded chicken on the baking tray and sprinkle the salt and pepper mixture over, turning to sprinkle on all sides. Spray with low calorie cooking spray.
7. Place in the oven for 25 - 30 minutes, turning once, until the chicken is golden and thoroughly cooked through. Test that the chicken is cooked by cutting a piece in half, the juices should run clear and there should be no signs of pinkness.

8.   Place a small frying pan on a medium heat and spray with low calorie cooking spray. Add the green pepper, red pepper and chilli and fry for 2-3 minutes, stirring. Add the spring onion and cook for a further 1-2 minutes, stirring well.

9.   Sprinkle the vegetable mixture over the cooked chicken nuggets and serve at once.

Air Fryer Turkey Tenderloin
Servings: 4
Cooking Time: 25 Minutes

Ingredients:
- (2) 1.5 pound turkey tenderloins
- 1 tablespoon Italian seasoning
- salt and pepper to taste
- OPTIONAL
- fresh parsley, to garnish

Directions:
1.   Preheat your air fryer to 350 degrees.
2.   Sprinkle the Italian seasoning, salt, and pepper evenly on the turkey.
3.   Place the turkey tenderloins inside the air fryer and cook for 25 minutes, flipping once. The internal temperature of the tenderloin should be 165 degrees.
4.   Remove the turkey from the air fryer, let rest for 5 minutes before slicing.

NOTES
HOW TO REHEAT TURKEY TENDERLOIN IN THE AIR FRYER:
Preheat your air fryer to 350 degrees.

Place leftover turkey tenderloin in the air fryer and cook for 4 to 5 minutes (2 to 3 minutes for slices).

Cook Frozen Turkey Tenderloin in the Air Fryer at 330 degrees until it reaches 165 degrees at its thickest point. This can take up to 40 to 50 minutes depending on thickness.

Air-fryer Chicken Legs
Servings: 8
Cooking Time: 15 Minutes

Ingredients:
- 2 cups ketchup
- 2/3 cup honey
- 1/3 cup packed brown sugar
- 2 tablespoons finely chopped sweet onion
- 2 tablespoons spicy brown mustard
- 4 garlic cloves, minced
- 1 tablespoon Worcestershire sauce
- 1 tablespoon cider vinegar
- 16 chicken drumsticks

Directions:
1.   In a large saucepan, mix the first 8 ingredients; bring to a boil. Reduce heat; simmer, uncovered, 15-20 minutes to allow flavors to blend, stirring occasionally. Reserve 2 cups sauce for serving.
2.   Preheat air fryer to 375°. In batches, place chicken in a single layer on greased tray in air-fryer basket. Cook until a thermometer reads 170°-175°, 15-20 minutes, turning occasionally and brushing generously with remaining sauce during the last 5 minutes. Serve with reserved sauce.

DESSERTS RECIPES

Air Fryer Cranberry White Chocolate Chip Cookies

Servings: 9
Cooking Time: 7 Minutes

Ingredients:

- 1/2 cup butter salted, softened
- 1/2 cup brown sugar
- 1/2 cup granulated white sugar
- 1 egg
- 1 teaspoon vanilla extract
- 1 1/2 cups all purpose flour
- 1/2 teaspoon baking soda
- 3/4 cup dried cranberries
- 1 cup white chocolate chips

Directions:

1. Add the flour and baking powder to a medium sized mixing bowl and set aside.
2. Cream together the sugar, brown sugar, and butter using a hand held mixer or a stand mixer.
3. Add the egg to the butter mixture and mix well. Stir in the vanilla.
4. Pour the sugar and butter mixture into the flour mixture and mix well. Pour in the cranberries and white chocolate chips until just combined.
5. Prepare the air fryer basket with a nonstick cooking spray or a piece of parchment paper.
6. Scoop the cookies into the air fryer basket using a small 1" cookie scoop. Make sure to keep room in between each cookie.
7. Air fry the cookies at 300 degrees Fahrenheit for 7-8 minutes, or until the cookies are a light golden brown.
NOTES
Note: All air fryers cook differently and you may need to add additional time or cook for less time. This recipe was made using a Cosori 5.8qt Air Fryer.
This recipe makes 3 batches of 9 cookies, or 27 cookies total.
Store leftover cookies in an airtight container at room temperature for up to 5 days.

Chocolate Chip Salted Caramel Cookie Skillets

Servings: 2
Cooking Time: 13 Minutes

Ingredients:

- For the Salted Caramel (optional):*
- 2 tbsp (30g) runny, smooth almond butter
- 2 tbsp (30ml) maple syrup
- 20ml (20g) coconut oil, melted
- Pinch of salt
- For the Cookies:
- 3 tbsp (45g) runny, smooth almond butter
- 1 tbsp coconut oil, melted
- 25g coconut or light brown sugar
- 2 tbsp (30ml) maple syrup
- 1 banana (half mashed till smooth and half chopped small)
- 1 tsp vanilla essence
- 50g ground almonds
- 25g oat flour
- 15g vegan vanilla protein powder
- 1/8 tsp bicarbonate of soda
- 30g dark chocolate chips, plus a few extra
- For the Bananas:
- 1 banana
- ¼ tsp cinnamon
- 1 tsp brown or coconut sugar
- Spray oil
- To serve:
- Dairy-free ice cream and maple syrup

Directions:

1. To prepare: grease and line two 4-inch ramekins with parchment paper. Cover one drawer of the Dual Air Fryer with parchment paper.
2. For the cookies: whisk together the almond butter, coconut oil, sugar, maple syrup, mashed banana and vanilla till smooth. Now add in the ground almonds, oat flour, protein powder, bicarbonate of soda and salt and stir to a sticky cookie dough. Fold in the chopped banana and chocolate chips.

3. To bake the cookies: press two ice cream scoops of cookie dough into each ramekin and make a small indent. Spoon 1 tbsp of the salted caramel in the middle and top with another scoop of cookie dough, making sure to seal in the edges. Smooth over the tops and sprinkle on a few more chocolate chips. Place both ramekins in one half of the air fryer.

4. For the caramelised bananas: slice the banana into coins and toss in a bowl with the cinnamon and sugar. Place in a single layer on top of the parchment paper in the second compartment.

5. Set up the air fryer to bake: for compartment one (the cookies) select manual function and set to 160ºC, setting the timer to 13 minutes. For compartment two (the bananas), select manual function, 160ºC and the timer for 8 minutes. Press the "sync" button and now press start. The cookies will begin cooking straight away and the bananas will cook with 8 minutes of time left, so they finish at the same time.

6. Once baked: remove carefully from the air fryer and allow to cool for 10-20 minutes.

7. To serve: use a palette knife or spatula to ease round the cookie skillets and lift them out onto plates. Top with the caramelised bananas, some ice cream, extra syrup and enjoy while the still warm. Or, allow to cool for longer and enjoy semi-warm or even cold.

8. To keep: once full cool, wrap tightly and chill in the fridge for 2-3 days or in the freezer for up to 1 month. Allow to defrost thoroughly and enjoy cold or warm back up in the air fryer for 5 minutes at 160ºC (the bananas are best eaten fresh).

Notes
*you can also use ready-made caramel, vegan Nutella, almond butter or jam for the middle for the cookie skillets.

Sesame Seed Balls
Servings: 4-5

Ingredients:
- 9 ounces red bean paste
- 2 cups glutinous rice flour
- 2 tablespoons wheat starch
- ½ cup granulated sugar
- A pinch kosher salt
- 1 teaspoon toasted sesame oil
- 1½ tablespoons canola oil, plus more for hands
- ¾ cup warm water
- ½ cup white sesame seeds

Directions:
1. Divide the red bean paste into nine 1-ounce balls. Place in the fridge for 5 minutes.
2. Whisk together rice flour, wheat starch, sugar, and kosher salt in a large bowl until well combined.
3. Whisk in the sesame oil and 1½ tablespoons of canola oil into the flour mixture.
4. Stir in the warm water until a dough forms.
5. Knead the dough until smooth, about 2 minutes.
6. Divide the dough into 9 equal balls and lightly coat with canola oil.
7. Flatten the dough balls into 3-inch circles and place a red bean paste ball in the center.
8. Pinch the edges of the dough together to cover the red bean ball and roll to make a ball.
9. Roll each ball into white sesame seeds.
10. Select the Preheat function on the Air Fryer, adjust to 350°F, and press Start/Pause.
11. Place the sesame seed balls into the preheated air fryer basket lined with parchment paper.
12. Adjust the temperature to 350°F, set time to 25 minutes, and press Start/Pause.
13. Remove from the air fryer and allow it to cool before serving or enjoy hot.

Air Fryer Brie En Croûte

Servings: 4
Cooking Time: 15 Minutes

Ingredients:
- 1 tablespoon unsalted butter
- ½ cup chopped walnuts
- ⅛ teaspoon ground cinnamon
- one (8-ounce) wheel brie cheese
- ¼ cup brown sugar
- 1 sheet frozen puff pastry (from 17.3-ounce package), thawed
- flour, for dusting
- 1 egg, beaten
- crackers, for serving

Directions:
1. In a saucepan over medium heat, melt butter. Add walnuts and sauté until golden brown, about 5 minutes. Add cinnamon and stir until walnuts are well coated. Place walnuts on top of Brie, and sprinkle brown sugar on top of nuts.
2. Unfold puff pastry and lay on a lightly floured surface. Place Brie in center of pastry. Gather up edges of pastry, pressing around Brie and gathering at top. Gently squeeze together excess dough and tie with kitchen twine. Brush beaten egg over top and sides of Brie.
3. Set temperature to 400 degrees and preheat air fryer for 5 minutes. Place Brie in air fryer basket lined with parchment paper and air fry for 10 minutes, or until golden brown. Serve warm with crackers.

Air Fryer Blackberry & Apple Crumble

Servings: 6
Cooking Time: 1 Hour

Ingredients:
- 1kg Bramley apples (about 4-6), peeled, cored and cut into 2cm chunks
- 200g blackberries
- 50g caster sugar
- ½ lemon, zest and juice
- vanilla ice cream, custard or double cream, to server
- Crumble
- 150g plain flour
- 100g chilled unsalted butter, cubed
- 75g caster sugar
- 50g porridge oats
- ½ tsp ground cinnamon

Directions:
1. First, make the crumble. In a medium bowl, use your fingertips to gently rub all the ingredients together until evenly combined (you'll have mostly small chunks with a few larger ones) and put in the fridge. .
2. Put the apple chunks and blackberries in the base of the air-fryer basket (without the rack). Toss through the sugar, lemon zest and juice, and 2 tbsp water with a pinch of salt; spread out evenly.
3. Scrunch the chilled crumble mix together then loosely scatter over the fruit to cover (this will help give you different-sized crumble pieces). Air-fry at 180°C for 1 hour, covering with foil after 25 minutes if needed, until golden and well cooked and the fruit is very tender and piping hot. Serve immediately with ice cream, custard or cream.

NOTES
Customer safety tips
Follow manufacturer's instructions and advice for specific foods
Pre-heat the air fryer to the correct temperature
If cooking different foods together, be aware that they may require different times and temperatures
Spread food evenly – do not overcrowd pan/chamber
Turn food midway through cooking
Check food is piping/steaming hot and cooked all the way through
Aim for golden colouring – do not overcook

Air Fryer Cookies
Servings: 18
Cooking Time: 8 Minutes

Ingredients:
- 1/2 cup unsalted butter {1 stick}
- 1/4 cup white sugar
- 1/2 cup brown sugar
- 1 egg {room temperature if possible}
- 1 tsp vanilla extract
- 1/2 tsp almond extract
- 1 tsp baking soda
- 1/2 tsp sea salt
- 1 1/2 cups all-purpose flour
- 2 cups semi-sweet chocolate chips

Directions:
1. In a microwave-safe bowl, microwave the butter for 20 seconds. You want some of it melted, but the vast majority of the butter should be soft but solid.
2. 1/2 cup unsalted butter
3. Add the brown and white sugar and mix.
4. 1/4 cup white sugar,1/2 cup brown sugar
5. Add the egg, vanilla, and almond extract. Mix.
6. 1 egg,1 tsp vanilla extract,1/2 tsp almond extract
7. Add the dry ingredients, and mix until everything is about 50% combined. Add the chocolate chips and mix. Optional: Refrigerate dough for an hour at this point.
8. 1 tsp baking soda,1/2 tsp sea salt,1 1/2 cups all-purpose flour,2 cups semi-sweet chocolate chips
9. Make dough balls about 2-inches wide.
10. Place a piece of parchment in the air fryer basket. Arrange cookies on parchment. Bake at 300 degrees F for 8 minutes.
11. Allow the cookies to rest on the pan for 4-5 minutes before removing.
Notes
Spoon flour into the measuring cup.
Egg should be at room temperature for optimal results.
You do not need to preheat your air fryer.
Add 1 minute to cooking time for frozen dough.

Air Fryer Frozen Waffle Cut Fries
Servings: 4
Cooking Time: 12 Minutes

Ingredients:
- 1 lb. (454 g) Frozen waffle cut fries
- salt , to taste
- black pepper , to taste

Directions:
1. Place the frozen waffle fries in the air fryer basket and spread out evenly. No oil spray is needed. We discuss this in the recipe write up on the website.
2. Air Fry at 400°F/205°C for 10 minutes. Shake and gently stir about halfway through cooking. If cooking larger batches, or if your waffle fries don't cook evenly, try turning them multiple times on following batches.
3. If needed air fry at 400°F/205°C for an additional 1-3 minutes or until crisped to your liking. Season with salt & pepper, if desired.
NOTES
No Oil Necessary. Cook Frozen - Do not thaw first.
Shake or turn if needed. Don't overcrowd the air fryer basket.
Recipe timing is based on a non-preheated air fryer. If cooking in multiple batches of fries back to back, the following batches may cook a little quicker.
Recipes were tested in 3.7 to 6 qt. air fryers. If using a larger air fryer, the waffle fries might cook quicker so adjust cooking time.
Remember to set a timer to shake/flip/toss as directed in recipe.

Air Fryer Cake
Servings: 6-8
Cooking Time: 25 Minutes

Ingredients:
- 1 cup granulated sugar
- ¾ cup plus 2 tablespoons all-purpose flour
- ½ cup unsweetened cocoa powder
- 1 teaspoon baking powder
- ½ teaspoon baking soda
- ½ teaspoon kosher salt

- 1 large egg
- ½ cup buttermilk
- ¼ cup vegetable oil
- 1 teaspoons vanilla extract
- ½ cup boiling water

Directions:

1. Preheat your air fryer to 350 degrees F.
2. Spray the inside of a 7-inch air fryer-safe cake pan with baking spray, then line with a 9-inch round piece of parchment paper, making sure it drapes up the sides a bit. Spray with more cooking spray and set aside.
3. In a large bowl, whisk together the sugar, flour, cocoa powder, baking powder, baking soda, and salt. Add the egg, buttermilk, vegetable oil, and vanilla extract. Mix for 2 minutes, until well combined. Stir in the boiling water to create a thin batter.
4. Pour the batter into the prepared pan and place it in the air fryer basket.
5. Cook for 25 minutes, or until the cake is baked through, leaving no crumbs on an inserted toothpick. Cool in the pan for 10 minutes, then remove to a wire rack to cool completely.
6. Decorate with frosting and sprinkles, if desired.

Air Fryer Cherry Pie Taquitos

Servings: 4
Cooking Time: 6 Minutes

Ingredients:

- 1 can cherry pie filling 21-ounce
- 12 medium soft flour tortillas
- 4 tablespoons butter melted
- 2 teaspoons powdered sugar optional

Directions:

1. Lay tortillas flat, and then spoon about 2 tablespoons of filling across the center of the tortilla. Roll tightly.
2. Brush the rolled taquito with melted butter.
3. Place in the air fryer basket, seam side down, without stacking or overlapping.
4. Air fry at 350 degrees F for 9-11 minutes, until the taquito is golden and crispy.

5. One can makes about 6 taquitos. Don't overfill-you should be able to roll it tightly.
6. Sprinkle with powdered sugar and serve.
NOTES
Add toppings - Let's be real and talk about the fact that toppings can make everything better. Adding a bit of cinnamon sugar mixture on top is the perfect sweet addition. You can also drizzle caramel sauce, sprinkle brown sugar, or top with some fresh fruit.
Change the fruit filling - I'm a fan of fruit pies, and this recipe makes it easy to change things up. If you want to give the cherry filling a break, try and make it again using blueberry pie filling, apple pie filling, or even fresh apples in this decadent dessert.

Cherry Cheesecake Egg Rolls

Servings: 8
Cooking Time: 15 Minutes

Ingredients:

- 4 ounces cream cheese softened
- 1 teaspoon lemon rind
- 3 tablespoons sugar
- ½ teaspoon lemon juice
- 1 can cherry pie filling
- 8 egg roll wrappers mine were 6"x6"
- oil for frying

Directions:

1. In a bowl, combine softened cream cheese, lemon rind, sugar and lemon juice until well mixed. Spoon into a Ziploc baggie. Cut off the corner of the bag.
2. Lay out the egg roll wrappers with one of the corners pointing towards you and pipe a line of cheese mixture across the wrapper. Add approx. 10 cherries on top of the cheese mixture.
3. Using water, wet the edges of the wrapper and roll up tightly ensuring the edges are sealed well. Let the rolls sit about 3-4 minutes allowing the water to dry and create a good seal.
4. Preheat oil to about 350°F and fry in small batches until brown and crispy (about 5-6 minutes). Serve warm.
Notes

Generously brush with vegetable oil before cooking.

Cook at 390°F for 8 minutes, flipping halfway through cooking.

Leftovers can be stored in an airtight container in the fridge for up to 3 days. Reheat in the air fryer or under the broiler.

Freeze cooled egg rolls on a baking sheet, then store in a ziptop bag for up to 4 weeks. Reheat in the air fryer or under the broiler.

Air Fryer Pumpkin Spice Muffins

Servings: 12
Cooking Time: 12 Minutes

Ingredients:
- 1 cup flour
- 1 teaspoon baking powder
- ⅓ cup sugar
- 1 teaspoon vanilla extract
- 1 tablespoon pumpkin spice
- ⅓ cup pumpkin puree
- 1 egg
- ¼ cup milk
- 3 tablespoon oil

Directions:
1. Preheat air fryer to 360°F on bake.
2. Place muffin liners into a muffin tray. Set aside.
3. In a bowl combine flour, baking powder and sugar. In another bowl combine vanilla extract, pumpkin spice, pumpkin puree, egg, milk and oil.
4. Slowly mix wet ingredients into dry ingredients, whipping until everything is well incorporated and there are no lumps.
5. Divide the batter between the muffin liners, place it in the air fryer basket.
6. Bake for 10-12 minutes or until a toothpick comes out clean from the centre of the muffin.
Notes
Store in an airtight container for 2-3 days on the counter or freeze in a zippered bag for up to 3 months.

Fried Banana Smores

Ingredients:
- 4 bananas
- 4 tbsp mini semi-sweet chocolate chips
- 4 tbsp mini peanut butter chips
- 4 tbsp mini marshmallows
- 4 tbsp graham cracker cereal

Directions:
1. Slice into the unpeeled banana lengthwise along the inside of the curve. Open the banana slightly to form a pocket.
2. Fill each pocket with chocolate chips, peanut butter chips and marshmallows. Poke the graham cracker cereal into the filling.
3. Place the bananas in the air fryer basket with perforated parchment paper (optional), resting them on each other to keep them upright.
4. Air fry at 400°F for 6 minutes, or until the bananas are soft to the touch, the peel has blackened, and the chocolate and marshmallows have melted and toasted. Allow your bananas to cool for a few minutes and enjoy!

Zucchini Cakes

Servings: 10

Ingredients:
- 2 large zucchini
- 2 large eggs
- 1/2 c. bread crumbs
- 1/2 c. ricotta
- 1/4 c. freshly grated Parmesan
- 1/2 tsp. garlic powder
- 1/4 tsp. crushed red pepper flakes
- Kosher salt
- Freshly ground black pepper
- Vegetable oil, for cooking

Directions:
1. FOR THE STOVETOP:
2. Grate zucchini on box grater, then use a clean kitchen towel to ring out as much excess water as possible. Work in batches as necessary.

3. In a large bowl, combine zucchini, eggs, bread crumbs, ricotta, Parmesan, garlic powder, and red pepper flakes. Season with salt and pepper.

4. In a large skillet over medium heat, add enough oil to come ½" up the sides. Scoop about a ¼ cup of zucchini mixture and add to skillet. Carefully flatten with a spatula and cook until golden, about 2 to 3 minutes per side. Place on a paper towel–lined plate, sprinkle with salt and serve.

5. FOR THE AIR FRYER:

6. Grate zucchini on box grater, then use a clean kitchen towel to ring out as much excess water as possible. Work in batches as necessary.

7. In a large bowl, combine zucchini, eggs, bread crumbs, ricotta, Parmesan, garlic powder, and red pepper flakes. Season with salt and pepper.

8. Using your hands, scoop up about 1/4 cup of zucchini mixture and flatten it into a patty. Place in air-fryer basket. Repeat to fill basket, spacing patties at least 1" apart.

9. Brush patties with oil, if using. Cook at 400° until golden, 15 minutes, flipping halfway through. Repeat with remaining ingredients.

10. Sprinkle with more salt before serving.

Air Fryer Strawberry French Toast Roll-ups

Cooking Time: 10 Minutes

Ingredients:
- 10 pieces bread
- 2 eggs
- 1 tbsp milk
- 1/2 cup strawberry preserves
- 1/2 tsp cinnamon
- 3 tbsp granulated white sugar
- 3-4 strawberries cut small to garnish

Directions:
1. Prepare the Air Fryer basket. I like to use a parchment paper with this recipe.
2. Mix together the cinnamon and sugar and set aside.

3. Whisk the eggs together and set them aside.

4. Cut the edges off of the bread. Take a glass or rolling pin and roll over the pieces of bread to flatten them.

5. Place a layer of strawberry preserves onto one end of the piece of bread and then roll up the bread. Continue with each piece of bread

6. Dip the rolled bread into the egg mixture.

7. Place the french toast roll ups into the prepared air fryer basket in a single layer, careful to leave room in between each one.

8. Air Fryer at 350 degrees Fahrenheit for 8-9 minutes, turning the roll-ups halfway through cooking.

9. Carefully remove the french toast roll ups from the air fryer and dip into the cinnamon and sugar mixture and top with fresh cut strawberries before serving.

NOTES

You want to lay the bread out to become stale. I find laying the bread out for an hour before cooking will do the trick, but you can even lay the bread out the night before if desired.

Here are a few changes you can make to this french toast recipe:

You can add 1 Tbsp of heavy cream in place of the milk to the egg mixture.

Dip the french toast roll-ups into the egg mixture and then directly into the cinnamon and sugar mixture before cooking for a more caramelized flavor.

Top the fully cooked dish with confectioners' sugar.

Air Fryer Caramelized Bananas Bananas

Servings: 12
Cooking Time: 6 Minutes

Ingredients:
- 2 bananas
- ¼ of a lemon, juiced
- 1 tablespoon coconut sugar
- optonal toppings: cinnamon, nuts, coconut cream, yogurt, granola... etc.

Directions:

1. Wash your bananas with the peel on, then slice them straight down the middle, length wise
2. Squeeze lemon juice over top of each banana
3. If using cinnamon mix with in with the coconut sugar, then sprinkle over top of the bananas until coated
4. Place into parchment lined air fryer for 6-8 minutes at 400F
5. Once taken out of the airfryer, eat as is or top with your favourite toppings and enjoy!

Easy 3-ingredient Air Fryer Bagels

Servings: 4
Cooking Time: 12 Minutes

Ingredients:
- FOR THE BAGELS:
- 1 cup (240 ML) plain, thick non-fat greek yogurt
- 1 cup (125 g) self rising flour , *if using all purpose flour, see note above.

- OPTIONAL TOP Ingredients:
- 1 (1) large egg , beaten * read note
- (optional) bagel toppings: Sesame seeds, pre-mixed bagel seasonings, poppy seeds, cheddar cheese, sliced jalapeños.
- EQUIPMENT
- Air Fryer

Directions:
1. Drain yogurt of excess liquid before you measure it out. Combine yogurt and flour until all the flour is mixed into the yogurt and dough forms a ball.
2. Sprinkle a light layer of flour on a cutting board. Knead the dough for about 30 seconds. Cut the dough into 4 equal parts. If dough is sticky lightly flour your hands. Don't add too much flour or the dough will become tough.
3. Roll each dough piece into a ball. Lightly flour your finger, then poke it in the center of the dough ball to create a hole. Look at the step by step photos on the website. These photos are helpful.

4. Gently stretch out the center hole to be about 1" wide opening and shape the the dough into a bagel shape.
5. Brush egg over the bagels. If adding seeds, sprinkle seeds or seasonings on top of bagels.
6. Spray air fryer basket or tray with oil to make sure bagel doesn't stick while cooking (you can also use air fryer parchment sheets).
7. Gently place bagels in your air fryer, leaving enough room between the bagels for the to expand. Don't crowd the basket or rack. Cook the bagels in batches.
8. Air Fry at 330°F for about 10-14 minutes, or until bagels are golden and cooked in the center.
9. Serve with cream cheese or make an awesome bagel sandwich out of it.
NOTES
We prefer the Stonyfield non-fat greek yogurt and Fage Total 0% Greek Yogurt. If you want to use whole milk yogurt, the Chobani whole milk greek yogurt is also thick and easy to work with.
These bagels have a wonderful yogurt taste so don't be surprise if there's a slight sour taste to the bagels.
The egg wash is optional and for folks who can't eat eggs feel free to leave it out. But if you can eat eggs, they add a great chewy and crisp, brown texture to the bagels. They also help the seeds to stick to the top of the bagels.
Read the recipe write up for all the different bagel topping ideas.

Air Fryer Banana Blueberry Muffins

Servings: 14

Ingredients:
- 3/4 c. all-purpose flour
- 3/4 c. whole wheat flour
- 1 tsp. baking powder
- 1 tsp. baking soda
- 1/4 tsp. kosher salt
- 3 large overripe bananas
- 1 large egg
- 3/4 c. packed light brown sugar
- 1/3 c. vegetable oil

- 1/4 c. sour cream
- 1 tsp. pure vanilla extract
- 1 c. fresh or frozen blueberries (unthawed if frozen)
- 14 banana chips

Directions:
1. In a medium bowl, whisk all-purpose flour, whole wheat flour, baking powder, baking soda, and salt.
2. In a large bowl, mash bananas with a fork. Add egg, brown sugar, oil, sour cream, and vanilla and whisk to combine.
3. Add dry ingredients to wet ingredients and stir until just combined. Fold in blueberries.
4. Scoop batter with a 2.5-oz. scoop or 1/3-cup measuring cup into 14 silicone muffin liners. Top with 1 banana chip.
5. Working in batches, in an air-fryer basket, arrange filled muffin liners, spacing about 1/2" apart. Cook at 350° for 7 minutes. Tent tops with foil to prevent overbrowning, then continue to cook until puffed and a tester inserted into center comes out clean, 5 to 7 minutes more.
6. Transfer muffins to a wire rack and let cool.

Air-fryer Cheesecake
Servings: 10
Cooking Time: 35 Minutes

Ingredients:
- 125g plain sweet biscuits, broken into pieces
- 60g unsalted butter, melted
- 750g cream cheese, softened
- 1 tsp vanilla extract
- 2/3 cup caster sugar
- 3 free range eggs
- 1/4 cup sour cream
- 125g raspberries
- 2 tbs maple syrup

Directions:
1. Grease a 19cm-round springform pan. Line side with baking paper, ensuring paper doesn't extend over the edge of pan.
2. Place biscuits in a food processor. Process until fine crumbs form. Add butter. Process until just combined. Press biscuit mixture over base of prepared pan. Refrigerate for 30 minutes.
3. Meanwhile, wash and dry food processor. Process cream cheese, vanilla and sugar until smooth. Add egg and sour cream. Process until just combined. Pour mixture into prepared pan.
4. Cover pan with foil. Place pan into the basket of a 12-litre air fryer. Set temperature to 180°C and cook cheesecake for 30 minutes. Uncover and cook for a further 5 minutes or until top is golden. Turn air fryer off and allow cheesecake to stand in air fryer for 30 minutes to cool. Remove from air fryer and refrigerate overnight. Serve topped with raspberry and drizzled with maple syrup.

Baked Apple Chips
Servings: 4
Cooking Time: 2 Hours 30 Minutes

Ingredients:
- 3 gala apples

Directions:
1. Preheat oven to 200 F. Line a large 1/2 pan baking sheet with a slipat mat or parchment paper.
2. From the bottom of the apples, slice into very thin slices, about 1/8 thick. Use a mandoline or a knife to slice. Place them down in a single even layer on the lined baking pan. You don't need to leave any space between them as they will shrink. For extra flavour, you can sprinkle some cinnamon on top.
3. Bake for 1 hour, then flip the apple slices over and bake for another 1.5 hours. If the apples aren't crispy enough, continue to bake, checking on them every 10-15 minutes.
NOTES
Equipment used: mandoline slicer, half sheet baking pan, and silpat liner.
How to cook in the air fryer: Preheat the air fryer to 200 F, about 3 minutes. Place apple slices in a single layer in the air fryer basket and air fry for 20 minutes until crispy.

How to slice apples super thin: I use a mandoline slicer on the thinest setting to slice the apples super thin and evenly. You can also use a knife. You want to slice the apples about 1/8-inch thick

How to make apple cinnamon chips: You can switch things up and add a little cinnamon on top for a different flavour. You can sprinkle about a teaspoon on cinnamon on top before popping the apples into the oven.

How to store: Store homemade apple chips in an airtight container for up to 1 week at room temperature.

Air Fryer Oreo Cheesecake

Servings: 8
Cooking Time: 18 Minutes

Ingredients:
• 1 Package Oreos 30 Cookies for the crust, and 10 cookies broken into large pieces, for the filling and topping.
• 1/2 cup unsalted butter melted One stick
• 24 ounces cream cheese softened
• 14 ounces sweetened condensed milk
• 2 large eggs
• 1 teaspoon vanilla

Directions:
1. Prepare the pan by lining the bottom with a circle of parchment paper, and then lightly butter the insides of the pan walls so the cheesecake will easily be removed after cooking.
2. Crush the Oreo Cookies in the food processor, until they are fine crumbs. (Or you can place them in a large bag and crush them with a rolling pin.
3. Pour the crushed cookies into a large bowl, and stir in the melted butter to mix with the crumbs.
4. Pour the mixture into the prepared springform pan, pressing the crust firmly to the bottom of the pan. Set the pan aside while making the filling.
5. In a large bowl, or using a stand mixer, beat the cream cheese until it is smooth.

6. Add in the eggs, sweetened condensed milk, and vanilla. Continue beating on medium speed until it is smooth and creamy.
7. Pour the filling over the crust and spread it evenly with a spatula or spoon. Push the large broken pieces of cookie into the filling until they are completely submerged. You can also pour half of the filling, then add broken pieces, then top with the remaining filling. Sprinkle any leftover crumbs on top of the cheesecake.
8. Place the springform pan in the basket of the air fryer. Cook at 300 degrees Fahrenheit for 15 minutes. If it still has a slight jiggle, return to air fryer and add an additional three minutes cook time.
9. Remove from the basket and allow the cheesecake to chill to set, for about 6-8 hours, or overnight
NOTES
Cooking times will vary, depending on your air fryer. Begin checking your cheesecake at 15 minutes, and if it still has a jiggle to it, add an additional three minutes of additional cooking time. Total cooking time should be 15-18 minutes in an 8 inch pan.
The cheesecake will be a little soft when it is done cooking. It will firm up once it cools.
Be sure to line the pan, and then butter the sides of the wall of the pan. The first time I made an air fryer cheesecake, I didn't butter the sides and the cheesecake stuck a little bit. If you forget, just slide a knife in between the cheesecake and the pan and go around until it is loosened.

Cheat's Air-fryer Churros

Servings: 8
Cooking Time: 5 Minutes

Ingredients:
• 8 Woolworths mini cinnamon doughnuts
• 100 dark chocolate, melted

Directions:
1. Preheat air fryer to 200°C. Place doughnuts in the air-fryer basket and cook for 4 minutes or until golden and crisp. Serve with melted chocolate.

Vortex Air Fryer Sweet Potato Orange Cups

Servings: 16
Cooking Time: 30 Minutes

Ingredients:
- 3 large sweet potatoes Can also use 2 cans of Yams
- ¼ cup brown sugar
- 2 tablespoons light cream
- 2 tablespoons butter
- ¾ cup miniature marshmallows
- 8 medium oranges

Directions:
1. Place sweet potatoes in a large saucepan and bring to a boil. Reduce heat and cover and cook just until tender, 25-30 minutes. Drain.
2. Preheat the Air Fryer to 350°F.
3. Mash sweet potatoes, sugar, cream, and butter in a large bowl until smooth.
4. Slice ¼ inch off each end of the orange and cut the oranges in half.
5. Remove the pulp from the oranges but leave the shells intact.
6. Place orange shells in the air fryer basket and fill with the sweet potato mixture. Top with the marshmallows.
7. Cook for 4-5 minutes or until marshmallows are golden brown.

Air Fryer Copycat Red Lobster Cheddar Bay Biscuits

Servings: 6
Cooking Time: 5 Minutes

Ingredients:
- 2 cups all purpose flour
- 4 teaspoon baking powder
- 1/2 teaspoon salt
- 1/2 teaspoon cream of tartar
- 2 teaspoon sugar
- 1/2 teaspoon garlic powder
- 1/2 cup unsalted butter
- 1 cup shredded cheddar cheese
- 2/3 cup milk
- Garlic Topping
- 2 tablespoon unsalted butter
- 1 large garlic clove, pressed
- 1/4 teaspoon garlic powder
- 1 teaspoon dried parsley flakes

Directions:
1. In a large bowl, stir together the flour, baking powder, salt, cream of tartar, sugar and garlic powder.
2. Add in the softened butter and stir with a fork until it is flaky.
3. Stir in the shredded cheese and the milk, until it forms into a dough.
4. Scoop or spoon a small amount of the dough into the basket, lined with parchment paper with holes in it, or a lightly sprayed with olive oil.
5. Cook at 400 degrees Fahrenheit if using a smaller basket for 5 minutes. If cooking more biscuits at a time in a larger basket, cook for 8 min.
6. Garlic Topping
7. Melt together the butter with garlic, garlic powder and parsley, and brush on the tops of the cooked biscuits. Serve warm.

Banana Split

Ingredients:
- 1 banana
- 1/4 tsp sugar
- 1/4 tsp cinnamon
- Toppings of choice :
- Yoghurt
- Bran flakes with barley
- Nuts

Directions:
1. Preheat airfryer to 180°C. Cut the banana lengthwise and cover inside of the banana with cinnamon and sugar. Air fry for 8 minutes until sugar caramelizes and banana is soft. Top with your favourite breakfast toppings and enjoy while the banana is still warm.
2. For a dessert option layer yoghurt, coconut flakes and some chocolate chips......

Air Fryer Snickerdoodle Cookies

Servings: 30
Cooking Time: 8 Minutes

Ingredients:

- 3/4 cup unsalted butter
- 1 cup granulated sugar
- 1/3 cup brown sugar
- 2 large eggs
- 1 teaspoon vanilla extract
- 2 cups all purpose flour
- 1 teaspoon ground cinnamon
- 1/2 teaspoon nutmeg
- 1/2 teaspoon salt
- 1/2 teaspoon baking soda
- Cinnamon Sugar Coating
- 1/2 cup sugar
- 2 tablespoons cinnamon

Directions:

1. To make these cookies from scratch, combine the butter, sugar, and brown sugar in a large mixing bowl.
2. Using a stand or had mixer, beat the butter with sugars until smooth and creamy.
3. Add eggs, vanilla, salt, baking soda, cinnamon, nutmeg, and half of the flour. Mix until the dry ingredients combine with the butter mixture.
4. Add the remaining half of the flour mixture to the wet ingredients and mix on medium speed until the cookie dough is thick and creamy. Scrape any remaining dough from the sides of the bowl to ensure even mixing.
5. In a small shallow bowl, combine the sugar and cinnamon for the coating, and mix.
6. Use a small cookie scoop or tablespoon to shape the equal-sized dough balls. Then gently roll the ball of dough in the bowl with cinnamon sugar mixture.
7. Place the dough in Air Fryer basket on parchment paper. Leave about an inch between dough balls. Air Fry at 300 degrees F for 8-10 minutes until edges golden brown. Allow cookies to sit in air fryer basket for an additional 1 to 2 minutes cooking time before transferring to a wire rack.

NOTES

Be careful not to overbake the cookies, or they will be tough. You want the cookies to look slightly undercooked when you pull them out to ensure they remain chewy.

To make these cookies a special dessert, place one or two in a small bowl, and top with vanilla ice cream.

This recipe makes 30-36 cookies.

SALADS & SIDE DISHES RECIPES

Air-fryer Nuggets Lunch Boxes
Servings: 4
Cooking Time: 20 Minutes

Ingredients:
- 4 slices Woolworths wholemeal bread, toasted
- 2 small carrots, grated
- 150g chicken mince
- 1 free range egg
- 5ml olive oil cooking spray
- 1 large Lebanese cucumber, cut into batons
- 80g light tasty cheese, diced
- 4 kiwi fruit, cut into wedges

Directions:
1. Preheat air fryer on 200°C for 4 minutes. Meanwhile, place bread into a food processor. Process for 15 seconds until fine crumbs form. Transfer to a bowl and set aside.
2. Place carrot in food processor. Process for 15 seconds or until finely chopped. Add chicken, egg and half of the breadcrumbs. Season with pepper. Pulse for 10 seconds or until just combined. Using damp hands, form tablespoonfuls of the chicken mixture into nuggets, then coat in remaining breadcrumbs.
3. Spray half the nuggets with oil and place, in a single layer, in air-fryer basket. Cook for 8 minutes, turning halfway, or until golden and cooked through. Repeat with remaining nuggets and oil. Serve nuggets in lunch boxes with cucumber, cheese and kiwi fruit.

Air Fryer Chimichangas
Servings: 4
Cooking Time: 10 Minutes

Ingredients:
- 1 tbsp unsalted butter melted
- ¼ cup onion diced
- 1 cup shredded chicken cooked
- 4 ounces cream cheese softened
- 3 tsp taco seasoning
- 1 cup mexican cheese blend shredded

- ¼ tsp ground black pepper
- 4 flour tortillas 8-inch

Directions:
1. Preheat the air fryer to 400 degrees Fahrenheit.
2. In a small bowl, combine the onion, chicken, cream cheese, taco seasoning, Mexican blend cheese, and ground black pepper. Mix well.
3. Brush one side of each tortilla with butter. Place the butter side down. Scoop 3 Tablespoons of chicken mixture into the center of the tortilla. Fold the tortilla in and roll it closed, then secure it with a toothpick.
4. Repeat for the remainder of the tortillas.
5. Place the chimichangas in a single layer in the basket of the air fryer. Air fry at 400 degrees Fahrenheit for 4 minutes, flip, and air fry for an additional 2 minutes.
6. Remove the toothpicks and serve with your favorite dipping sauce.
NOTES
I make this recipe in my Cosori 5.8 qt. air fryer or 6.8 quart air fryer. Depending on your air fryer, size and wattages, cooking time may need to be adjusted 1-2 minutes.
Store remainder chimichangas in the refrigerator in an airtight container for up to 3 days.

Buffalo Chicken Salad
Servings: 2
Cooking Time: 0 Minutes

Ingredients:
- 6 1/2 ounces cooked chicken breast or canned (from an 8 oz breast, cubed)
- 1/4 cup red onion (plus more for garnish)
- 1/2 celery stalk (plus leaves for garnish)
- 1 baby carrot
- 1/4 cup mayo
- 1/4 cup Frank's hot sauce (or more to taste)
- 6 baby romaine lettuce leaves (or your favorite lettuce for wraps)

- light blue cheese dressing (optional for topping)

Directions:
1. If you need to cook the chicken in the slow cooker, cover it with water 4 hours on low then shred. Use a rotisserie chicken breast or even canned chicken works here.
2. In a mini chopper, chop all the veggies, then add the chicken and pulse a few times.
3. Transfer to a bowl and mix with the mayo and hot sauce, adding more to taste.
4. To serve, spoon into lettuce wraps and garnish with red onion, celery leaves and more hot sauce.

Air Fryer Roasted Garlic
Servings: 1
Cooking Time: 19 Minutes

Ingredients:
- 1 garlic bulb
- 1 tablespoon olive oil

Directions:
1. On a cutting board with a sharp knife carefully slice off the bottom part of whole head of garlic.
2. Place the fresh garlic head on a piece of aluminum foil.
3. Use a pastry brush to coat the entire bulb of garlic with olive oil or drizzle olive oil over bulb and gently roll bulb of garlic in aluminum foil to cover bulb evenly.
4. Next pull all edges of aluminum foil over garlic head. Sealing all exposed parts of bulb.
5. Air fry at 380 degrees F for 20-25 minutes, air fry until garlic softens and is golden brown.
6. Allow garlic to cool prior to removing individual garlic cloves. The best way to remove each clove of garlic is to gently squeeze top of bulb and they will easily slide out of garlic bulb.
NOTES
Optional seasonings after cooking: Pinch of salt & pepper, parmesan cheese, hand grated loose cheese, red pepper flakes, onion or garlic powder. Fresh herbs like chopped rosemary,

thyme or dill will add a brightness to this recipe.

Air Fryer Egg Salad
Servings: 4
Cooking Time: 15 Minutes

Ingredients:
- 8 large eggs
- 4 tablespoons mayonnaise
- 1 tablespoon finely chopped chives or scallions (plus more for garnish)
- 1/4 teaspoon kosher salt
- fresh black pepper (to taste)
- 1/8 teaspoon sweet paprika (for garnish)

Directions:
1. Place the eggs in the air fryer basket and set the temperature to 250°F.
2. Cook for 15 to 16 minutes, depending on your air fryer until the eggs are hard-boiled (time may vary depending on the make and model of your air fryer), play around with 1 egg to see how your air fryer cooks before making a whole batch.
3. Once the eggs are cooked, remove them from the air fryer and run under cold water.
4. Peel the eggs and chop them into small pieces.
5. In a separate bowl, mix together the mayonnaise, salt, and pepper.
6. Add the chopped eggs, chives to the bowl with the mayonnaise mixture. Stir until everything is well combined.
7. Top with paprika and chives, for garnish.
8. Serve the egg salad on top of your favorite bread, crackers, or lettuce leaves, or use it to make a sandwich. Enjoy!

Air Fryer Artichoke

Servings: 4
Cooking Time: 15 Minutes

Ingredients:
- 2 medium artichoke
- 1 Tablespoon lemon juice fresh
- 1 Tablespoon olive oil
- 1 teaspoon kosher salt
- 1/2 teaspoon ground black pepper

Directions:
1. Rinse and clean the artichokes.
2. Remove outer leaves, cut the tips and shorten the stem with a sharp knife or kitchen scissors.
3. Cut them in half, lengthwise, and turn the artichoke halves so they are flat side up.
4. Place them in a baking dish.
5. Drizzle fresh lemon juice generously over entire artichoke half.
6. Next drizzle all 4 halves with olive oil, then season with salt and pepper.
7. Place each halved artichoke in air fryer basket, in a single layer, flat side down.
8. Air fry artichokes at 340 degrees F for 12-15 minutes until cooked (a knife should be able to cut through the flesh easily and they will have soft leaves).
9. Serve artichokes while hot.
NOTES
This recipe was made in a 1700 watt 5.8 quart Cosori air fryer. All air fryers can cook a little differently depending on the wattage and size. Use this recipe as a guide for best results if you are using a different air fryer.
Optional Favorite Dipping Sauce: Lemony garlic aioli sauce, feta dip, honey mustard, ranch dressing, pepper garlic aioli dip, Greek yogurt with fresh dill or ancho chili aioli.
Creamy Dipping Sauce: In a medium bowl measure 1 cup of mayonnaise with any spices, citrus juices, vinegars or herbs that you are craving.
Kitchen Tips: You can also use kitchen shears or a serrated knife to cut the artichokes. You may have to cook artichokes in batches depending on the size.

Substitutions: Avocado oil, grapeseed oil or refined coconut oil. Use a few tablespoons lemon juice to make artichokes extra tangy.

Teriyaki Root Vegetable Salad With Crispy Tofu

Servings: 2
Cooking Time: 10-30 Minutes

Ingredients:
- For the teriyaki dressing
- 60ml/2¼fl oz dark soy sauce
- 2 tbsp honey
- 1 tbsp sesame oil
- 1 tbsp rice vinegar or white wine vinegar
- 1 tsp cornflour
- 2 garlic cloves, crushed
- For the salad
- 200g/7oz firm tofu, cut into 2cm/¾in cubes and patted dry with kitchen paper
- 1 tbsp olive oil
- 1 tbsp cornflour
- 300g/10½oz celeriac, julienned
- 2 carrots, julienned
- 1 parsnip, julienned
- 100g/3½oz kale, stems removed and leaves torn
- pinch sesame seeds
- salt

Directions:
1. Preheat the oven to 200C/180C Fan/Gas 6 and put a baking tray on the middle shelf to heat up. (Or see Recipe Tip for air fryer instructions)
2. To make the dressing, whisk all of the ingredients together in a small saucepan, then bring to the boil. Cook for 2 minutes until thick and glossy, then remove from the heat and leave to cool.
3. Put the tofu in a large bowl, add 1 tablespoon of the dressing and drizzle over the olive oil. Stir to coat. Sprinkle over the cornflour, stir again, then tip onto the preheated baking tray. Roast for 25 minutes, turning halfway through cooking.
4. Meanwhile, tip the vegetables into a large bowl, add a pinch of salt and massage together

for a couple of minutes – this helps to soften them, and in turn soak up more dressing. Once the vegetables are soft, pour in 3–4 tablespoons of the dressing and toss to coat.

5. Divide the salad between 2 serving bowls, top with the crispy tofu and sprinkle over the sesame seeds.

NOTES

Use a julienne peeler to shred the vegetables. They are relatively cheap and make prepping salads like this really easy. If you don't have one you can grate the vegetables.

Plan ahead and prepare the tofu the night before. Cut into cubes, pat dry, then sandwich between a few sheets of kitchen paper. Weigh down with a plate on top and chill overnight. The more moisture you can remove in advance, the crispier the tofu will be.

You can cook the tofu in an air fryer. Just coat in cornflour then drizzle or spray with oil and air fry for 10 minutes at 180C.

Any leftover dressing will keep for up to a week in an airtight container in the fridge.

Air Fryer Portobello Mushroom
Servings: 3-4
Cooking Time: 12 Minutes

Ingredients:
- 3 to 4 portobello mushroom caps
- Juice and zest of 1 lemon
- ¼ cup parsley, loosely packed
- ¼ cup oregano, loosely packed
- 2 tablespoons loosely packed thyme
- 1 tablespoon garlic, minced
- 3 tablespoons olive oil, divided

Directions:
1. Preheat your air fryer to 350 degres.
2. Remove the stem from your mushroom cap by carefully pulling the cap to the side and it will pop out.
3. Hold your mushroom cap under slowly running water and gently rub to remove any dirt from the outside and inside of the cap. Pat them dry with paper towels.
4. Zest your lemon with a zester or grater. Then cut your lemon in half to juice it.
5. Wash your herbs and pat them dry.

6. In a small food processor or blender, place your herbs, garlic, lemon zest and juice, and olive oil. Blend until smooth.
7. Using a basting brush, brush the mushrooms on the top and bottom till they are covered.
8. Place the mushroom caps top side down and cook at 350 degrees F for 10 minutes. Then flip the caps for an additional 2 minutes.

NOTES

HOW TO REHEAT PORTOBELLO MUSHROOMS IN THE AIR FRYER

Place the leftover mushroom caps in the air fryer basket.

Cook at 350 degrees F for 3 to 4 minutes until warmed through.

Air Fryer Lemon Pepper Wings
Servings: 4
Cooking Time: 20 Minutes

Ingredients:
- 24 drummies
- 1 Tablespoon olive oil
- 1 Tablespoon cornstarch
- 1 teaspoon smoked paprika
- 1 teaspoon ground black pepper
- 1 teaspoon lemon pepper
- 1/2 teaspoon lemon zest

Directions:
1. Preheat the Air Fryer to 380° Fahrenheit. Prepare the Air Fryer basket with olive oil spray.
2. Rinse and pat the wings with paper towels until they are completely dry.
3. Add the chicken wings, olive oil, cornstarch, ground black pepper, paprika, lemon pepper seasoning, and lemon zest to a large Ziploc bag.
4. Seal the bag and toss to coat the wings with the oil and seasonings.
5. Place wings in a single layer in the basket of your Air Fryer.
6. Cook at 380°F for 16 minutes, flipping every 4 minutes. Increase the heat to 400°F and cook for an additional 4 minutes. Use a meat thermometer to ensure the wings have

reached 165°F. Add 1-2 minutes at 400°F if needed.

7. Remove the crispy wings from the Air Fryer basket and place them on a serving dish.

8. Serve with your favorite dipping sauce and sides.

NOTES

If you don't have cornstarch, you can use flour instead! Just make sure to use twice as much flour as cornstarch for best results.

If you're cutting up whole wings, cut off the small wing tip, and then use a sharp knife to cut the wings in the joint to make the wings and drummettes.

If you want some added lemon flavor, squeeze a little lemon juice on the wings just before serving.

Fried Eggplant With Spicy Goat Cheese Dip

Servings: 4

Ingredients:

- 1 globe eggplant
- ½ cup all-purpose flour
- 2 teaspoons kosher salt, plus more to taste
- 1 teaspoon paprika
- 3 large eggs, beaten
- 1 teaspoon dried oregano leave
- 3 cups panko breadcrumbs
- Oil spray
- Cinnamon stick
- Items Needed
- Food processor
- Spicy Goat Cheese Dip
- ¼ cup pine nuts
- 1/3 cup fresh basil leaves
- ¼ cup fresh parsley leaves
- 4 or 5 Calabrian chili peppers
- 3 garlic cloves
- 1 lemon, zested and juiced
- 2 tablespoons chili oil
- ½ cup olive oil
- Kosher salt, to taste
- Freshly ground black pepper, to taste
- 4 ounces goat cheese
- 2 tablespoons heavy cream

Directions:

1. Place the crisper plate into the Smart Air Fryer basket.

2. Select the Preheat function, adjust the temperature to 385°F, then press Start/Pause

3. Cut the eggplant into ½-inch thick planks, then cut the bottom and top ends off. Cut each plank into ½-inch thick strips.

4. Set up a breading station with the flour, 2 teaspoons salt, and paprika in one bowl, the eggs in a second bowl, and the panko and oregano in a third bowl.

5. Dredge the eggplant pieces in the flour, followed by the egg, then the panko, shaking off the excess after each step.

6. Place the breaded eggplant pieces onto the crisper plate and spray with oil spray.

7. Set the temperature to 385°F and time to 8 minutes, press Shake, then press Start/Pause.

8. Flip the eggplant over halfway through the cooking time and spray again with oil spray. The Shake Reminder will let you know when.

9. Place the pine nuts, basil, parsley, Calabrian chilis, garlic, lemon zest, lemon juice, and chili oil in the bowl of a food processor fitted with the blade attachment. Blend on high for 20 seconds, then add in ½ cup of the olive oil while the motor is running on low speed. Season to taste with salt and pepper, then transfer the pesto to a bowl.

10. Wipe out the food processor, then place the goat cheese and heavy cream into it and blend until very smooth and whipped, then season with salt and pepper and transfer to another bowl. Pour the pesto over the goat cheese and set aside until ready to serve.

11. Remove the fried eggplant when done, season to taste with salt, and let cool, then serve with the spicy pesto and whipped goat cheese.

Air Fryer Tempeh

Servings: 3
Cooking Time: 14 Minutes

Ingredients:

- 1- 8 ounce package of Tempeh
- ½ cup of your favorite BBQ Sauce
- 2 tablespoon of olive oil

Directions:

1. Cut your Tempeh into ½ inch strips. Then turn them on their side to cut again, making thinner strips.
2. Tempeh is fermented soy and can be bitter. To help make them tender and to take some of the bitterness away you will want to steam your tempeh before air frying it. To do this fill a pot with about 2 inches of water in it. Bring it to a boil. Place your tempeh in a steaming basket and steam for 10 minutes. If you do not have a steaming basket, you can place it in the water and hard boil it for 10 minutes, but you will need to pat them dry before the next step.
3. Preheat your air fryer to 380 degrees.
4. Place your steamed tempeh on a cutting board and brush both sides of it with olive oil. Brush the inside of your air fryer with olive oil as well. Then place your tempeh in the basket, leaving a little room around each of them.
5. Cook for 7 minutes and then flip them. Place them back in the air fryer for 4 more minutes and then remove the basket. Brush the tops of your tempeh with BBQ sauce and then place it back in the air fryer for an additional 3 minutes. (14 minutes total) This allows that BBQ sauce to caramelize and get a delicious sticky texture to it.
6. When they are cooked and are crispy, then place them back on the cutting board and brush them with BBQ sauce again, covering them. Enjoy immediately.

NOTES

HOW TO REHEAT TEMPEH IN THE AIR FRYER:

Preheat your air fryer to 350 degrees.

Place tempeh in your air fryer and cook for 3-4 minutes or until warmed thoroughly.

Brush with additional BBQ sauce if desired and serve.

Green Goddess Carrot Salad

Servings: 4

Ingredients:

- 1 lb. slim baby carrots, trimmed and cut lengthwise in half (or in quarters if large)
- 1 tbsp. olive oil
- 1 c. Green Goddess Dressing
- 1 head Bibb lettuce, leaves separated and torn
- GREEN GODDESS DRESSING
- 3/4 c. buttermilk
- 1/2 c. mayonnaise
- 1/3 c. plain Greek yogurt
- 4 anchovies or 2 tsp. anchovy paste
- 2 tbsp. fresh lemon juice
- 1 tbsp. Dijon mustard
- 1 small clove garlic
- Pinch of sugar
- 3/4 tsp. salt
- 1/4 tsp. pepper
- 1/2 c. loosely packed fresh parsley
- 1/4 c. packed fresh basil
- 3 tbsp. fresh tarragon
- 2 tbsp. snipped fresh chives

Directions:

1. Heat air fryer to 400°F. Toss carrots with 1 tablespoon olive oil and 1/2 teaspoon salt. Add carrots to air-fryer basket and air-fry until crisp-tender and edges are slightly caramelized, 15 to 17 minutes. Cool completely.
2. Meanwhile, prepare Green Goddess Dressing: In blender, puree buttermilk, mayonnaise, Greek yogurt, anchovies or anchovy paste, lemon juice, Dijon mustard, garlic, pinch sugar, salt and pepper until smooth. Add parsley, basil, tarragon and chives; pulse until herbs are finely chopped. Makes about 2 cups; can be refrigerated up to 1 week.
3. To serve, arrange carrots over lettuce. Drizzle with dressing.

Homemade Tortilla Chips & Salsa

Servings: 2
Cooking Time: 8 Minutes

Ingredients:
- 6 corn tortillas (6-inch), cut into 6 pieces each
- Spray oil
- Salt, to taste
- Salsa, for serving

Directions:
1. Select the Preheat function on the Air Fryer, adjust the temperature to 330°F, then press Start/Pause.
2. Spray the tortilla chips with oil so they are evenly coated on both sides, then season lightly with salt.
3. Place the tortillas chips in the preheated air fryer basket.
4. Set the temperature to 330°F and the timer to 8 minutes, then press Start/Pause.
5. Shake the basket halfway through the cooking time.
6. Remove the chips when done, season with additional salt if desired, then serve with salsa.

Chestnut Stuffing

Servings: 5

Ingredients:
- 2 ounces onion, minced
- 2 ounces carrots, minced
- 2 ounces celery, minced
- 2 ounces white button mushrooms, minced
- 1½ tablespoons unsalted butter or bacon fat
- 12 ounces day-old bread, cubed
- 4 fluid ounces chicken stock, hot
- 1 egg, whisked
- 2 tablespoons parsley
- ½ teaspoon sage, chopped
- 6 ounces shelled, peeled, roasted chestnuts, quartered
- 1 teaspoon kosher salt
- ½ teaspoon ground black pepper
- 1 teaspoon ground nutmeg
- ¼ teaspoon ground ginger
- ¼ teaspoon ground mustard
- Gravy, for serving (optional)

Directions:
1. Sauté the onions, carrots, celery, and mushrooms in the butter (or bacon fat) until tender, about 5 minutes.
2. Combine the bread, chicken stock, egg, and sauteed vegetables in a large bowl.
3. Add the parsley, sage, chestnuts, salt, pepper, nutmeg, ginger, and mustard and mix until fully combined.
4. Select the Preheat function on the Air Fryer, set temperature to 330°F, and press Start/Pause.
5. Line the preheated air fryer basket with foil, being careful not to touch the hot surfaces.
6. Transfer the stuffing into the lined air fryer basket.
7. Select the Bake function, adjust temperature to 330°F and time to 30 minutes, press Shake, then press Start/Pause.
8. Cover the top of the stuffing with foil halfway through cooking. The Shake Reminder will let you know when.
9. Let the stuffing cool for 5 minutes inside the air fryer basket, then transfer to a serving dish.
10. Scoop the stuffing out into a dish or flip the stuffing out onto a cutting board and cut into individual servings.
11. Serve alongside your Thanksgiving dinner with gravy, if desired.

SANDWICHES & BURGERS RECIPES

Beyond Burger In The Air Fryer
Servings: 4
Cooking Time: 10 Minutes

Ingredients:
- 2-4 Beyond Burger Patties
- 2 tsp of Weber Steak 'N Chop Seasoning

Directions:
1. Preheat your air fryer to 350 degrees and season your patties with ¼ tsp of seasoning on each side of the burger.
2. Place your burgers in the air fryer.
3. Cook at 350 for 9-11 minutes till the internal temperature is 165 degrees. Flip it half way through the cooking time.
4. Serve and enjoy!
NOTES
HOW TO REHEAT BEYOND BURGERS:
Add Beyond burger patties to the air fryer basket.
Air fry at 380 degrees for 3-4 minutes or until hot.

Air Fryer Hamburgers
Servings: 4
Cooking Time: 10 Minutes

Ingredients:
- 1 pound 90% lean ground beef
- 1 tablespoon extra-virgin olive oil
- 2 teaspoons Dijon mustard optional
- 1/2 teaspoon garlic powder
- 1/2 teaspoon kosher salt
- 1/2 teaspoon ground black pepper
- For Serving
- 4 hamburger buns we like brioche or pretzel buns, split, toasted if desired
- Toppings of choice: lettuce, sliced tomato, avocado, Barbecue Sauce, ketchup, etc.

Directions:
1. Place the beef in a large mixing bowl. Add the oil, mustard, garlic powder, salt, and pepper.

2. With a fork, gently stir to combine, being careful not to compact the meat (handle it as little as possible for the most tender burgers). Gently shape it into 4 equal patties that are 1/2-inch thick. With your thumb, gently press an indentation in the center.
3. Preheat the air fryer to 375 degrees F. Place the patties in the basket, leaving some space around each (cook in batches if needed). Air fry the burgers for 6 minutes, then flip and continue cooking until the internal temperature of the burger reaches 155 degrees F, about 2 to 4 minutes more. DO NOT overcook, or the burgers will be dry. If you'll be adding cheese, do so during the last minute of cooking. Serve hot on buns with your favorite toppings.
Notes
TO STORE: Store leftover burger patties in an airtight container for up to 3 days in the refrigerator.
TO REHEAT: Warm patties in a skillet, covered, with a bit of water to keep them from drying out.
TO FREEZE: Cooked burger patties can be frozen for up to 3 months in a freezer-safe container. Let thaw overnight in the refrigerator prior to reheating.

Air Fryer Falafel With Vegan Yogurt Tahini Sauce
Servings: 18
Cooking Time: 10 Minutes

Ingredients:
- For the Falafel
- 1 15 oz can chickpeas drained
- 1 cup chopped white onion
- 6 small cloves garlic
- 1 tablespoon lemon juice
- 1 cup lightly packed parsley leaves
- ½ cup lightly packed cilantro leaves
- ¼ cup lightly packed fresh dill leaves
- 1 teaspoon baking powder
- 2 teaspoons cumin

- 1 teaspoon salt
- ½ cup flour (either all-purpose flour or 1:1 gluten free flour)
- For the Vegan Yogurt Tahini Sauce
- 1 cup vegan plain yogurt (not vanilla flavored)
- 1 tablespoons tahini (see notes)
- 2 tablespoons lemon juice

Directions:
1. Add chickpeas, onion, garlic, lemon juice, parsley, cilantro, dill, flour, baking powder, cumin, and salt to a food processor. Pulse until a coarse crumb texture is formed. Stop to scrape down the sides of the bowl as needed.
2. Transfer the falafel mixture to a bowl, cover, and refrigerate for 1 hour (or up to 2 days before cooking).
3. While the falafel mixture sets, prepare the vegan tahini sauce. Whisk together the vegan yogurt, tahini, and lemon juice until combined. Add salt and pepper and stir to combine. Cover and refrigerate until time to serve.
4. Once the falafel mixture is chilled, use a spoon or cookie dough scooper to measure out 1 tablespoon of the dough. Form into balls. Place falafel balls on a plate. Repeat until all the batter has been used.
5. Spray the air fryer basket with vegetable cooking spray. Preheat air fryer to 375°F.
6. Use tongs to place raw falafel in the basket, arranging them on the bottom of the basket. Return basket to air fryer and cook for 15 minutes, removing the basket and using tongs to turn falafel once or twice during cooking time. Once done, remove falafel from the air fryer basket. Allow them to cool slightly.
7. To serve, place falafel on a plate and serve with tahini sauce for dipping. Or add 3–4 falafel inside a halved, pita along with hummus, chopped romaine lettuce, and chopped onions. Drizzle with the tahini sauce.
Notes
Tahini is ground sesame seeds. If you don't have this, you can substitute almond butter or Sun Butter (made from ground sunflower seeds).

Air-fryer Chicken Katsu Sandwiches
Servings: 4

Ingredients:
- 2 8 ounce skinless, boneless chicken breast halves, halved crosswise
- ¼ cup reduced-sodium soy sauce
- 1 tablespoon toasted sesame oil, plus more for serving
- 1 tablespoon mirin (optional)
- 2 garlic cloves, minced
- ¼ cup all-purpose flour
- 1 teaspoon kosher salt
- ⅛ teaspoon black pepper
- 1 egg, lightly beaten
- 2 tablespoon mayonnaise or sour cream
- 1 teaspoon honey mustard or hot mustard (optional)
- 1 cup panko
- 1 - 2 tablespoon black and/or white sesame seeds
- Olive oil cooking spray
- 8 slices milk bread or 4 hamburger buns, split
- Desired toppers, such as shredded cabbage, bottled tonkatsu sauce*, chopped green onion, and/or mayonnaise (optional)

Directions:
1. Using the flat side of a meat mallet, lightly flatten chicken pieces between two pieces of plastic wrap to an even thickness. In a bowl or resealable bag combine soy sauce, the 1 Tbsp. sesame oil, mirin (if using), and garlic. Add chicken; turn to coat. Cover or seal, and chill 30 to 90 minutes.
2. In a shallow dish stir together flour, 1 tsp. kosher salt, and 1/8 tsp. ground black pepper. In a shallow bowl whisk together egg, mayonnaise, and mustard (if using). In another shallow dish combine panko and sesame seeds.
3. Remove chicken pieces from marinade; discard marinade. Coat chicken pieces with flour mixture, then dip in egg mixture. Coat with panko mixture, pressing to adhere. Coat one side of chicken pieces with olive oil nonstick cooking spray.

4. Preheat air fryer to 400°F.** Add chicken to basket, oil spray side up, and cook 4 minutes. Turn chicken, coat with additional olive oil cooking spray, and cook 4 to 5 minutes more or until golden brown and chicken reaches 165°F.

5. Serve chicken between slices of bread or on buns with desired toppers. lf you like, drizzle with additional sesame oil to serve. Makes 4 sandwiches.

6. If you can't find bottled tonkatsu sauce, a sweet and savory Japanese condiment usually served with pork, you can make your own: In a small saucepan combine 1/2 cup ketchup, 2 Tbsp. soy sauce, 1 Tbsp. packed brown sugar, 1 Tbsp. mirin or rice vinegar, 1 1/2 tsp. Worcestershire sauce, 1 tsp. grated fresh ginger, and 2 cloves minced garlic. Heat over medium, stirring to dissolve sugar. Let cool. Refrigerate up to 1 week. Makes 3/4 cup.

7. Sheet Pan Variation

8. If you don't have an air fryer, preheat oven to 450°F. Place a wire rack in a sheet pan. Prepare chicken as directed through Step 3. Place chicken pieces on rack in prepared pan. Bake 15 minutes or until golden brown and chicken reaches 165°F. Serve as directed.

Air Fryer Mozzarella Mushroom Burgers

Servings: 4
Cooking Time: 25 Minutes

Ingredients:
- 8 portobello mushrooms (400g)
- 1 tablespoon balsamic vinegar
- 1 tablespoon extra virgin olive oil
- 4 large brioche buns (400g), split
- ¼ cup (75g) aioli
- 40 grams mixed salad leaves
- 1 large tomato (220g), sliced thinly
- 125 grams fresh mozzarella ball, cut into 4 slices
- 1/3 cup (90g) basil pesto
- to serve: shoestring fries and low-sugar tomato sauce

Directions:

1. Place mushrooms, vinegar and oil in a medium bowl; toss to coat. Season.

2. Preheat a 7-litre air fryer to 180°C/350°F for 3 minutes.

3. Taking care, place mushrooms in air fryer basket; at 180°C/350°F, cook for 12 minutes, turning halfway through cooking time, until tender.

4. Spread bun bases with aioli, then top with salad leaves, tomato, mozzarella, mushrooms and pesto; sandwich together with bun tops.

5. Serve mushroom burgers with shoestring fries and tomato sauce.

6 Ingredient Veggie Burgers

Servings: 6
Cooking Time: 10 Minutes

Ingredients:
- 1 tin black beans, drained and rinsed
- 1 onion finely chopped
- 2 garlic cloves, grated
- 1/3 cup roasted walnuts, roughly chopped
- 1/3 cup Oat flour*
- 1 Aubergine cut into bite-sized chunks
- Oat flour? Oat flour is simply porridge oats, popped into a blender, and ground until a fine powder. If you do not have oats, substitute this quantity for ¼ cup of wheat flour.

Directions:

1. Place the rinsed black beans into the basket of the Instant Pot Vortex, and air-fry on 205C for 5 minutes, until bursting and blistered.

2. While the beans cook, sprinkle ½ tsp of salt evenly over your aubergine and place it in a colander, to allow any bitter juices to drain out. Add the chopped onion to a frying pan with a little oil and cook until soft and translucent on a medium heat (about 4 minutes).

3. Once the beans have finished cooking, remove them from the basket and pop them into the bowl of a food processor.

4. Toss the aubergines in a little oil, then air fry them at 205C for 7 minutes, until golden and soft.

5. To the beans, add the grated garlic, cooked onions, walnuts, oat flour, and cooked aubergine. Pulse the mixture until the mixture comes together and starts forming a chunky paste. Then divide the mixture into 5 balls and shape them into patties.

6. Set the patties aside for 10 minutes to firm up. This is an important step, as the oat flour will absorb excess moisture in the patties, making them easier to cook and handle.

7. Set the Vortex air fryer to 190C. Brush the patties in olive oil, then place them into the air fryer for 6-9 minutes, until crisped and brown to your desired level.

8. Serve your veggie burgers with your favorite toppings on a soft roll (we love rocket, vegan aioli, and tomato) or omit the bun, and add your toppings to the patty, before wrapping it in butter lettuce, for a low carb alternative.

Air Fryer Frozen Impossible™ Burgers

Servings: 4
Cooking Time: 15 Minutes

Ingredients:
- 4 frozen Impossible™ Burger patties , 1/4lb (113g) patties
- salt , to taste
- black pepper , to taste
- oil spray , for coating
- BURGER ASSEMBLY:
- 4 Buns
- Optional - cheese, pickles, lettuce, onion, tomato, avocado, cooked bacon etc.
- EQUIPMENT
- Air Fryer
- Instant Read Thermometer (optional)

Directions:
1. Spray or brush both sides of the frozen patties with oil and season with salt and pepper.
2. Spray air fryer basket or rack with oil. Place the frozen patties in the air fryer basket/tray in a single layer. Air Fry at 380°F/193°C for 8 minutes.

3. Flip the patties and continue cooking for about 3-6 minutes or until cooked through and internal temperature is 160°F/71°C. Timing will vary depending on thickness of patties and individual air fryer model.
4. For Cheeseburgers: add the slices of cheese on top of the cooked patties. Air fry at 380°F/193°C for about 30 seconds to 1 minute to melt the cheese.
5. Warm the buns in the air fryer at 380°F/193°C for about 1 minute.
6. Serve on buns, topped with your favorite burger toppings.

Frozen Burgers In The Air Fryer

Servings: 2
Cooking Time: 10 Minutes

Ingredients:
- 2 frozen burger patties
- 2 slices cheddar cheese
- salt and pepper to taste
- toppings as desired

Directions:
1. Preheat your air fryer to 375°F.
2. Place the frozen burgers in the air fryer basket and cook for 5 minutes.
3. Flip the patties and cook for an additional 5 minutes. Add cheese in the last minute of cooking.
4. Top as desired and serve.
Notes
Avoid overcrowding the air fryer so the burger can cook evenly!

Homestyle Cheeseburgers

Servings: 4
Cooking Time: 15 Minutes

Ingredients:
- 1 pound ground beef chuck
- 1 ½ teaspoon kosher salt
- 1 teaspoon freshly ground black pepper
- 4 slices American cheese
- 4 sesame seed buns
- Ketchup, for serving
- 4 sesame seed buns

- Ketchup, for serving
- Yellow mustard, for serving
- Pickles, for serving

Directions:
1. Select Preheat on the Air Fryer, adjust the temperature to 400°F, then press Start/Pause.
2. Form the ground beef into 4 equally sized patties, a little less than ¾-inch thick. Season with the salt and pepper.
3. Place the beef patties into the preheated air fryer basket.
4. Set the temperature to 400°F and time to 14 minutes, then press Start/Pause.
5. Flip the burger patties over halfway through cooking.
6. Open the basket and top each patty with a slice of American cheese.
7. Set the temperature to 400°F and time to 1 minute, then press Start/Pause.
8. Remove the burger patties when done.
9. Place each patty on a sesame seed bun, dress the burgers with the condiments and pickles, then serve.

Air Fryer Burgers
Servings: 4
Cooking Time: 8 Minutes

Ingredients:
- 1 lb ground beef
- ¼ cup seasoned bread crumbs
- 2 tablespoons barbecue sauce
- 1 egg
- ¾ teaspoon seasoning salt
- ¼ teaspoon onion powder
- ¼ teaspoon garlic powder

Directions:
1. Preheat air fryer to 375 degrees F.
2. In a large bowl, combine beef, bread crumbs, barbecue sauce, egg, seasoning salt, onion powder and garlic powder.
3. Divide beef mixture into 4 sections and shape into patties (keep in mind they will shrink, so try to make them on the larger side).
4. Add patties to air fryer basket (you may have to work in batches depending on the size of your air fryer) and cook for 4-5 minutes per side (you don't have to flip, but they will brown evenly on both sides if you do), until an internal temperature of 160 degrees F is reached.
5. Serve on buns and with desired toppings.

Air Fryer Grilled Cheese Sandwiches
Servings: 2
Cooking Time: 8 Minutes

Ingredients:
- 2 tablespoons mayonnaise
- 4 thick slices country or sourdough bread
- 3 slices bacon halved crosswise
- 1 cup shredded Mexican blend or cheddar cheese

Directions:
1. Spread the mayonnaise on one side of each of the slices of bread. Place two slices of bread in the air fryer basket, mayo side facing down. Divide the shredded cheese over the tops of the two slices of bread. Cover the cheese with the remaining slices of bread, mayo side up.
2. Set the air fryer to 350°F for 6 to 8 minutes, or until the cheese is melted and the bread is crispy – it may not brown all that much. Cut in half and serve hot.
Notes
Other possible add-ins are:
Prosciutto
James, jellies and preserves
Pesto
Caramelized onions or shallots
Pickled Things (try sliced or chopped pickled brussels sprouts!)
Sliced Roasted Turkey Breast or Roast Chicken
Green Olive Tapenade
Roasted Peppers

All-american Grilled Burgers

Servings: 4

Ingredients:

- 2 teaspoons (10 grams) kosher salt
- 1 teaspoon (5 grams) ground black pepper
- ½ teaspoon (3 grams) onion powder
- ½ teaspoon (3 grams) garlic powder
- 1½ pounds (680 grams) ground beef
- Oil spray
- 4 slices cheese of choice, optional
- Mayonnaise, as needed
- 4 brioche burger buns, sliced
- Lettuce, as needed
- Tomato slices, as needed
- Ketchup, for serving
- Yellow mustard, for serving

Directions:

1. Combine the kosher salt, pepper, onion powder, and garlic powder together in a large bowl.
2. Add the ground beef to the spices, mix until well combined, and shape into 4 quarter-pound patties, about a ⅓-inch (8 millimeters) thick.
3. Place the cooking pot into the base of the Smart Indoor Grill, followed by the grill grate.
4. Select the Air Grill function on high heat, adjust temperature to 500°F (260°C) and time to 6 minutes, press Shake, then press Start/Pause to preheat.
5. Spray the grill grate lightly with oil spray once the grill is done preheating.
6. Place the burger patties onto the preheated grill grate, then close the lid.
7. Flip the patties halfway through cooking. The Shake Reminder will let you know when.
8. Place a cheese slice over each patty, close the lid, and let sit for 2 minutes for the cheese to melt.
9. Remove the patties when done and set aside.
10. Spread mayonnaise inside the sliced burger buns.
11. Select the Broil function, adjust temperature to 415°F (210°C) and time to 3 minutes, then press the Preheat button to bypass preheating.
12. Place the buns mayonnaise-side down onto the grill grate, then press Start/Pause to begin cooking.
13. Remove the buns when done and set aside until cool to the touch.
14. Assemble the burgers by topping the bottom halves of the brioche buns with lettuce and tomato, placing the burger patty on top, and finishing with the top bun.
15. Serve immediately with condiments on the side.

FAVORITE AIR FRYER RECIPES

Air-fryer Brats With Beer Gravy
Servings: 5

Ingredients:
- 1 package uncooked bratwurst links (20 ounces)
- 2 tablespoons butter
- 1 medium onion, thinly sliced
- 2 tablespoons all-purpose flour
- 1/8 teaspoon dill weed
- 1/8 teaspoon pepper
- 1 bottle (12 ounces) beer or nonalcoholic beer
- 5 slices thick bread

Directions:
1. Preheat air fryer to 400°. Place bratwurst in a single layer in a greased air fryer. Cook until no longer pink, 8-10 minutes.
2. Meanwhile, in a large saucepan, heat butter over medium-high heat. Add onion; cook and stir until onions start to brown and soften. Add flour, dill weed and pepper; stir until smooth. Stir in beer. Bring to a boil. Reduce heat; simmer, stirring constantly until thickened, 3-5 minutes. To serve, place 1 brat on each slice of bread; top evenly with onion mixture.

Air Fryer Taquitos And Charred Salsa
Servings: 4-6

Ingredients:
- Deselect All
- Salsa:
- 1 pound Roma tomatoes
- 1 small onion, cut into 8 wedges
- 1 serrano chile
- 1 clove garlic
- 1 tablespoon extra-virgin olive oil
- Kosher salt
- Taquitos:
- 1 cup chopped rotisserie chicken
- 1 cup (about 4 ounces) shredded Colby Jack
- One 4-ounce jar diced pimientos, drained
- 1 teaspoon dried oregano
- 1/2 teaspoon ground cumin
- 1/2 teaspoon paprika
- 1/4 teaspoon chili powder
- Kosher salt
- One 12.6-ounce package small "street-size" corn tortillas (24 tortillas)
- 1 cup refried beans
- Butter-flavored nonstick cooking spray
- Sour cream, for serving
- Shredded romaine lettuce, for serving

Directions:
1. Special equipment: A 6-quart air fryer
2. For the salsa: Preheat a 6-quart air fryer to 350 degrees F (see Cook's Note).
3. Combine the tomatoes, onion, chile, garlic and oil in a large bowl and toss to coat. Transfer to the basket of the air fryer and cook until the skin of the tomatoes and the chile are wrinkled and the onion and garlic are charred, about 10 minutes. Cool slightly.
4. When cool enough to handle, peel the skins from the tomatoes and discard. Remove the stem, seeds and skin from the chile and discard. Place the tomatoes, chile, garlic, onion and 1/4 teaspoon salt in a blender. Pulse until smooth. Set aside until ready to serve.
5. For the taquitos: Combine the chicken, cheese, pimientos, oregano, cumin, paprika, chili powder and 1/4 teaspoon salt in a large bowl and toss.
6. Working in batches, quickly run 4 tortillas under running water. Shake off excess water and place in the air fryer basket. Fry until softened and pliable, 15 to 30 seconds. Fill them while they are still warm: Spread 2 teaspoons refried beans over a tortilla, reserving a bit of bean to dab on the seal. Spread 1 1/2 tablespoons of the chicken filling over the beans. Roll the tortilla over the filling and seal tightly with a little refried bean. Repeat with the remaining tortillas, beans and chicken.

7. Spray all sides of the taquitos generously with cooking spray. Place in the air fryer basket (work in batches if needed) and fry until golden brown and crispy, about 8 minutes. Serve warm topped with some of the salsa and sour cream and shredded lettuce.

8. Cook's Note

9. Depending on the size of the air fryer, you may need to cook the taquitos in batches. Extra salsa can be refrigerated in an airtight container for up to 2 weeks. The taquitos can be prepared in advance: Air fry them until lightly golden brown, about 4 minutes. Allow to cool. Place in a resealable freezer bag and freeze for up to 1 month. To reheat, wrap in a moist paper towel and microwave for 1 minute to defrost the filling. Place in the basket of a 6-quart air fryer preheated to 350 degrees and cook until crispy and golden brown, about 6 minutes.

Pepperoni Pizza

Ingredients:
- 11 oz. Pre-made pizza dough
- 5 Tbsp. Pizza sauce
- 1 cup Mozzarella cheese
- 10-12 Pepperonis

Directions:
1. Use your hands to stretch the pre-made dough out into a shape that will fit in air fryer.
2. Spread sauce over dough, leaving a ¼-inch border. Sprinkle mozzarella cheese over sauce and place pepperonis on top.
3. Cook pizza at 400 degrees for 15 minutes, depending on desired level of crispiness.
4. Plate, serve, and enjoy!

Air Fryer Churros Twists

Servings: 2
Cooking Time: 12 Minutes

Ingredients:
- 1 and 3/4 cups of The Pantry Self Raising Flour
- 100g of Everyday Essentials Milk Chocolate

- 1 cup of Brooklea Greek Style Natural Yogurt
- 2 tablespoons of Sugar
- 1 tablespoon of Ground Cinnamon

Directions:
1. Makes 6 large or 12 small churros.
2. Add 1 and 3/4 of a cup of self raising flour to a bowl with 1 cup of Greek yoghurt.
3. Mix together with your hands. If the mixture is sticking to your hands after all flour has been mixed in, add more flour, tablespoons at a time.
4. Place some more flour on your kitchen surface and roll mixture into a large sausage shape. Divide this into either 6 or 12.
5. Roll your smaller pieces into long sausage shapes and bend them in half at the middle. Plait each side over each other to create a twist.
6. Brush with plenty of oil and place in the airfryer for 12 minutes on 200 degrees until golden brown.
7. Meanwhile, on a plate put 2 tablespoons of sugar and 1 tablespoon of ground cinnamon and mix together.
8. Remove churros and place in the sugar, ensuring all sides are coated.
9. Melt chocolate in the microwave and serve with churros.

Peanut Sauce Soba With Crispy Tofu

Servings: 4

Ingredients:
- 2 12.3-oz. packages extra-firm tofu, drained
- 3 tbsp. canola oil
- 2 tsp. grated garlic, divided
- 2 1/2 tbsp. low-sodium soy sauce, divided
- 3 tbsp. natural smooth peanut butter
- 1 tbsp. agave or honey
- 1 tbsp. fresh lime juice
- 1/4 c. hot water
- 1/4 tsp. grated ginger
- 1 tsp. sriracha
- 1 tbsp. toasted sesame oil
- 2/3 c. cornstarch

- 8 oz. soba noodles, cooked per package
Directions:
- 5 oz. baby spinach

Directions:
1. Pat tofu dry with paper towels and cut into 3/4-inch cubes.
2. In small bowl, whisk together canola oil, half of garlic, and 1 tablespoon soy sauce. Transfer one-third to small baking dish, coating bottom evenly. Add tofu and pour remaining marinade on top. Gently turn tofu to coat and let sit at room temp 45 minutes.
3. In medium bowl, combine peanut butter, agave, and lime juice with remaining 1 1/2 tablespoons soy sauce. Gradually whisk in hot water to emulsify. Whisk in ginger, sriracha, sesame oil, and remaining garlic. Set aside.
4. Heat air fryer to 400°F. Carefully dredge marinated tofu in cornstarch, coating evenly and shaking off excess. Add tofu to air fryer basket, spacing apart. Air-fry, shaking basket twice, until golden brown and crisp, 15 to 18 minutes.
5. Meanwhile, in large bowl, toss warm soba noodles with baby spinach and peanut sauce. Serve topped with crispy tofu.

Reheat Pizza In Air Fryer
Cooking Time: 5 Minutes

Ingredients:
- 2-3 slices pizza (see description in notes)

Directions:
1. Set the Air Fryer to 325 degrees Fahrenheit and reheat the pizza according to thickness and size. 4-6 minutes for thick crust, 3-5 minutes for medium crust, and 2-4 minutes for thin crust.
2. Add additional increments of 1-2 minutes if needed.
NOTES
Click here to print out the infographic on how to reheat pizza in an Air Fryer.
Thick Crust: 325 degrees for 4-6 minutes, adding increments of 1-2 minutes if needed.
Medium Crust: 325 degrees for 3-5 minutes, adding increments of 1-2 minutes if needed.
Thin Crust: 325 degrees for 2-4 minutes, adding increments of 1-2 minutes if needed.
It's ok to open and check the food while cooking with an Air Fryer. Always make sure you are cooking and reheating the food evenly and not over cooking or over browning.

Carrot Chip Dog Treats
Servings: 50
Cooking Time: 4 Hr

Ingredients:
- 6 large carrots, washed
- ½ teaspoon dried parsley (optional)
- ½ teaspoon dried turmeric (optional)
- ½ teaspoon dried dill (optional)
- Items Needed
- Mandolin (optional)

Directions:
1. Slice the carrots into ¼-inch-thick rounds or strips using a sharp knife or mandolin.
2. Steam the carrots: Place a steamer rack in a large pot filled with 2 inches of water. Bring the water to a simmer, then add the carrots. Cover the pot and steam for 4 minutes, or until just tender but not falling apart. Remove the carrots when done and allow them to cool.
3. Combine the herbs in a small bowl, then sprinkle over the carrots.
4. Place the carrots evenly between the Food Dehydrator trays.
5. Set temperature to 135°F and time to 4 hours, then press Start/Stop.
6. Remove when done, cool to room temperature on the trays, then serve to your pet.

Curried Parsnip Soup

Servings: 4
Cooking Time: 20 Minutes

Ingredients:
- 3 large parsnips peeled
- 1 large potato peeled
- 2 cloves garlic crushed
- 1 large onion diced
- 1-2 tbsp medium curry powder (use hot or mild if preferred)
- 1 vegetable stock pot
- 1 bunch fresh coriander
- 1.5 litres boiling water
- low calorie cooking spray

Directions:
1. Keep half of one parsnip aside. Chop the rest of the parsnips into 1 inch pieces. Add to a saucepan with the diced potato, onion, garlic, curry powder and stock pot. Stir in the boiling water and simmer for 10 minutes.
2. Chop the half parsnip you put aside, into 0.5cm dice. Add to an air fryer with some low calorie cooking spray and cook for 10 minutes until crisp.
3. After 10 minutes, finely chop the leafy part of the fresh coriander and add half to the sauce pan. Simmer for a further 10 minutes.
4. Blitz the soup until thick and creamy - you may need to add some extra boiling water if it is too thick. Add the remaining coriander leaves and blitz for a further few seconds.
5. Serve immediately, topped with the parsnip croutons and a sprinkle of curry powder!

Italian Sausage In Air Fryer

Servings: 4
Cooking Time: 22 Minutes

Ingredients:
- 1 medium red bell pepper
- 1 medium green bell pepper
- 1 small onion
- 4 Italian Sausage links
- 4 sausage rolls or hamburger buns

Directions:

1. Slice the bell peppers and onion into long strips and set aside.
2. Preheat the air fryer to 320 degrees Fahrenheit for 2-3 minutes.
3. Add peppers and onions into the basket of the air fryer and use the air fry function to cook at 320 degrees Fahrenheit for 10-12 minutes, tossing halfway through the cooking process.
4. Remove peppers and onions from the air fryer basket and set them aside.
5. Increase the temperature of the air fryer to 370 degrees Fahrenheit and add Italian sausage links to the basket.
6. Air fry at 370 degrees F for 10-12 minutes, flipping the links halfway through the cooking process. 7. Remove the sausage links from the air fryer and set them aside.
7. Slice open the sausage rolls, place them into the basket, and carefully add the sausage links and top them with the cooked peppers and onions. 8. Cook at 370 degrees F for 1-2 minutes.
8. Serve.
NOTES
This recipe was made in a 5.8 qt Cosori Air Fryer so make sure to adjust your total cooking time depending on the size of your air fryer.
If you want to add the sausage to hot dog buns, you can easily make killer sausage, onion, and pepper sandwiches!
If you want to skip the carbs, skip the buns!
Add a bit of heat and spice to your serving only by sprinkling on some cayenne pepper to the mixture!
If you're a fan of dips, a tad bit of marinara sauce goes a long way!

Nana's Macaroni

Ingredients:
- 12 oz. tomato sauce
- 6 oz. Colby cheese, grated
- ¾ stick of butter, cut into chunks
- ¾ of a lb. macaroni elbows, cooked
- 1 cup milk
- salt and pepper to taste

Directions:
1. Cook your pasta and then grate your cheese. Put the cooked pasta and some of the cheese into your dish. Add in the tomato sauce, butter and milk. Sprinkle salt and pepper to taste. Or add "one cross" salt and pepper, according to Rachel's Nana. Then, add in the rest of the cheese, mixing thoroughly.
2. Cover your dish with tinfoil and place it in your Air Fryer Oven. Using the Manual mode, bake it at 350°F for 30 minutes. Once the timer goes off, give it good stir. If desired, replace the tinfoil and place the dish back in the Air Fryer Oven. Cook for an additional 5-10 minutes and enjoy!

Air Fryer Brats

Servings: 5
Cooking Time: 13 Minutes

Ingredients:
- 1 pound uncooked bratwurst
- 5 hoagie rolls optional

Directions:
1. Preheat the air fryer to 360°F.
2. Place the brats in a single layer in the air fryer.
3. Cook for 8 minutes. Flip the brats over and cook an additional 5-7 minutes or until cooked through and the internal temperature reaches 165°F.
4. Serve in rolls with desired toppings.
Notes
Keep brats warm in a dish covered with foil in the oven until ready to serve.

Air Fryer Oven Corn Dogs

Ingredients:
- 3/4 cup yellow corn meal
- 3/4 cup all-purpose flour (plus some extra on a plate for coating hot dogs)
- 1 1/2 tablespoons sweetener
- 1 1/2 teaspoons baking powder
- 1/4 teaspoon salt
- 1 egg
- 1 cup buttermilk
- 1 1/2 tablespoons melted butter
- 8-12 hot dogs
- 8-12 wooden skewers

Directions:
1. Spray cooking oil Combine dry ingredients into a large bowl and whisk. Add wet ingredients and mix thoroughly.
2. Transfer the batter to a tall drinking glass. Grease the mesh rack with cooking spa. Or use perforated parchment paper, if available.
3. Dry the hot dogs with a paper towel. Roll in flour, lightly coating. Stick the skewer into the hotdog then submerge in the batter.
4. Place the hot dogs onto the mesh rack and cook for 12 minutes at 400 degrees.
5. Cool before serving.

Air Fryer Hot Dogs

Servings: 2
Cooking Time: 10 Minutes

Ingredients:
- Nonstick cooking spray
- 4 hot dogs
- 4 hot dog buns (top cut is best)
- 4 slices cheddar cheese, optional
- For serving
- Mustard
- Ketchup
- Pickles

Directions:
1. Spray the basket of an air fryer with nonstick spray.
2. Air fry the hot dogs:
3. Add your 4 hot dogs to the air fryer basket, leaving some space between each hot dog.

4. Air fry at 350°F for 5 minutes. When the hot dogs are done, they should be glistening hot and slightly browned in spots.

5. Toast the buns in the air fryer:

6. Remove hot dogs from air fryer basket using tongs or a fork and place each hot dog in a bun.

7. Simple Tip!

8. I prefer top-cut buns for this recipe. The buns stand up easier for better toasting.

9. Place 2 assembled hot dogs in the air fryer and cook for 90 seconds to toast the bun. The finished toasted bun will have a light toast on it and be slightly crispy on the edges.

10. If you are adding cheese to your hot dogs—add a slice of cheese in the middle each bun and top with hot dog. Air fry for 90 seconds and cheese will be melted, and the buns toasted.

11. Repeat with remaining hot dogs.

12. To serve:

13. Serve hot dogs immediately topped with your favorite hot dog toppings including mustard, ketchup, and pickles.

Easy Air Fryer Pepperoni Pizza

Servings: 1
Cooking Time: 8 Minutes

Ingredients:

- 1 whole wheat pita
- 2 tbsp pizza sauce or marinara If you don't like thick sauce, you can use 1 tbsp
- 1/8th cup mozzarella cheese, shredded
- 1/8th cup cheddar cheese, shredded If you prefer only mozzarella cheese, omit and use 1/4th cup mozzarella
- 8 slices pepperoni
- olive oil spray
- 1 tbsp chopped parsley, optional to garnish the pizza when it has cooled

Directions:

1. Standard Directions:

2. Drizzle the sauce on top of the pita bread, then load the pepperoni and shredded cheese on top.

3. Spray the top of the pizza with olive oil spray.

4. Place in the Air Fryer for 8 minutes on 400 degrees. Check in on the pizza at the 6-7 minute mark, to ensure it does not overcook to your liking.

5. Remove the pizza from the Air Fryer. I used a spatula. Cool before serving.

6. Crispy Crust Directions:

7. For a more crisp crust, spray one side of the pita bread with the olive oil. Place in the Air Fryer for 4 minutes on 400 degrees. This will allow the pita to fully crisp on one side.

8. Remove the pita bread from the Air Fryer. Turn the pita over to the side that is less crisp. This should be the side that was face-down in the Air Fryer.

9. Drizzle the sauce throughout, then load the pepperoni and shredded cheese on top.

10. Place the pizza back in the Air Fryer for 3-4 minutes until the cheese has melted. Use your judgment. You may need to allow the pizza to cook for an additional couple of minutes to reach your desired texture.

11. Remove the pizza from the Air Fryer. I used a spatula. Cool before serving.

Notes

Topping ideas: grated parmesan, crushed red pepper, and ranch dressing

If you prefer homemade marinara on your pizza. Be sure to check out my homemade marinara recipe here.

I prefer to purchase my cheese in the deli section by the block. I grate my own cheese. It melts so much better than pre-shredded cheese that you buy from a store that comes in a bag. If you want to keep this recipe quick and easy, you can use pre-shredded cheese. Grating your own cheese is simply an option.

Air Fryer Fig And Camembert Phyllo Parcel

Servings: 4
Cooking Time: 10 Minutes

Ingredients:
- 1 camembert round
- 2 TBSP fig jam
- 5 sheets phyllo pastry
- ½ cup melted butter
- Preserved figs and flaked almonds to serve

Directions:
1. Score the top of the camembert then top with fig jam.
2. Brush each sheet of phyllo pastry with butter, and lay the 3 pieces one on top of another.
3. Wrap the camembert in the pastry.
4. Brush the remaining 2 sheets of phyllo with butter and tear into strips.
5. Arrange in rosettes on top of the camembert.
6. Bake at 160°C for 10 mins until golden.
7. Remove from the Vortex / Duo Crisp and serve with preserved figs and lightly drizzle with fig syrup.

Air Fryer Mozzarella Sticks

Servings: 4
Cooking Time: 10 Minutes

Ingredients:
- 8 mozzarella string cheese
- 2 eggs
- ½ cup seasoned bread crumbs
- ½ cup Panko bread crumbs
- 1 tablespoon vegetable oil
- ½ teaspoon garlic powder
- ⅓ cup flour
- salt & pepper to taste

Directions:
1. Cut mozzarella sticks in half.
2. Whisk eggs with 1 tablespoon water. In a separate bowl combine bread crumbs, Panko bread crumbs, vegetable oil, and garlic powder. Place flour in a 3rd bowl and season with salt & pepper.

3. Dip each mozzarella stick into the eggs and then into the flour mixture. Dip back into the eggs and finally into the bread crumb mixture.
4. Place on a baking sheet and freeze at least 30 minutes (or up to 6 months).
5. Preheat air fryer to 390°F.
6. Generously spray mozzarella sticks with oil or cooking spray. Place in the air fryer basket in a single layer and cook for 5-7 minutes or until crisp.
7. Serve immediately.
Notes
No Air Fryer? No Problem! These can be baked in a preheated oven at 400°F for 9-11 minutes.
These are frozen before cooking to allow the crumbs to crisp up without the cheese melting out.
Be sure to preheat the air fryer and keep in mind that air fryers can vary. Check them early at about 4 minutes. Once you see cheese starting to bubble, they're ready.
Purchased frozen mozzarella sticks will cook for about 5-7 minutes at 390°F.

Air Fryer Pizza Quesadilla

Servings: 2
Cooking Time: 8 Minutes

Ingredients:
- 2 flour tortillas 8-inch
- 1 cup mozzarella cheese shredded
- 10 slices pepperoni
- 2 tbsp pizza sauce
- ½ tsp Italian seasoning
- ½ tsp butter melted and unsalted
- ½ tsp Parmesan cheese

Directions:
1. Remove tortillas from packaging and brush one side of each tortilla with melted butter.
2. Place each tortilla in air fryer basket, brushed side down. 3. Spread a thin layer of pizza sauce, pepperoni slices, shredded cheese, and Italian seasoning on top of tortilla.
3. Fold each tortilla in half and gently press together or seal them with a toothpick.

4. Air fry at 350 degrees F for 8-10 minutes, flipping the tortilla halfway through cooking time, until you have a crispy tortilla that is golden brown. After two minutes of air frying, open basket and if tortillas have opened, gently press together. The melted cheese will now keep them sealed.

5. Remove tortillas and brush again with a light coat of butter then sprinkle with parmesan cheese before serving.

NOTES

I make this recipe in my Cosori 5.8 qt. air fryer or 6.8 quart air fryer. Depending on your air fryer, size and wattages, cooking time may need to be adjusted 1-2 minutes.

An easy way to store leftovers is to let them cool after cooking and then place quesadillas in an airtight container to save for later. Leftovers of this make for a quick dinner. You can also wrap leftovers in plastic wrap and store them in the fridge as well.

Air Fryer Gnocchi, Sausage, And Green Beans

Servings: 4
Cooking Time: 10 Minutes

Ingredients:

- 1/2 pound green beans, washed, trimmed, and cut in half
- 4 Italian sausages
- 12 ounces gnocchi (frozen or refrigerated both work great)
- 1 teaspoon Italian seasoning
- 1 tablespoon extra-virgin olive oil
- salt and pepper to taste

Directions:

1. Preheat your air fryer to 380 degrees.
2. Cut the Italian sausage into 1-inch slices and place aside.
3. Place green beans and gnocchi into a bowl and mix with extra-virgin olive oil, Italian seasoning, salt, and pepper.
4. Add sausage slices to the air fryer then place the green beans and gnocchi on top. Do not shake or stir!
5. Cook for 10-12 minutes until the Italian sausage reaches an internal temperature of 160 degrees, shaking the basket halfway through.
6. Remove from the air fryer and enjoy!

Air Fryer Frozen Jalapeño Poppers

Servings: 2
Cooking Time: 8 Minutes

Ingredients:

- 6 Frozen Jalapeño Poppers
- EQUIPMENT
- Air Fryer

Directions:

1. Place the frozen jalapeño poppers in the air fryer basket and spread out evenly in a single layer. No oil spray is needed.
2. Air Fry at 380°F/193°C for 5 minutes. Gently shake or turn. Continue to Air Fry at 380°F/193°C for another 2-4 minutes or until the cheese just starts to ooze out.
3. Make sure to let them cool a little before eating. The filling can be super hot.

NOTES

Nutrition:

- based on using Frozen Cauliflower Veggie Tots.
- Air Frying Tips and Notes
- No Oil Necessary. Cook Frozen - Do not thaw first.
- Shake or turn if needed. Don't overcrowd the air fryer basket.
- Recipe timing is based on a non-preheated air fryer. If cooking in multiple batches back to back, the following batches may cook a little quicker.
- Recipes were tested in 3.7 to 6 qt. air fryers. If using a larger air fryer, they might cook quicker so adjust cooking time.
- Remember to set a timer to shake/flip/toss as directed in recipe.

Garlic Parmesan Pull-apart Rolls

Air Fryer Pizza

Servings: 2
Cooking Time: 10 Minutes

Ingredients:

- 1 pkg pizza dough mix 6.5 oz. , used Betty Crocker mix with water
- 1/4 c spaghetti sauce
- 1/2-3/4 c mozzarella cheese
- pepperoni optional
- olives optional
- olive oil spray

Directions:

1. Preheat your air fryer at 320 degrees for 3 minutes.
2. Make your pizza dough. Spray 7" springform pan and spread dough inside so it is level across the pan.
3. Put into air fryer and spray top of raw pizza dough with olive oil.
4. Close lid/drawer and set to 320 degrees for 3 minutes so dough can cook a bit.
5. Open and add pizza sauce, cheese, pepperoni and other toppings.
6. Close lid/drawer again and reset to 320 degrees for 7 minutes. Add 1 more minute if you want top crispier. Enjoy!

Air Fryer Sausage And Peppers

Servings: 4
Cooking Time: 10 Minutes

Ingredients:

- 1 onion sliced
- 1 bell pepper sliced
- 1 pound sausage of your choice
- 2 tablespoons olive oil

Directions:

1. Preheat your air fryer to 400°F.
2. Toss peppers and onions with the oil and season with salt and pepper to taste. Place in the air fryer basket.
3. Nestle the sausage between the vegetables and cook for 10 minutes, flipping the sausages halfway through the cooking time.

Rice Paper Dumplings

Servings: 8
Cooking Time: 15 Minutes

Ingredients:

- 8 medium sheets of rice paper
- 2 nori sheets quartered
- 16 oz (453 g) extra firm tofu (see notes)
- 1 (120 g) carrot thinly sliced
- ½ (120 g) zucchini or cucumber, thinly sliced
- ¼ of a small (120 g) red cabbage thinly sliced
- 2½ cups (450 g) cooked sushi rice (about 1 cup dry)
- Sesame oil to fry
- Sesame seeds
- Tofu glaze
- 2 Tbsp tamari or coconut aminos
- 1½ Tbsp maple syrup
- 1½ Tbsp lemon juice or rice vinegar
- ¼ tsp garlic powder
- ¼ tsp ginger powder
- ¼ tsp black pepper

Directions:

1. You can watch the video in the post for visual instructions.
2. Prepare the Fillings
3. First, soak the sushi rice in water, drain it, then cook it with fresh water according to its package instructions.
4. Meanwhile, thinly slice the carrot and zucchini into matchstick pieces (or use the julienne blade on a mandoline), and shred the cabbage into thin strips (slice it in half and remove the tough core first). Also, cut the nori sheets into quarters.
5. Then, combine all the tofu glaze ingredients in a separate bowl and slice the tofu into even-sized rectangles.
6. In a large skillet, heat a swirl of the oil over medium heat. Once hot, add the tofu and pan-fry it until golden brown on every side.
7. Don't move it around too much while it cooks to get a nice crispy sear. 2-3 minutes per side should work great.

8. Pour the tofu sauce into the pan and continue to cook, occasionally stirring, until the sauce thickens.

9. Assemble the Rice Paper Wraps

10. To assemble the rice paper dumplings, first -working one at a time - soak a rice paper sheet in cold water for 3-4 seconds, then transfer it to a slightly damp (to stop it from sticking) wooden board.

11. Place one of the cut nori pieces into the center of the rice paper. Top that with some cooked sushi rice, pan-fried tofu, and, finally, the veggies on top.

12. To seal the dumpling, fold all the corners in over the filling into the center, sealing it with your fingers. Then dip the flat surface of the dumpling into a plate of sesame seeds for a seedy crust.

13. I find it easiest to fold the wrap one side at a time. I start with the bottom-half, folding it up to cover the filling, then I fold the top half over the filling and finally the right and left sides.

14. Repeat these steps with the remaining rice paper and filling.

15. Cook the Dumplings

16. Clean out the skillet and add a little more oil, heating it over medium heat.

17. Once hot, add a single layer of rice paper dumplings (not touching) and pan-fry them on all sides for about 3-4 minutes, or until golden and crispy.

18. For air fryer rice paper dumplings: Cook in batches, placing a single layer of dumpling in the bottom of your air fryer basket and cooking for 8-10 minutes at 360F/182C (up to 12 minutes for large dumplings/super crispy results), flipping them over halfway.

19. Serve the crispy dumplings immediately with the dip of your choice. I like to either double the tofu marinade ingredients for a dipping sauce, use Chinese Garlic Sauce, or even sometimes Hoisin Sauce. Then, enjoy!

Notes

Tofu: For a soy-free option, you could use my Chickpea Tofu, adding 1-1 ½ tsp of agar powder for firmer tofu.

Sicilian Pizza

Servings: 8
Cooking Time: 25 Minutes

Ingredients:

- For the Dough
- 4 cups all purpose flour
- 3 tsp kosher salt
- 1 tsp granulated sugar
- 0.75 oz Fleischmann's® RapidRise® Yeast packet
- 1 1/2 cup lukewarm water up to 1 3/4 cup
- 6 tbsp quality oil to coat the bowl plus more for the pan
- For the Assembly
- 1 lb mozzarella cheese sliced (up to 2 lbs)
- 3/4 cup pizza sauce up to 1 cup
- 1 lb crumbled cooked Italian sausage
- pepperoni slices
- cooked bacon in bits
- 1 green pepper chopped
- 1/2 medium onion chopped
- grated parmesan cheese
- dried Italian seasoning

Directions:

1. For the Pizza Dough

2. Add all-purpose flour, salt, sugar and yeast to a large bowl and stir to combine.

3. Next, add 2 tbsp of oil to the lukewarm water then add enough water to dry ingredients until it becomes elastic and soft but not too sticky. Remove from the bowl and knead with a little flour and form a ball.

4. Take another large bowl and coat with 1-2 tbsp of olive oil. Add the dough to the bowl, cover with plastic wrap, and let rise in a warm area for an hour.

5. After an hour, add remaining 3 tbsp of olive oil to a 11x17 inch pan. Remove the dough from the covered bowl and, using your finger tips, press and spread out the dough allowing some of the oil to get on the top of the dough in the dimples. Add plastic wrap over the pan and allow it to rest again in a warm area for another hour.

6. To Assemble Pizza

7. Preheat the oven to 500 degrees or as high as your oven will go and set your rack on the lowest bottom position.

8. Top your pizza dough with mozzarella cheese leaving a 1 inch border uncovered. Add as much cheese as you prefer.

9. Spoon pizza sauce over the cheese in diagonal rows or in various spots on top of the dough.

10. Sprinkle sausage, pepperoni, bacon, green pepper and onion on top of cheese and sauce.

11. Finally sprinkle with grated parmesan cheese making sure to sprinkle even on the 1 inch border.

12. Sprinkle with a tiny bit of Italian seasoning.

13. Bake for 20-25 minutes or until the dough is very crisp and browned and the cheese is totally melted and golden and slightly browned bubbly (don't' burn!).

Notes

To Store: After you've had your fill, allow the remaining slices to cool down until the cheese has slightly hardened. Next, stack the slices in a large resealable bag and store in the refrigerator. Alternatively, you can stack the slices in between sheets of wax or parchment paper and then, wrap the pizza pile in plastic wrap. Pizza will stay fresh for up to 4 days.

To Reheat: My first suggestion is to use an air fryer! Yes, an air fryer. It returns the dough to the perfect crisp exterior that you remember from the first dining experience. Secondly I suggest using a conventional oven for a perfectly crisp outside, warm, saucy inside and a gooey layer of cheese. Preheat the oven to 350 degrees, line a baking sheet with parchment paper and arrange the slices on top. Mist or drizzle a bit of water (to add moisture) and cover loosely with foil. Bake until hot and melt, about 15-20 minutes.

Air Fryer Toasted Perogies Recipe
Servings: 6
Cooking Time: 12 Minutes

Ingredients:
- 1 bag store bought frozen Perogies
- 2 cups Italian-style bread crumbs
- 1 egg
- 1 cup buttermilk
- Olive Oil Spray
- Parmesan cheese optional

Directions:
1. Whisk together egg and buttermilk. Dip Perogi in the egg/milk mixture and then cover with breadcrumbs. Repeat with all perogies.
2. Add perogies to the air fryer basket and spray with olive oil spray. Close the fryer basket and press power. Set the temperature to 400 degrees F and time to 12 minutes. Halfway through, pause and turn the perogies over. Add additional spray, if needed.
3. Garnish with additional Parmesan cheese and serve hot.

Air-fryer Pizza
Servings: 4
Cooking Time: 10 Minutes

Ingredients:
- 1 leftover refrigerated pizza

Directions:
1. Preheat air fryer to 180°C. Place pizza slices in a single layer into air fryer and
2. cook in batches for 3 minutes or until crisp and heated through. Serve.

VEGETABLE & & VEGETARIAN RECIPES

Poblano And Black Bean Loaded Baked Potato

Servings: 4

Ingredients:

- 4 medium russet potatoes (about 8 oz each), scrubbed and dried
- Olive oil
- Kosher salt
- 2 poblano peppers, cut into small pieces
- 1 15.5-oz can black beans (including liquid)
- 1/2 tsp. ground cumin
- 1/4 tsp. smoked paprika
- 1/3 c. sour cream
- 1/2 tsp. tsp lime zest, plus 2 tsp lime juice and more for serving
- 1 large plum tomato, seeded and chopped
- Grated Cheddar, for serving

Directions:

1. Heat oven to 400°F. Prick potatoes and microwave on High 10 minutes. Brush potatoes with 1 tablespoon oil, sprinkle with 1/4 teaspoon kosher salt, place directly on middle oven rack (with baking sheet on rack below to catch oil drippings), and bake until tender, 18 to 20 minutes.
2. Meanwhile, heat 1 tablespoon oil in large skillet on medium. Add peppers and cook, covered, stirring occasionally, until tender, 5 to 7 minutes; transfer to plate.
3. To skillet, add black beans, cumin, smoked paprika, and 1/4 teaspoon salt and cook, stirring occasionally, until beans are slightly thickened, 4 to 5 minutes. Fold in poblanos.
4. In bowl, combine sour cream and lime zest. In second bowl, toss tomato with lime juice and a pinch of salt.
5. Split potatoes, top with Cheddar if desired, then top with beans, tomatoes, and sour cream. Sprinkle with additional lime zest if desired.
6. AIR FRYER:
7. Air fry potatoes (do not microwave) at 400°F until tender, 35 to 40 minutes, flipping once. Meanwhile, toss poblanos with 1 teaspoon oil and 1/4 teaspoon salt. In another bowl, toss the beans with cumin, paprika, 1/4 teaspoon salt and 1/2 teaspoon oil. Remove potatoes from air-fryer and transfer to a plate. Add poblanos to air fryer and air-fry until tender, 5 to 6 minutes. Transfer to bowl with black beans and fold to combine. Split potatoes, top with cheese, then bean-poblano mixture. Return potatoes to air fryer and air-fry just until cheese melts and bean mixture is warmed through, 1 to 2 minutes. Serve topped with tomatoes, sour cream and more lime zest.

Mushroom Fajitas

Servings: 3
Cooking Time: 10 Minutes

Ingredients:

- 2 portobello mushrooms, gills removed and sliced into ¼-inch thick strips
- 2 bell peppers, any color, ribs removed and cut into ¼-inch-thick slices
- ½ red onion, thinly sliced
- 3 garlic cloves, minced
- ½ jalapeno, seeded and minced
- 2 tablespoons neutral oil
- 2 limes, zested and juiced
- 2 teaspoons dried oregano
- 2 teaspoons kosher salt
- 1 teaspoon ground coriander
- 1 teaspoon paprika
- For Serving:
- Warm tortillas (flour or corn)
- Lime wedges

Directions:

1. Select the Preheat function on the Air Fryer, adjust the temperature to 380°F, then press Start/Pause.
2. Combine the sliced portobellos, bell peppers, red onion, garlic, jalapeno, oil, lime zest, lime juice, oregano, salt, coriander, and paprika in a large bowl and mix well.
3. Place the vegetables into the preheated air fryer basket.

4. Set the temperature to 380°F and adjust the timer to 10 minutes and press Start/Pause.
5. Shake the vegetables halfway through the cooking time.
6. Remove the vegetables when done, then serve them with the tortillas and lime wedges.

Air Fryer Buffalo Cauliflower Wings
Servings: 6
Cooking Time: 30 Minutes

Ingredients:
- For the Cauliflower
- 4 cups cauliflower florets ~1 medium head
- 1 cup blanched superfine almond meal
- 1 tablespoon garlic powder
- 1/2 teaspoon smoked paprika
- 1/2 teaspoon salt
- 1/2 teaspoon ground pepper
- 2 large eggs
- For the Buffalo Sauce
- 3 tablespoons melted butter
- 1/2 cup Franks Hot Sauce
- 2 tablespoons honey

Directions:
1. First, prepare cauliflower by cutting it into small, bite-sized pieces.
2. Next, place almond meal, garlic powder, paprika, salt, and pepper into a medium bowl and whisk to combine. Whisk 2 eggs in another medium bowl.
3. Prepare cauliflower wings by tossing cauliflower pieces in the egg wash to fully coat them. Then, place a couple of pieces of cauliflower into the almond meal bowl at a time. Use a spoon to carefully spoon the mixture on top of the cauliflower, coating it fully. Repeat until all cauliflower is coated in the mixture.
4. Preheat the air fryer to 370°F and spray the pan with nonstick cooking spray. Once preheated, place half of your cauliflower wings onto the bottom of the pan and spray the tops with nonstick cooking spray. It's okay if they are touching, but you'll have to cook these wings in 2 separate batches.

5. Air fry cauliflower wings at 370°F (or 375°F depending on the air fryer) for 12-15 minutes, tossing halfway through. You know your wings are done when they begin to brown and crisp up.
6. While your wings are air frying, prepare buffalo sauce. Melt 3 tablespoons of butter and then mix it with Frank's Hot Sauce and honey. Stir to combine.
7. Once your wings are done air frying, toss them in the buffalo sauce.
8. Serve immediately with your favorite dipping sauce.

Air-fryer Mushrooms With Balsamic, Thyme, And Goat Cheese
Servings: 4
Cooking Time: 8 Minutes

Ingredients:
- 16 ounce fresh button or cremini mushrooms, halved or quartered
- 1 tablespoon olive oil
- 2 cloves garlic, minced
- ¼ teaspoon kosher salt
- ¼ teaspoon black pepper
- 1 tablespoon balsamic glaze
- 2 tablespoon crumbled goat cheese (chevre)
- 2 teaspoon chopped fresh thyme

Directions:
1. Preheat air fryer at 375°F. In a medium bowl toss together mushrooms, oil, garlic, salt, and pepper.
2. Working in batches if needed, arrange mushrooms in a single layer in air-fryer basket. Cook 8 to 10 minutes or until tender and golden, stirring once.
3. While still warm, transfer mushrooms to a serving bowl. Drizzle with balsamic glaze; toss to coat. Sprinkle with cheese and thyme.

Lamb Chops With Roast Potatoes And Chilli Mint Sauce

Servings: 3-4
Cooking Time: 25 Minutes

Ingredients:
- Potatoes
- 750g baby potatoes, halved
- 1 Tbsp olive oil
- 1 Tbsp chopped rosemary
- salt and pepper to taste
- Chops
- 6 lamb rib chops
- 1 Tbsp olive oil
- 1 Tbsp thyme leaves
- 1/2 Tbsp lemon juice
- 1 clove garlic, minced
- 1 tsp cumin seeds
- 1 tsp lemon zest
- salt and pepper to taste
- Sauce
- 50g fresh mint
- 5 rosemary sprigs
- 1/4 cup olive oil
- 2 Tbsp lemon juice
- 1/2 tsp chili flakes
- salt and pepper to taste
- To serve
- 250g tenderstem broccoli

Directions:
1. On the Vortex Plus ClearCook Dual, set drawer 1 to Grill* mode at 8 min and drawer 2 to Air Fry at 200C at 20 minutes; press Sync Finish so both drawers finish at the same time. Press Start and allow preheating to commence.
2. For the potatoes toss all the ingredients together to coat. When drawer 2 is ready, add the potatoes and allow to cook, tossing halfway.
3. In the meantime, mix all the ingredients for the chops and coat them well. When drawer 1 is ready, add the chops and Grill for 8 minutes, turning halfway.
4. Blitz together all ingredients for the sauce to achieve a chunky consistency. When they are done, remove the chops from the drawer.

5. Reset this drawer to Air Fry at 180C for 5 minutes and add the broccoli. Cook the broccoli while the chops rest, tossing through the left-over lamb spices in the basket.
6. Serve the chops with crispy roast potatoes, broccoli, and a drizzle of chilli mint sauce. Enjoy!
7. *Grill mode automatically sets the Vortex to the highest temperature 205C for best results.

Air Fryer Garlic Zucchini

Servings: 2
Cooking Time: 15 Minutes

Ingredients:
- 2 zucchini (@ 1 lb. or 455g total)
- Olive oil or cooking spray
- 1 teaspoon (5 g) garlic powder
- salt , to taste
- black pepper , to taste

Directions:
1. Wash and dry the zucchini. Cut the ends of the zucchini, if desired. Cut the zucchini into 1/2" thick slices (either into lengthwise slices or into coins). If cutting into lengthwise slices, cut to length to fit the width of your air fryer basket if needed.
2. Lightly oil or spray the zucchini slices on both sides and then season with garlic powder, salt and pepper.
3. Air Fry at 400°F for 8-14 minutes or until browned and cooked through.

Air Fryer Cauliflower Recipe

Servings: 4
Cooking Time: 15 Minutes

Ingredients:
- 2 tablespoons olive oil
- 3/4 teaspoon kosher salt
- 1/2 teaspoon dried thyme
- 1/4 teaspoon garlic powder
- 1/4 teaspoon freshly ground black pepper
- 1 medium head cauliflower (1 1/2 to 2 pounds)

Directions:

1. Place 2 tablespoons olive oil, 3/4 teaspoon kosher salt, 1/2 teaspoon dried thyme, 1/4 teaspoon garlic powder, and 1/4 teaspoon black pepper in a large bowl and whisk to combine.

2. Cut 1 head cauliflower in half and cut out the tough core. Cut the florets into 1- to 1 1/2-inch pieces (6 to 7 cups). Transfer to the bowl and toss until evenly coated.

3. Heat an air fryer to 390°F to 400°F. Arrange the cauliflower florets in an even layer in the basket or tray of a 5 1/2-quart or larger air fryer. Air fry, tossing every 5 minutes, until the cauliflower is tender with browned and crispy edges, about 15 minutes total.

NOTES

Make ahead: The cauliflower can be cut into florets up to 3 days in advance and refrigerated.

Storage: Leftovers can be refrigerated in an airtight container for up to 4 days.

Air Fryer Zucchini

Servings: 4

Ingredients:
- 2 medium zucchini, sliced into 1/4" rounds
- 2 large eggs
- 3/4 c. panko bread crumbs
- 1/3 c. cornmeal
- 1/3 c. freshly grated Parmesan
- 1 tsp. dried oregano
- 1/4 tsp. garlic powder
- Pinch of crushed red pepper flakes
- Kosher salt
- Freshly ground black pepper
- Marinara, for serving

Directions:
1. Place zucchini on a plate lined with paper towels and pat dry.
2. In a shallow bowl, beat eggs to blend. In another shallow bowl, combine panko, cornmeal, Parmesan, oregano, garlic powder, and red pepper flakes; season with salt and black pepper.

3. Working one at a time, dip zucchini rounds into egg, then into panko mixture, pressing to adhere.
4. Working in batches, in an air-fryer basket, arrange zucchini in an single layer. Cook at 400°, flipping halfway through, until crispy on both sides, about 18 minutes. Serve warm with marinara.

Air Fryer Stuffed Peppers

Servings: 4
Cooking Time: 25 Minutes

Ingredients:
- 2 large bell peppers or 4 small bell peppers
- 1 pound lean ground beef
- ½ onion diced
- 2 cloves garlic minced
- ½ cup instant rice or minute rice
- ½ teaspoon Italian seasoning
- ½ cup water
- 2 cups pasta sauce divided
- ½ cup mozzarella cheese shredded

Directions:
1. Preheat air fryer to 320°F.
2. Cut bell peppers in half lengthwise and scrape out seeds (if using small peppers, cut off tops instead).
3. Brush peppers with olive oil and place in the air fryer basket. Cook 5-6 minutes.
4. While peppers are cooking, brown beef, onion, and garlic in a medium saucepan until no pink remains. Drain fat.
5. Add instant rice, Italian seasoning, water, and 1 cup pasta sauce. Bring to a boil, reduce heat, and simmer 3-4 minutes.
6. Scoop the mixture into the peppers and top with remaining sauce. Turn air fryer up to 350°F and cook 8-10 minutes or until heated through and peppers are soft. Top with cheese and cook an additional 1-2 minutes.

Notes

Leave the stems on the peppers while air frying to make them look pretty.

If your peppers don't sit flat, use a little bit of bunched up foil to hold them in place.

If your peppers are small you may need a few extra.

If you happen to have leftover filling, it's great in tomato soup or stuffed inside zucchini as well.

To brown the cheese add it a little bit earlier.

Air Fryer Tofu
Servings: 4
Cooking Time: 16 Minutes

Ingredients:
- 16 ounces Extra firm tofu
- 2 tablespoons cornstarch
- Tofu Marinade
- 1/4 cup soy sauce or low sodium soy sauce or liquid aminos
- 1 tablespoon sesame oil
- 2 teaspoons garlic minced

Directions:
1. Before you cut tofu into cubes, press and drain tofu to remove excess moisture, for 30 minutes. If you don't have tofu press, you can wrap the block of tofu with layers of paper towel or a clean dish towel, then place a heavy object on top and let the tofu sit for about 15-30 minutes.
2. Once drained, slice tofu into 1 inch cubes, then place tofu cubes into a medium bowl and add ingredients for tofu marinade. Gently toss until the tofu is coated.
3. Set bowl aside to allow the tofu to marinate for about 15-30 minutes. Once marinated, toss tofu in cornstarch.
4. Spread cubed tofu pieces in a single layer in air fryer basket, without stacking or overlapping. Air fry at 380 degrees F for 16-20 minutes, gently tossing halfway through cooking time.
5. Eat tofu cubes themselves, with vegetables, or toss with sesame seeds and serve with pasta or rice.
NOTES
Optional Sauces: You can serve this tofu with any of your favorite dipping sauce. I love hot sauce, barbecue sauce, or for a sweet tofu, substitute a little bit of maple syrup.

Air Fryer Broccoli Recipe
Servings: 4
Cooking Time: 10-12 Minutes

Ingredients:
- 1 1/2 pounds broccoli (2 medium)
- 2 tablespoons olive oil
- 1/2 teaspoon kosher salt
- 1/4 teaspoon red pepper flakes
- Finely grated Parmesan cheese or nutritional yeast, for serving (optional)

Directions:
1. Cut the stalks off 1 1/2 pounds broccoli. Cut the florets into 1- to 1 1/2-inch pieces. Trim the tough, woody ends of the stems, peel until you get to the lighter smooth parts of the stems, then slice crosswise into 1/4-inch pieces.
2. Place the florets and stems (7 to 8 cups) in a large bowl. Drizzle with 2 tablespoons olive oil, 1/2 teaspoon kosher salt, and 1/4 teaspoon red pepper flakes, and toss to combine.
3. Heat an air fryer to 390°F to 400°F. Arrange the broccoli florets and stems in an even layer in the basket or tray of a 5 1/2-quart or larger air fryer. Air fry, tossing every 5 minutes, until the broccoli is tender with brown and crispy edges, 10 to 12 minutes total.
4. Transfer the broccoli to a serving platter and top with finely grated Parmesan cheese or nutritional yeast if desired.
NOTES
Make ahead: The broccoli can be cut into florets up to 3 days in advance.
Storage: Leftovers can be refrigerated in an airtight container for up to 4 days.

Air Fryer Acorn Squash
Servings: 2
Cooking Time: 25 Minutes

Ingredients:
- 1 whole acorn squash
- 1 tablespoon olive oil
- ½ teaspoon kosher salt
- Black pepper, to taste
- 2 tablespoons unsalted butter (optional)

Directions:
1. Preheat your air fryer to 350 degrees F. Wash and dry the acorn squash, then use a sharp knife to cut it in half lengthwise. Use a spoon to scoop out the seeds, then discard them.
2. Brush the cut sides with olive oil, then season with salt and pepper to taste. Place the two halves of the squash, cut side down, in the basket of the air fryer.
3. Air fry for 15 minutes. Carefully flip the squash, so the cut sides face up. Place 1 tablespoon of butter in the cavity of each one, then air fry at 400 degrees F for about 5-10 more minutes, until the squash flesh is browned and fork tender.

Air Fryer Veggie Dippers
Servings: 4
Cooking Time: 20 Minutes

Ingredients:
- For the Dippers
- 1 medium potato approx 200g, peeled and diced
- 1 medium carrot peeled and diced
- 60 g red pepper deseeded and diced
- 30 g canned sweetcorn drained
- 30 g frozen peas, no need to defrost
- 60 g cooked Basmati rice
- 1/4 tsp garlic granules
- 1/4 tsp onion granules
- 1/4 tsp smoked paprika
- 1 tbsp tomato puree
- 50 g panko breadcrumbs
- 100 ml dairy free coconut milk alternative
- salt and pepper to taste
- low calorie cooking spray
- For the ketchup
- 3 tbsp reduced sugar and salt tomato ketchup
- 1 tbsp honey
- 1/4 tsp chipotle paste

Directions:
1. Add the potato and carrot to a small saucepan of boiling water and set on a medium heat. Cook for 10 minutes until the potato and carrot are soft but holding their shape. Run under cold water and drain.
2. Add the rice, red pepper, sweetcorn, frozen peas, carrot and potato to a food processor and pulse. The vegetables should still be chunky, but some bits mashed.
3. Tip the vegetable mix into a mixing bowl and add the garlic granules, onion granules, smoked paprika and tomato purée. Give it a good mix and season with salt and black pepper.
4. Line a baking tray with greaseproof paper. Take a small amount of mixture in your hands and shape into a rough dipper shape. Place onto the baking tray and further shape the dippers. The mixture should make 12 dippers.
5. Place the baking tray into the freezer for one hour until the dippers are firm.
6. Pre-heat the air fryer to 200°C and pour the panko breadcrumbs and coconut milk alternative into 2 small bowls.
7. Take the first dipper and dip into the coconut milk alternative then into the panko forming a coating all over. Repeat with all dippers.
8. Add the dippers to the air fryer, spray with a little low calorie cooking spray and cook for 20 minutes until crispy and golden.
9. To make the ketchup, mix the ketchup, honey and chipotle paste in a small bowl and serve alongside the dippers.

Air Fryer Mushrooms
Servings: 2
Cooking Time: 35 Minutes

Ingredients:
- 4 large flat mushrooms
- 2 tsp chopped fresh tarragon
- 50g garlic butter, chopped

- Select all Ingredients:

Directions:
1. Heat air fryer to 180°C. Place the mushrooms, base-side up, in the air fryer basket. Sprinkle with fresh tarragon. Spray with oil and place the garlic butter on the gills of the mushrooms. Cook for 5 minutes.

Sausage And Cabbage

Ingredients:
- 12 oz smoked sausage, cut into coins
- 1 yellow onion, sliced
- 1 head of green cabbage, chopped
- 3 cloves garlic, minced
- Pinch of red pepper flakes
- Salt and pepper, to taste

Directions:
1. Add the sausage and onion into the air fryer basket. Spray with a little oil spray and season with salt and pepper to taste.
2. Cook at 400F for about 12 minutes, getting the sausage and onion a bit crispy.
3. Once done, remove the sausage and onion to a clean plate.
4. Without cleaning the basket, add in the cabbage. This adds a little flavor to the cabbage.
5. Steam at 212F for about 6 minutes. You want the cabbage to still have a bit to it.
6. Remove the basket and season the cabbage with salt, pepper, red pepper flakes and the 3 cloves of minced garlic.
7. Add in the sausage and onions and give it a nice mix.
8. Cook all together at 400F for 5 minutes or so.
9. Plate and enjoy!

Mini Air Fryer Hasselback Potatoes

Servings: 4
Cooking Time: 10 Minutes

Ingredients:
- 1 pound small golden potatoes (about 1.5" long)
- olive oil spray

Directions:
1. Slice each potato ~10 times, making sure not to cut all the way through the potato. You want to have no larger than ¼" slices that go no more than ¾ of the way through the potato.
2. Add the potatoes cut side up to the air fryer (make sure not to overcrowd the air fryer basket) and spray them with olive oil spray. Season as desired (see notes for flavor suggestions).
3. Cook at 400°F for 10-12 minutes or until the potatoes are crisp and golden brown. Serve warm or store in an airtight container in the fridge for up to two days.

Notes

Serving Suggestions

Ranch: Sprinkle a pinch (about ¼ teaspoon) of dried ranch seasoning over each potato in Step 2.

Garlic Parmesan: Combine ½ cup grated parmesan and ¾ teaspoon garlic powder in a small bowl. Top each potato with 1 teaspoon of the mixture in Step 2.

Plain: Sprinkle a small pinch (about ⅛ teaspoon) of kosher salt over each potato in Step 2.

These potatoes will keep in the refrigerator for up to 4 days.

Loaded Air Fryer Smashed Potatoes

Servings: 4
Cooking Time: 20 Minutes

Ingredients:
- 1 pound baby potatoes
- 2 slices uncooked bacon
- ½ cup cheddar cheese shredded
- 1 green onion sliced
- ¼ cup sour cream
- salt and pepper to taste

Directions:
1. Preheat the air fryer to 390°F.
2. Place the bacon in the air fryer basket and cook for 6-7 minutes or until crispy.
3. Remove from the basket and place on a paper towel don't discard the bacon grease. Crumble the bacon and set aside for later.
4. Toss the potatoes in a medium bowl with the seasonings and bacon grease.
5. Place the potatoes in the air fryer basket and cook for 10-13 minutes or until fork-tender.

6. Using the bottom side of a measuring cup or glass gently crush the potatoes and top with cheese.

7. Cook for 2 more minutes or until cheese is melted.

8. Garnish with sour cream, bacon bits, and green onions.

Notes

Don't overfill the air fryer basket with potatoes as they will take up more space once smashed. Cook in batches if needed. Heat all batches together before serving for 3 minutes.

Air Fryer Blooming Onion Recipe

Servings: 4
Cooking Time: 30-35 Minutes

Ingredients:

- FOR THE ONION:
- 1 large sweet onion (about 1 pound), such as Vidalia
- 1 cup all-purpose flour
- 1 tablespoon paprika
- 2 teaspoons kosher salt
- 1 teaspoon ground cumin
- 1/2 teaspoon garlic powder
- 1/4 teaspoon freshly ground black pepper
- 2 large eggs
- 1/2 cups whole or 2% milk
- Cooking spray
- FOR THE SAUCE:
- 2 tablespoons mayonnaise
- 2 tablespoons sour cream
- 1 tablespoon ketchup
- 1 teaspoon Worcestershire sauce
- 1/2 teaspoon paprika
- 1/2 teaspoon garlic powder
- 1/2 teaspoon kosher salt
- 1/8 teaspoon cayenne pepper

Directions:

1. Cut off about 1/2 inch from the stem end of 1 large sweet onion. Peel and discard the outer skin. Place the onion cut-side down on the cutting board. Starting about 1/2 inch from the root, make a downward cut to the bottom of the onion. Repeat to make 3 more evenly-spaced cuts around the onion. Make 3 additional cuts between each section until you have 16 evenly spaced cuts.

2. Flip the onion over and use your fingers to gently pull back and separate the onion sections to separate the petals.

3. Place 1 cup all-purpose flour, 1 tablespoon paprika, 2 teaspoons kosher salt, 1/2 teaspoon garlic powder, 1/2 teaspoon ground cumin, and 1/4 teaspoon black pepper in a large, wide bowl, and whisk to combine. Place 2 large eggs and 1/2 cup milk in a medium bowl and whisk to combine.

4. Heat an air fryer to 375°F. Meanwhile, coat the onion.

5. Transfer the flour mixture to a rimmed baking sheet and place the onion on top. Use your hands or a spoon to sprinkle the flour mixture over the onion, separating the petals as needed, so that the onion is well-coated all over. Shake off any excess flour if needed, then pour the remaining flour mixture back into the bowl.

6. Dip the onion in the egg mixture, moving the petals as needed so that it's coated all over. Allow any excess to drip off. Return the onion to the baking sheet. Working your way around the onion, use your hands or a spoon to sprinkle the remaining flour mixture all over the onion and in between each petal, so that the onion is well-coated all over. Shake off any excess to avoid clumping.

7. Generously coat the onion all over, including in between the petals, with cooking spray. Lightly coat the air fryer basket with cooking spray. Use a thin metal spatula to place the onion in the basket. Air fry until crispy and golden brown all over, 30 to 35 minutes. Meanwhile, make the dipping sauce.

8. Place 2 tablespoons mayonnaise, 2 tablespoons sour cream, 1 tablespoon ketchup, 1 teaspoon Worcestershire sauce, 1/2 teaspoon paprika, 1/2 teaspoon garlic powder, 1/2 teaspoon kosher salt, and 1/8 teaspoon cayenne pepper in a small bowl, and stir to combine.

9. Remove the blooming onion from basket and serve immediately with the dipping sauce.

NOTES

Make ahead: The dipping sauce can be made up to 1 day in advance and refrigerated in an airtight container.

Air Fryer Fingerling Potatoes
Servings: 4
Cooking Time: 18 Minutes

Ingredients:
- 1.5 pounds fingerling potatoes, washed and sliced in half lengthwise
- 2 tablespoons olive oil
- 1 teaspoon garlic powder
- 1 teaspoon Italian seasoning
- ½ teaspoon salt (or to taste)

Directions:
1. Preheat your air fryer to 400 F.
2. In a large bowl, toss the halved potatoes with oil, garlic powder, italian seasoning, and salt until all potatoes are evenly coated.
3. Transfer the mixture to the preheated air fryer and cook 15-18 minutes, shaking the basket halfway through, or until cooked through.
NOTES
HOW TO REHEAT FINGERLING POTATOES:
Preheat your air fryer to 350 degrees.
Add potatoes and cook for 3-5 minutes or until they are hot all the way through.

Cauliflower Tots
Servings: 6

Ingredients:
- Cooking spray
- 4 c. cauliflower florets, steamed (about 1/2 large cauliflower)
- 1 large egg, lightly beaten
- 1 c. shredded cheddar
- 1 c. freshly grated Parmesan
- 2/3 c. panko breadcrumbs
- 2 tbsp. freshly chopped chives
- Kosher salt
- Freshly ground black pepper
- 1/2 c. ketchup
- 2 tbsp. Sriracha

Directions:
1. FOR OVEN
2. Preheat oven to 375°. Grease a large baking sheet with cooking spray.
3. In a food processor, pulse steamed cauliflower until riced. Place riced cauliflower on a clean kitchen towel and squeeze to drain water.
4. Transfer cauliflower to a large bowl with egg, cheddar, Parmesan, Panko, and chives and mix until combined. Season with salt and pepper to taste.
5. Spoon about 1 tablespoon mixture and roll it into a tater-tot shape with your hands. Place on prepared baking sheet and bake for 15 to 20 minutes, until tots are golden.
6. Meanwhile, make spicy ketchup: Combine ketchup and Sriracha in a small serving bowl and stir to combine.
7. Serve warm cauliflower tots with spicy ketchup.
8. FOR AIR FRYER
9. In a food processor, pulse steamed cauliflower until riced. Place riced cauliflower on a clean kitchen towel and squeeze to drain water.
10. Transfer cauliflower to a large bowl with egg, cheddar, Parmesan, Panko, and chives and mix until combined. Season with salt and pepper to taste.
11. Spoon about 1 tablespoon mixture and roll it into a tater-tot shape with your hands. Working in batches, arrange in basket of air fryer in a single layer and cook at 375° for 10, until tots are golden.
12. Meanwhile, make spicy ketchup: Combine ketchup and Sriracha in a small serving bowl and stir to combine.
13. Serve warm cauliflower tots with spicy ketchup.

Crispy, Cheesy Cauliflower Balls

Ingredients:
- 300g cauliflower florets - steamed
- Handful Freshly chopped Spring Onion
- 2 cloves garlic - crushed
- 1 cup grated Mozzarella

- 60g Hard grated Cheese / Parmesan
- 1 Large Egg
- 1/2 cup breadcrumbs
- 1 T smoked Chilli flakes
- Salt & Pepper

Directions:

1. Steam the cauliflower - Once cooked place in a bowl and mash with a fork. You could use a food processor or mash until your desired consistency is reached. I prefer them to have a bit of integrity so I lightly mashed mine.

2. Add all the ingredients to the bowl and mix well. Mould the batter into balls - I suggest golf ball size. Using your Instant Pot Air Fryer - Preheat to 191C and bake for 20min - turning the balls halfway through. Serve with a dip or as a side and enjoy!

Air Fried Crunchy Onion Rings

Servings: 6
Cooking Time: 20 Minutes

Ingredients:
- 1 cup all-purpose flour
- 1 teaspoon paprika
- 1 teaspoon salt, divided
- 1 cup buttermilk
- 2 eggs
- 2 cups panko breadcrumbs
- 2 large sweet onions, sliced 1/2-inch thick and separated into rings
- Oil Spray

Directions:

1. In a shallow bowl combine flour, paprika, and ½ teaspoon salt. In another bowl combine buttermilk and egg. In the third combine panko breadcrumbs and remaining ½ teaspoon salt.

2. Pat dry the onion rings with paper towels to remove excessive moisture. Dredge the onions in the flour mixture, drop them in the egg mixture and then dredge them in the panko mixture.

3. Arrange in a single layer on a dark-coated, non-stick baking sheet. Coat liberally with oil spray.

4. Air Fry at 400°F for 10 minutes, flip, cook 5 minutes more. Serve immediately with dipping sauce of your choice.

Air Fryer Pickles

Servings: 8
Cooking Time: 5 Minutes

Ingredients:
- 4 large dill pickles
- 1/4 cup flour
- For the batter
- 1 large egg
- 1 tablespoon mustard
- 1 tablespoon mayonnaise
- 1/2 cup water
- 1/3 cup flour
- For the dry mix
- 1/2 cup breadcrumbs
- 1/2 cup panko breadcrumbs
- 1/2 teaspoon smoked paprika
- 1/4 teaspoon salt

Directions:

1. Preheat the air fryer to 200C/400F.

2. Slice the pickles in ½ inch slices and toss them in the flour.

3. In a small bowl, whisk together the egg, mustard, mayonnaise, and water. Slowly fold in the flour, until a smooth pancake-like batter remains. In a separate bowl, whisk together the dry mix.

4. Dip the pickles in the first batter, then the dry mix. Place the battered pickles on a plate lined with parchment paper.

5. Generously grease an air fryer basket. Place the pickles in a single layer and air fry for 4-5 minutes, or until golden brown.

6. Remove them from the air fryer and repeat the process until all the pickles are air fried.

Notes

TO STORE: Place leftovers in a shallow container and store them in the refrigerator for up to three days.

TO FREEZE: Place the cooled air fried pickles in a ziplock bag and store them in the freezer for up to two months.

TO REHEAT: These pickles are supposed to be crispy, so do not reheat them in the microwave. Instead, use a preheated oven or back in the air fryer.

Air Fryer Spinach-artichoke Crescent Bites

Servings: 16

Ingredients:
- 1 package (10 oz) frozen chopped spinach
- 3 oz (from 8-oz package) cream cheese, softened
- 1 tablespoon plus 1 teaspoon grated Parmesan cheese
- 1/4 teaspoon salt
- 1/8 teaspoon garlic powder
- 1/4 cup artichoke hearts, drained, chopped and patted dry (from 14-oz can)
- 1 can (8 oz) refrigerated Pillsbury™ Original Crescent Rolls (8 Count)
- 1 tablespoon butter, melted

Directions:
1. Cook spinach as directed on package; drain. Cool 15 minutes. With hands, squeeze excess liquid from spinach. Measure 1/4 cup of the spinach; set aside for filling. Cover and refrigerate remaining spinach for another use.
2. Cut 8-inch round of cooking parchment paper. Place in bottom of air fryer basket.
3. In medium bowl, stir cream cheese, 1 tablespoon of the Parmesan cheese, the salt and garlic powder with spatula until blended. Stir in the 1/4 cup spinach and the artichoke hearts until mixed well.
4. Unroll dough; separate into 8 triangles. With pizza cutter or sharp knife, cut each triangle in half lengthwise to 16 triangles. Spoon approximately 2 teaspoons cream cheese mixture onto each triangle. Roll up, starting at shortest side and rolling to opposite point. Place 8 crescents on parchment in air fryer basket point side down, spacing apart
5. In small bowl, stir melted butter with remaining 1 teaspoon Parmesan cheese. Brush half of the mixture over tops of crescents in air fryer basket.
6. Set air fryer to 325°F; cook 5 to 6 minutes or until crescent tops are light brown. With tongs, turn over each one; cook 4 to 5 minutes or until golden brown and cooked through. Remove from air fryer. Repeat with remaining crescents, brushing tops with remaining butter mixture before cooking.

Roasted Tomato Bruschetta

Servings: 4
Cooking Time: 10 Minutes

Ingredients:
- 3 cups cherry tomatoes, halved
- 3 garlic cloves, minced
- 1 shallot, minced
- 1 tablespoon olive oil, plus more as needed
- 1 tablespoon fresh thyme leaves, chopped
- 1 teaspoon kosher salt
- ½ teaspoon freshly ground black pepper
- 1 baguette, cut into ½-inch rounds
- 1 tablespoon fresh basil leaves, for garnish

Directions:
1. Select the Air Fry function on the Air Fryer Oven, adjust time to 10 minutes, then tap Start/Pause to preheat.
2. Combine the tomatoes, garlic, shallot, olive oil, thyme, salt, and pepper in a medium bowl and stir to combine, then transfer to the food tray.
3. Place the baguette slices onto the air fryer tray and drizzle them with olive oil.
4. Insert the food tray at position 3 and the air fryer tray at position 2 in the preheated air fryer oven.
5. Remove the toasts after 4 minutes.
6. Remove the tomato topping when done, then spoon onto the toasts and serve garnished with basil.

Air Fryer Tomatoes

Servings: 4
Cooking Time: 8 Minutes

Ingredients:

- 4 medium Roma tomatoes
- 1 tablespoon olive oil
- 1 clove garlic minced
- 1 teaspoon rosemary freshly chopped
- 1 teaspoon thyme freshly chopped
- Salt and Pepper to taste

Directions:

1. Wash and pat dry each tomato with paper towels. Then slice in half with a sharp knife, lengthwise.
2. In a medium bowl, or laying flat on a baking sheet, toss tomatoes with olive oil, then season with garlic, rosemary, and thyme.
3. Brush the bottom of the Air Fryer basket with olive oil, spritz with cooking spray, or line with a piece of parchment paper. Place tomato slices in the air fryer basket in a single layer.
4. Air fry at 380 degrees Fahrenheit for 8-10 minutes. If you want crispier tomatoes, depending on size of tomatoes, add a few additional minutes of cook time.

NOTES

Seasonings and Flavors: Sprinkle some parmesan cheese, fresh herbs, blue cheese, garlic powder, or Italian seasoning!

Varieties of Tomatoes: You can use several kinds of tomatoes for this recipe. For example, you can use grape tomatoes, beefsteak tomatoes, Campari tomatoes, plum tomatoes, cherry tomatoes, or whatever type of tomato you like!

Flavorful Tomatoes: To get super flavorful tomatoes, make sure you thoroughly coat the tomatoes in seasonings so that the flavor can meld with the tomato's juices. In addition, using seasonal tomatoes gives you an amazing flavor on top of added seasonings!

SNACKS & APPETIZERS RECIPES

Tater Tots In The Air Fryer
Servings: 4
Cooking Time: 7 Minutes

Ingredients:
- 16 ounces frozen tater tots

Directions:
1. Preheat your air fryer to 400 degrees.
2. Place the frozen tater tots into the air fryer filling the basket no more than halfway.
3. Cook tater tots for 7 to 9 minutes, shaking the basket halfway through.
4. Remove tots from the air fryer and enjoy immediately with your favorite dipping sauce.

Avocado Fries
Servings: 35
Cooking Time: 20 Minutes

Ingredients:
- 2 large avocados
- ½ cup unsweetened almond milk , may also sub with 1 large egg if not vegan
- ½ cup superfine blanched almond flour
- For the coating:
- 1 cup unsweetened toasted shredded coconut , OR sub with crushed Simple Mills Grain-Free Sea Salt Almond Flour Crackers (or other favorite grain-free crackers like Hu's Kitchen Grain-Free Crackers)
- 1.5 tbsp Cajun seasoning spice mix OR smoked paprika
- Salt and pepper
- For the optional dip:
- ⅓ cup vegan mayo
- 1 tbsp lemon juice
- ½ tbsp Cajun seasoning
- Salt and pepper to taste

Directions:
1. Use a large knife to cut your avocados in half and remove the pit from the middle. Cut the avocado into wedges or "fries".
2. Oven Directions:
3. Preheat oven to 400F. Line a large baking sheet with parchment paper.
4. Gather three wide shallow bowls. Place the almond milk in one bowl, the almond flour in the next bowl and combine the coating ingredients in the the third bowl.
5. Take one avocado slice, place it in the flour. Make sure it is fully coated in flour then gently shake to get rid of any excess flour.
6. Place it in the almond milk and again make sure it is fully coated and wet. You will find it easier if you use one hand for the first two steps and then the other hand for the breading, so you don't get too messy!
7. Finally place it in the coconut breading, making sure it is fully coated, then place on the baking pan.
8. Repeat until all the slices are coated. Place the baking sheet in the oven for 15-20 minutes until turning golden brown.
9. FOR THE DIP:
10. Make the dip by mixing all the ingredients together. Enjoy with the avocado fries!
11. Air Fryer Directions:
12. Place the breaded avocado sticks in a single layer in the air fryer basket, you will have to work in batches.
13. Lightly coat with cooking spray and cook for 8-12 minutes at 375F, or until golden and crispy, flipping halfway through.

Air Fryer Green Beans
Servings: 4
Cooking Time: 10 Minutes

Ingredients:
- 1 pound Green Beans
- 1 tbsp olive oil
- 1 tsp salt
- 1/2 tsp black pepper

Directions:
1. Trim the ends of the green beans, then rinse in water.
2. In a large bowl combine the beans with olive oil, salt and optional black pepper. Toss

the ingredients together until they beans are coated.

3.   Next, transfer them to the air fryer basket, and then lay them in a single layer. Work in batches if necessary. (One pound green beans is usually two batches.)

4.   Cook at 400 degrees F for 8-10 minutes, tossing one or two times during cooking, until they reach the desired crispness you prefer.

5.   Remove the beans with tongs, and add additional salt, parmesan cheese, or your favorite extra seasonings.

NOTES

Depending on your air fryer, cooking times may vary. Add 1-2 minutes if necessary.

Air Fryer Baked Sweet Potatoes

Servings: 3
Cooking Time: 40 Minutes

Ingredients:
*   3 small sweet potatoes
*   1 tablespoon olive oil
*   1 teaspoon kosher salt

Directions:
1.   Preheat the air fryer to 390°F.

2.   Use a fork to poke holes all over the sweet potato. Rub the skin evenly with olive oil and sprinkle with salt.

3.   Cook for 35-40 minutes or until sweet potatoes are tender when pierced with a fork.

4.   Cut potatoes open and top with butter (and brown sugar if desired).

Air Fryer Kale Chips

Servings: 4
Cooking Time: 3 Minutes

Ingredients:
*   1 bunch kale
*   2 teaspoons olive oil
*   1/2 teaspoon salt

Directions:
1.   Wash the kale and pat dry until completely dry. Roughly tear the leaves into bite sized pieces.

2.   Add the kale to a mixing bowl, then drizzle with olive oil. Using your hands, rub the leaves to ensure they have some oil on them. Sprinkle the salt all over.

3.   Transfer the kale to the air fryer basket and air fry at 190C/375F for 3-4 minutes, ensuring they don't burn.

4.   Repeat the process until all the kale chips are cooked.

Notes

TO STORE: It's best to store the cooled kale chips in a paper bag at room temperature to prevent them from becoming soggy. They should stay crisp for up to 3 days.

Air-fried Chips

Servings: 4
Cooking Time: 35 Minutes

Ingredients:
*   4-5 large potatoes, about 1kg
*   1 tbsp sunflower or olive oil

Directions:
1.   To make straight, neat chips, peel the potatoes and trim away all the rounded edges so they become rectangular blocks. Cut the blocks into batons – they should be somewhere between fries and thick chips, as if they're too thin, they might break; too thick, and they won't cook through (if you like, save the offcuts to make mash or add to soups). Alternatively, cut the unpeeled potatoes into chips without trimming, if you're not bothered by neatness. Rinse the chips and pat dry with a clean tea towel.

2.   Tip the chips into the bottom of an air fryer (the part with the paddle), add the oil, and toss the chips in the oil so they are evenly coated. Program the fryer to cook for 30 mins using the paddle. After this time, check that the chips are tender and cooked through. If they're not, cook for a further 5 mins. Season well.

Air Fryer Crispy Herbed Chickpeas

Servings: 1 1/2

Ingredients:

- 1 (15-ounce) can chickpeas, rinsed and dried with paper towels
- 1 tablespoon olive oil
- 1/2 teaspoon dried rosemary
- 1/2 teaspoon dried parsley
- 1/2 teaspoon dried chives
- 1/4 teaspoon mustard powder
- 1/4 teaspoon sweet paprika
- 1/4 teaspoon cayenne pepper
- Kosher salt and freshly ground black pepper

Directions:

1. In a large bowl, combine all the ingredients except the kosher salt and black pepper and toss until the chickpeas are evenly coated in the herbs and spices. Scrape the chickpeas and seasonings into the air fryer and cook at 350°F until browned and crisp, 6 to 12 minutes, shaking the basket halfway through. Transfer the crispy chickpeas to a bowl, sprinkle with kosher salt and black pepper, and serve warm.
2. Cooks' Note
3. During testing, I found that different brands of canned chickpeas "fry" up at wildly different rates. Some brands only took 6 minutes to get crisp, while other brands, where the chickpeas were comparatively larger in size and meatier, took almost double that. Hence, the range in cooking time for this recipe. Start out with your favorite go-to brand and cook them for 6 minutes. If they're not crisp enough after that, continue cooking in 2-minute intervals until they are. Then you'll know the correct amount of time for that specific brand.

Sesame Air Fryer Green Beans

Servings: 4
Cooking Time: 10 Minutes

Ingredients:

- 1 ½ pounds green beans washed and trimmed
- 1 tablespoon sesame oil
- 1 tablespoon honey
- 2 teaspoons sesame seeds
- 1 clove garlic minced
- ¼ teaspoon red chili flakes or to taste, optional
- ¼ teaspoon salt

Directions:

1. Preheat air fryer to 390°F.
2. Combine sesame oil, honey, sesame seeds, garlic, red chili flakes, and salt in a small bowl. Toss with green beans.
3. Place in the air fryer and cook 9-11 minutes shaking the basket after 6 minutes.

Air Fryer Loaded Tater Tots

Servings: 4
Cooking Time: 15 Minutes

Ingredients:

- 1 bag tater tots
- 3 tablespoons bacon bits
- ½ cup cheddar cheese shredded
- ¼ cup green onions sliced
- ½ cup sour cream

Directions:

1. Heat the air fryer to 400°F.
2. Add tater tots to the basket and cook for five minutes. Flip, and cook for another 3 minutes or until crispy.
3. Sprinkle with the shredded cheese and bacon bits.
4. Return tater tots to the air fryer and bake for another 2-3 minutes until the cheese is melted. Remove.
5. Top with green onion and serve with sour cream.

Air Fryer Tater Tots

Servings: 55

Ingredients:

- 3 lb. russet potatoes, peeled
- 1 1/2 tsp. kosher salt, plus more for finishing
- 1/2 tsp. garlic powder
- 1/4 tsp. onion powder
- Freshly ground black pepper

Directions:

1. In a large pot of boiling water, add potatoes and boil until potatoes are met with only a little resistance when poked with a knife, about 7 minutes. Drain and let cool.
2. When potatoes are cool enough to handle, use medium holes on a box grater to shred potatoes. In a large bowl, combine shredded potatoes, salt, garlic powder, onion powder, and pepper. Use your hands to form about 2 tablespoons worth of mixture into a tater tot shape, gently squeezing mixture as necessary.
3. Working in batches, place tater tots in basket of air fryer. Cook on 375° for 20 minutes, stopping to shake basket halfway through, until golden.
4. Remove from basket and sprinkle with salt.

Air Fryer Potato Chips

Servings: 4
Cooking Time: 30 Minutes

Ingredients:

- 2 baking potatoes
- olive oil
- salt & seasonings to taste

Directions:

1. Scrub potatoes and thinly slice into ⅛" slices using a mandolin.
2. Place potato slices in a bowl of cold water and let soak 15-30 minutes. Drain well and dab dry with a towel.
3. Preheat air fryer to 370°F. Toss potatoes with oil and season with salt to taste.
4. Add potatoes to the air fryer and cook 10 minutes. Toss and continue to cook an additional 12-17 minutes stirring and tossing every few minutes or so.
5. Once the potatoes begin to crisp, remove the browned potatoes so they don't burn. Continue cooking until all chips are crisp and browned.

Notes

Use a mandolin or the 'slice side' on a box grater if possible.

Soaking chips in cold water prevents discoloration and makes them extra crispy,

Dry them as much as possible before cooking.

As individual chips begin to crisp/get slightly brown, remove immediately so they don't burn.

Storage

Store at room temperature in a bowl. If they are sealed, they can sometimes soften. A brown bag with a clip works well too.

If chips lose crispiness, just pop them back in the air fryer for a few minutes until they are hot and crunchy again! Or, place in a single layer on a cookie tray and crisp under the oven broiler for 3-5 minutes.

Fries

Servings: 4
Cooking Time: 8 Minutes

Ingredients:

- 6 Potatoes, sliced into chips
- Olive oil, to toss
- Chilli seasoning, to season
- Salt, to season

Directions:

1. Rinse and dry the chips well, toss in olive oil, chilli and salt.
2. Spray the basket with olive oil spray and layer the chips (if using Duo Crisp) or lie flat across the Vortex drawer.
3. Bake at 200°C for 5-8 minutes, turning / tossing halfway when prompted.

Yuca Fries Recipe

Servings: 6
Cooking Time: 30 Minutes

Ingredients:

- 1 large (900 g) yuca root (cassava)
- ½ tsp salt
- ½ tsp paprika
- ½ tsp garlic powder
- ½ tsp onion powder
- Black pepper to taste
- 2 tbsp oil

Directions:

1. Peel and slice it
2. You can watch the short video for visual instructions.
3. To peel the yuca root, start by cutting off both ends. If the root has a thin peel (like mine had), simply use a peeler. If not, then make a thin slice down the length of the root. You can then dig a finger underneath the peel and peel it away by hand.
4. Slice the yuca root into sticks: Cut it into 3 to 4-inch-long sections and then slice it into batons/wedges (refer to images/video in the post).
5. Boil it
6. Soak in cold water for about 5 minutes, then drain the water.
7. Boil the sticks in plenty of fresh salted water for about 20 minutes, or until fork-tender.
8. Drain the water very well (optionally pat-dry with a kitchen towel), then add the cooked yuca sticks to a large bowl together with all other ingredients.
9. Toss to combine until well coated.
10. Cook it (air fryer method)
11. Finally, transfer the fries to your air fryer basket in a single layer, with space in between (cook in batches if necessary). Depending on the thickness of the yuca fries, cook at 380 °F (190 °C) for about 15-18 minutes or, until golden brown and crispy.
12. Check the recipe notes below for the oven and skillet method.
13. Enjoy with a dip of choice like this yum yum sauce or vegan mayonnaise!

Notes
Skillet Directions:
Prepare the yuca root as written (minus seasoning the fries). Meanwhile, heat a large, wide skillet with at-least ½-1 inch of oil over medium-high heat.
Once hot (around 375F/190C), transfer the fries in batches and cook, flipping halfway, until golden-brown and crispy.
Use a slotted spoon to transfer the cooked cassava fries to paper towels to drain excess oil, then season and enjoy.
Oven Directions:
Follow the recipe, but instead of transferring them to an air fryer, spread them across a parchment paper-lined baking sheet.
Bake in a preheated oven at 425F/220C for about 25 minutes, turning halfway. Baked yuca fries won't be as crispy, but are delicious. Cooking time will vary: Based on how thick you cut the fries.

Air Fryer Chickpeas

Servings: 1
Cooking Time: 15 Minutes

Ingredients:

- 1 x 400g tin chickpeas, drained and rinsed
- 1 tbsp olive oil
- 2 tsp spice or herb seasoning*

Directions:

1. Drain and rinse the chickpeas.
2. Add the oil and your choice of spices or herbs (see notes).
3. Toss the chickpeas until they are coated in the oil and seasoning.
4. Transfer to the air fryer basket and set off at 200°C (190°F), and air fry for 15 minutes, shaking two or three times.
5. The chickpeas should be hard and crispy when they are ready. If they are still a little soft, air fry them for a few more minutes. Add extra seasoning if required.

Air Fryer Sweet Potato Fries

Servings: 2
Cooking Time: 10-30 Minutes

Ingredients:

- 325–350g/11½–12oz small–medium sweet potatoes, scrubbed clean
- 2 tsp light rapeseed, sunflower or vegetable oil
- ¼ tsp dried oregano
- ¼ tsp paprika or smoked paprika, plus a pinch to serve (optional)
- salt and freshly ground black pepper

Directions:

1. Preheat the air fryer to 200C. Cut the sweet potatoes into 1cm/½in thick chips: try to cut evenly to ensure even cooking and crispness, and keep in mind that shorter chips are easier to fit into the air fryer.
2. Tip the chips into a bowl, drizzle over the oil and sprinkle with the dried oregano and paprika, if using. Season with salt – it will help the fries crisp up – and pepper.
3. Put a single layer of chips in the base of the air fryer – don't overcrowd or they won't cook evenly. Air-fry for 8 minutes, using tongs to turn them halfway through, until golden and crisp on the outside, and soft on the inside. If they're not quite done, continue to cook for a minute at a time before checking again.
4. Cook in two or three batches until all the fries are ready, then put them all back into the air fryer to heat through for 30 seconds. Serve immediately, sprinkled with more seasoning and a pinch more paprika, if using.

NOTES

If you find your fries aren't crisp enough, try cutting them more finely the next time you make them.

If your oven is on for something else, you can keep the first batches of fries warm while you air-fry the rest.

If your air fryer is fitted with a stirring paddle, you won't need to turn the fries during cooking.

Pumpkin Tortilla Chips

Ingredients:

- Chips:
- 2 tbsp olive oil
- 1 tbsp nutmeg
- 2 cups plain flour
- 3 tbsp butter
- 2 tbsp pumpkin pie puree
- 1/3 cup whole milk
- ½ tsp salt, plus more for sprinkling
- 1 tsp baking powder
- pumpkin pie spice, for sprinkling
- pepper to taste

Directions:

1. In a large mixing bowl, combine the salt, flour, and baking powder. Add in the butter, pumpkin pie puree and milk, kneading to combine.
2. Divide the mixture into handfuls and roll out. Fry the wraps over medium heat until they bubble. Then, brush oil on one side of each of the tortilla wraps. Stack them and cut into tortilla chip shapes.
3. Sprinkle them with pumpkin pie spice and salt and pepper to taste and place them on the mesh trays in the Air Fryer Oven.
4. Air fry them at 400°F for 6-8 minutes or until golden brown. Remove them from the Air Fryer Oven and serve with your favorite Fall dipping sauce!

Air Fryer Green Bean Casserole With Toasted Fried Onions

Servings: 4-6
Cooking Time: 25 Minutes

Ingredients:
- 1 lb. (454 g) fresh green beans
- 14 oz. (397 g) cream of mushroom soup (1 can)
- 1/2 cup (120 ml) milk
- 1 Tablespoon (15 ml) Worcestershire sauce
- 1/2 teaspoon (2.5 ml) garlic powder
- Optional - salt , to taste - depending on seasoning of your cream of mushroom soup
- 1/4 teaspoon (1.25 ml) black pepper
- 1 cup (56 g) fried onions
- 1/4 cup (30 g) cheese (optional)
- EQUIPMENT
- Air Fryer
- 8" square Baking Pan
- 7" Accessory Cake Bucket Pan

Directions:
1. Cut green beans into bite sized pieces. Place in an 8" baking dish or a 7" Bucket-style Baking Pan, whichever fits your air fryer best (we recommend the baking dish for oven style air fryers, and at the bucket with the handles for the basket style air fryers). Spray green beans with oil. Place the baking dish in the air fryer middle rack or basket.
2. Air Fry at 340°F/170°C for 12 minutes, stirring halfway through cooking *see note below recipe. If needed, stir 3 times during cooking and continue cooking until the green beans are to your preferred texture.
3. In bowl, whisk together the cream of mushroom soup, milk, Worcestershire sauce, garlic powder and black pepper. Taste for seasoning and add salt or other seasonings if needed. Pour over the air fried green beans and gently stir.
4. Air Fry at 340°F/170°C for 11-13 minutes, stirring halfway through cooking. Cook green beans until tender and sauce is bubbly.
5. Top with the fried onions, then cheese and Air Fry at 340°F/170°C for 1-2 minutes or until the cheese is melted.

NOTES
Note about Green Beans: Smaller french green beans will cook quicker. Reduce time by a few minutes and check that they are done to your preference. The opposite goes for older or large green beans. You may need to add several minutes more to have them cooked to your preference. Adjust as needed.

Air Fryer Pumpkin Seeds Recipe

Servings: 4
Cooking Time: 10-15 Minutes

Ingredients:
- 1 (10- to 15-pound) large pumpkin
- 1 teaspoon olive oil
- 1/4 teaspoon ground chipotle pepper
- 1/4 teaspoon kosher salt, plus more as needed
- 1/8 teaspoon cayenne pepper

Directions:
1. Cut the top off a large pumpkin and scoop out the seeds. Rinse in a colander under running water to separate from the pulp. Lay the seeds out on paper towels and pat dry. Let sit for 30 minutes to remove any excess moisture. You should have about 1 cup pumpkin seeds.
2. Heat the air fryer to 350°F. Transfer the dried pumpkin seeds to a medium bowl. Add 1 teaspoon olive oil, 1/4 teaspoon ground chipotle pepper, 1/4 teaspoon kosher salt, and 1/8 teaspoon cayenne pepper. Toss to combine.
3. Spread the seeds evenly in the basket of the air fryer. Cook, shaking the basket halfway through cooking, until the seeds are golden and crispy, 10 to 15 minutes total. Transfer to a bowl and let cool. Taste and season with more salt as needed.
RECIPE NOTES
Yield: If your pumpkin yields more than 1 cup seeds, adjust the oil and seasonings as necessary. If you are making a larger quantity of pumpkin seeds, they will likely need to be cooked in batches for even roasting.

Baked Chipotle Sweet Potato Fries

Servings: 1
Cooking Time: 25 Minutes

Ingredients:
- 1 medium sweet potato ((about 6 ounces) peeled)
- 1 teaspoon olive oil
- 1/4 teaspoon kosher salt
- 1/4 teaspoon garlic powder
- 1/4 teaspoon ground chipotle chile powder
- olive oil spray

Directions:
1. Oven Directions:
2. Preheat oven to 425F.
3. In a medium bowl, toss sweet potatoes with olive oil, salt, garlic powder and chipotle chile powder.
4. Spread potatoes on a baking sheet. Avoid crowding so potatoes get crisp. Bake 15 minutes. Turn and bake an additional 10-15 minutes. Ovens may vary so keep an eye on them and be sure to cut all the potatoes the same size to ensure even cooking.
5. Air Fryer Directions:
6. Preheat air fryer to 400°F.
7. Slice the potato into even 1/4 inch thick fries. Toss with oil, salt, garlic powder, and chipotle chile powder.
8. Transfer to the air fryer basket, spritz the top with olive oil then cook 400F in a single layer without overcrowding the basket until golden brown and crisp on the outside, about 7 to 8 minutes, turning half way.

Air Fryer Potato Skins

Servings: 4
Cooking Time: 5 Minutes

Ingredients:
- 4 medium baked potatoes
- 1/2 cup shredded cheddar cheese
- 4 strips cooked bacon crumbled
- 1/2 cup sour cream

Directions:

1. Slice each baked potato in half. Scoop out most of the inside of the potato, leaving about ¼ inch of potato.
2. Sprinkle each half with cheddar cheese and bacon crumbles.
3. Place the potatoes in the air fryer basket, and air fry at 350 degrees F for about 3-5 minutes, until the cheese melts.
4. Serve with your favorite toppings!

Air Fryer Tortilla Chips

Servings: 2
Cooking Time: 5 Minutes

Ingredients:
- 12 corn tortillas
- 1 tablespoon olive oil
- 2 teaspoons kosher salt
- 1 tablespoon McCormick® TASTY Jazzy Spice Blend
- guacamole, for serving

Directions:
1. Preheat the air fryer to 350°F (180°C).
2. Lightly brush the tortillas with olive oil on both sides.
3. Sprinkle the tortillas with the salt and Tasty Jazzy Spice Blend on both sides.
4. Cut each tortilla into 6 wedges.
5. Working in batches, add the tortilla wedges to the air fryer in a single layer and "fry" for about 5 minutes, or until golden brown and crispy.
6. Serve with guacamole.
7. Enjoy!

Sweet Potato Wedges

Servings: 4
Cooking Time: 12 Minutes

Ingredients:
- 2 small sweet potatoes cut into wedges (peeling optional)
- 2 tablespoons olive oil
- ¼ teaspoon salt and pepper each
- ¼ teaspoon smoked paprika
- ¼ teaspoon cumin

Directions:
1. Preheat the air fryer to 400°F.
2. Cut sweet potatoes into wedges and soak in cold water for 15-30 minutes.
3. When done soaking pat dry with paper towel and toss with olive oil and seasonings.
4. Place in the air fryer basket and cook for 11-12 minutes or until cooked.

Notes

Cut sweet potatoes to the same thickness to ensure they cook at the same rate.

Soaking sweet potatoes in cold water removes the starch and it is critical to getting that crispy exterior.

Crispy Air Fryer Potato Skins

Ingredients:
- Potato skins
- Olive oil
- Salt
- Pepper
- Potato spice

Directions:
1. In a bowl, drizzle potato skins with olive oil, salt, pepper, potato spice and mix. Place the potato skins in the air fryer at 180 degrees for 10 minutes, time will also depend on how crispy you like your potato skins and enjoy!

Peri Peri Fries Recipe

Ingredients:
- 4 potatoes (or sweet potatoes)
- ¼ tsp paprika
- ¼ tsp oregano
- ¼ tsp ginger powder
- ¼ tsp ground cardamom
- ¼ tsp garlic powder
- ¼ tsp onion powder
- Cooking spray
- Salt and cayenne pepper, to taste

Directions:
1. For the chips:
2. Peel the potatoes and slice into chips.
3. Add the potatoes to a pan of cold salted water and bring to the boil.
4. Once the boiling point has been reached, drain and place into a large bowl.
5. For the Seasoning:
6. To create the spice mix, mix the dry ingredients together in a large bowl.
7. Spray the fries on all sides with cooking spray and dust with spice mix.
8. Plug in and switch on the air fryer at the mains power supply.
9. Select the 'CHIP' function.
10. Carefully place the fries into the relevant cooking compartment.
11. Check that the fries are crispy before serving.
12. Serve immediately with your choice of dipping sauce.

Air Fryer Waffle Fries

Servings: 4
Cooking Time: 10 Minutes

Ingredients:
- 1 pound frozen waffle fries
- ½ teaspoon seasoned salt (optional)

Directions:
1. Preheat Air Fryer to 400°F.
2. Add the waffle fries to the air fryer basket, filling about ½ full.
3. Cook for 10-12 minutes, shaking the basket after 5 minutes to prevent sticking.
4. Toss waffle fries with seasoned salt (if desired) and serve immediately.

Notes

To prevent the waffle fries from sticking to each other, lightly spray with pan release or a high smoke point cooking oil before cooking.

Spiced Air Fryer Chickpeas

Servings: 4
Cooking Time: 15 Minutes

Ingredients:
- 14 ounces canned chickpeas drained and rinsed
- 1 tablespoon olive oil
- ½ teaspoon cumin
- ½ teaspoon garlic powder
- 1 teaspoon kosher salt or to taste
- ¼ teaspoon smoked paprika
- ⅛ teaspoon cayenne pepper or to taste

Directions:
1. Preheat air fryer to 400°F.
2. Dab drained chickpeas dry with a paper towel.
3. Toss chickpeas with oil and seasonings. Toss to coat.
4. Place in a single layer in the air fryer basket.
5. Cook chickpeas 14-16 minutes or until crisp.

Notes

Oil and seasonings adhere better to chickpeas that are really dry. Lay them in a single layer on a clean kitchen towel and fold one end over the top of them and thoroughly pat them dry. Easily and evenly season oiled chickpeas in a zippered bag by shaking them before pouring them into the air fryer basket.
For crisper chickpeas, cook longer.

Air Fryer Carrot Fries

Servings: 2
Cooking Time: 8 Minutes

Ingredients:
- 3 medium carrots sliced into sticks
- 1 tablespoon olive oil
- ½ teaspoon salt
- ½ teaspoon pepper
- ¼ teaspoon garlic powder
- Dipping Sauce
- ¼ cup mayonnaise
- 1 tablespoon honey
- ½ teaspoon Sriracha

Directions:
1. Preheat air fryer to 400°F.
2. Slice carrots into fries and toss with oil and seasonings.
3. Place in a single layer in air fryer basket and cook for 5-6 minutes, shaking basket halfway through cooking.
4. Combine mayonnaise, honey, and sriracha in a small bowl and whisk till combined.

Notes

Leftover air fryer carrot fries can be kept in a covered container in the refrigerator for up to 3 days. Reheat fries in the air fryer and season before serving.

Chunky Chips

Servings: 2
Cooking Time: 30 Minutes

Ingredients:
- 2 medium potatoes approx. 425g/15oz total
- low calorie cooking spray
- 2 pinches garlic salt
- 1 pinch salt

Directions:
1. Preheat the oven to 200-210°C.
2. Peel the potatoes and cut them into chunky chips (the chunkier the better).
3. Place the potatoes in a pan and cover with boiling water, add a good pinch of salt.
4. Bring back up to the boil and let it boil for 2 minutes.
5. Drain the potatoes and place them in a large bowl.
6. Spray generously with low calorie cooking spray and add a good pinch of garlic salt. Toss them in the bowl to make sure they are evenly coated, then repeat (spray, sprinkle and toss).
7. Spray an oven tray with low calorie cooking spray then tip on the potatoes and spread them out evenly.
8. Cook in oven for around 30 minutes. Halfway through cooking, flip the chips over so they colour evenly.

Roasted Garlic Hummus

Ingredients:
- 1 bulb of garlic cloves, separated and unpeeled
- 5 tbsp olive oil, divided
- can of tinned chickpeas in water
- 2 tbsp light tahini
- sea salt
- 1 pinch of white pepper
- 1 tsp lemon juice
- 2 tbsp water
- fresh parsley to garnish

Directions:
1. Preheat air fryer oven to 350°F. Place the separated, unpeeled garlic cloves into a small oven-safe dish. Cover in 2 tbsp olive oil and roast for 20 minutes.
2. Remove the dish from the oven and leave to cool for 1 hour. While you wait, drain and rinse the chickpeas well and remove any skins they might have. Place the chickpeas into the blender. Squeeze the cooled roasted garlic into the blender, as well.
3. Then, add in the remaining olive oil, tahini, sea salt, white pepper, lemon juice and 1 tbsp of water. Blend until creamy. Add more water if needed and garnish with chopped parsley and an extra drizzle of olive oil. Serve with your desired crackers or chips.

Air Fryer Cream Cheese Wontons
Servings: 4
Cooking Time: 10 Minutes

Ingredients:
- 8 ounce cream cheese softened
- 2 Tablespoons green onion finely chopped
- 1/2 teaspoon garlic powder
- 1/4 teaspoon salt
- wonton wrappers
- olive oil spray

Directions:
1. In a small bowl add the cream cheese, green onions, garlic powder and salt and beat until creamy.
2. Lay a wonton wrapper on a non stick surface. With your finger wet the edges of the wonton wrapper. Add about a teaspoon of the cream cheese filling and bring up each corner creating a star and seal tightly.
3. Spray the basket of an air fryer with olive oil spray. Add the wontons to the basket and lightly spray with olive oil. Cook at 370 degrees for 8 minutes. Check to see if they are golden and cook for an additional 2 minutes if needed.

Printed in Great Britain
by Amazon

28464969R00064

Herefordshire's Postcard Past

Herefordshire's
Postcard
Past

by

Tim Ward

Logaston Press

LOGASTON PRESS
Little Logaston Woonton Almeley
Herefordshire HR3 6QH

First published by Logaston Press 2003
Copyright © Tim Ward 2003

ISBN 1 904396 00 3

Set in Times New Roman by Logaston Press
and printed in Great Britain by
Bell & Bain Ltd, Glasgow

This book is dedicated to my grandchildren, Reuben and Lottie,
in the hopes that they continue enjoying Herefordshire
as much as their grandparents

Acknowledgements

I gratefully acknowledge the contents of all the books on the county I have read, all the directories, newspapers and records I have studied, the places I have visited and all the people I have quizzed for information on this my adopted county. My thanks and appreciation to them all for the knowledge they have generously given me.

Especial thanks to Susan Probert for providing biographical details of her grandfather G.W. Young and permission to use some of his postcards.

By the same author

Herefordshire on old Postcards, Volume One
Herefordshire on old Postcards, Volume Two
Around Newent
Ledbury
Images of Childhood (with Colin Ward)

Introduction

The past century witnessed more fundamental changes to our world and way of life than any before. Improvements in health, hygiene, food, transportation and housing have transformed our lives beyond our grandparents' wildest dreams. On the debit side we have witnessed and survived the two most costly wars ever and now global warming, caused by pollution, poses both known and unknown threats.

Fortunately the social changes of the last century were recorded for us by thousands of photographers and postcard publishers nationwide, whose photographs are now regarded as important historical documents. In this book I have tried to show how some of these national and international trends and events have affected Herefordshire and its people in cards chosen from my own collection. Although I might seem to hanker for the 'Good old Days', I recognise that the past contained a mixture of good and bad features and it really depended on your position in society just how good or bad those days were. Consumerism has replaced poverty, but perhaps our greatest loss is the 'Freedom of the Streets' now relinquished to the ubiquitous motor car.

Picture postcards have been with us since 1894 and provide an insight into the social life of the last century like nothing else achieves. They illustrate changing times and places as well as reflecting the outlook and character of their photographers and publishers. As my collection of Herefordshire postcards has grown, I have developed more interest in the photographers and publishers involved. With the help of friends and fellow collectors I have been able to assemble a list of over 600 nationwide publishers of Herefordshire related postcards. Of these about 325 lived and worked in the county. They cover the entire period of postcard production up to the present day and are listed at the back of the book. If anyone can identify any of the initials listed I would be very grateful. I would also appreciate any comments, additions and extra information which would add to our knowledge of these people who created such a wealth of postcards for us to collect, enjoy and, when time allows, research.

Tim Ward, 2003

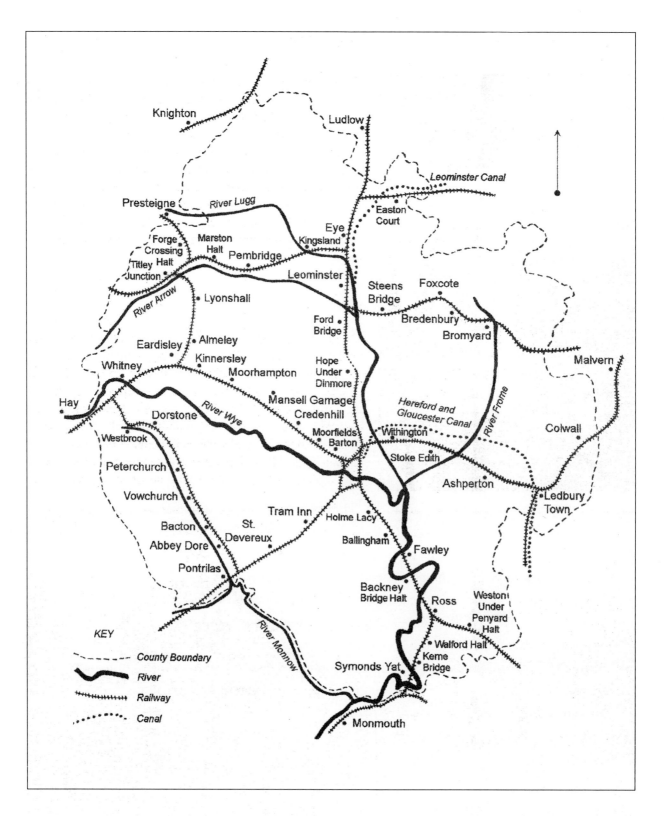

Map of Herefordshire showing rivers, canals and railways

Ledbury

Who could resist the charms of this young lady so attractively wearing the 8 April 1913 edition of the *Ledbury Reporter*? The *Ledbury Reporter and Farmer's Gazette*, to give its full title, was published every Friday by Thomas Vaughan at 1d. Like the *Times,* and other newspapers of the period, the front page was filled with advertisements, in this case for local businesses. To enhance her appeal further this unknown young lady wears *Ledbury Reporter* ribbons in her hair and on her shoes, before leaving John Tilley's studio to take her place in a fancy dress parade through the town.

Market day in Ledbury about 1926, when only a few motor vehicles were parked in the street, allowing plenty of space for people and the stalls clustered around the Market House. Farmers had sufficient parking space along the St. Katherine's side of the High Street for their horse drawn carts and gigs. The few cars demonstrate the transition in transport to the internal combustion engine that was to alter all our lives. The unknown photographer has provided us with a picture of a period we shall never see again.

HIGH St. LEDBURY.

Ledbury

On a hot sunny morning in August 1937 Mr. Fowler of New Mills Dairy drives his horse up Church Lane to deliver the last of the morning's milk. The football final between Ashperton and Ross All Whites at Ledbury Football Club is advertised on the board at the bottom of Church Lane. Just in front, a man wearing shorts shows the latest fashion for walkers, a pastime gaining popularity at the time.

A sparse crowd look over the stalls around the Market House about 1900. It is just possible to make out the names of the shops behind. At No. 1 was Robert Edy, family grocer and maltster. Mrs. Emma Baker was at No. 2. Mrs. Charlotte Parr sold china, glass and seeds at Nos. 3 & 4 and at No. 5 Mr. Suter sold clothing. To the extreme right of the photograph stands an extending fire escape and other ladders hang in the shelter of the Market House for use in the event of a fire, which was an ever present risk with Ledbury's wooden framed houses.

Farming & Elections

Hops have been an essential part of Herefordshire's rural economy since brewers started using them for flavouring their beer. Hop-picking provided much needed money and a spell in the open air for families from the Black Country, the Midlands and the mining communities of South Wales. Hop money also gave a much needed boost to country people's income, while better off families used it as an excuse for a picnic as can be seen here. Cups of tea properly presented on a tray with a cloth must have caused raised eyebrows from the men in cloth caps, though the man with the bow tie expected nothing else!

This typical agricultural show scene could almost be repeated today, except that most Hereford cattle are now polled, i.e. hornless. These placid prize-winning bulls, sporting their rosettes, parade past the corn and feed merchants' tents at Hazle Farm just outside Ledbury during the Herefordshire and Worcestershire Agricultural Show on 7, 8 and 9 June 1911. The Three Counties Show now has a permanent site at Malvern, but for many years the old Show found a new venue in alternate counties each year.

Social changes and poor living standards in Edwardian years were reflected in the interest in politics, even County Council elections, although not everyone was entitled to vote. A good number of ladies as well as men attended this evening meeting to hear Charles Stephens, who had an ironmonger's business at the Cross, express his thanks at being re-elected after 21 years service to the district. John Tilley was a very competent photographer as well as an enterprising businessman and had invested in flashlight apparatus, thinking it would bring him a profit. To get above people's heads he probably used a step-ladder and successfully photographed over 100 people listening to Mr. Stephens' speech in the dim light of the gas flares under the centre of the Market House.

Dedication of the New Church at The Wyche, Colwall

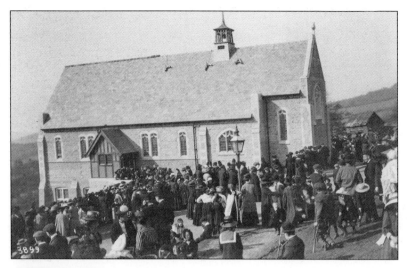

A large crowd of parishioners, friends and relations flocked to the opening of the new church at the Wyche, Upper Colwall in bright, fine, spring weather on 29 March 1910. Once there everyone awaited the arrival of the long procession from the village below the hill. After 90 years of religious use the church became redundant and, like several others in the area, is now a private house.

During the late Victorian and Edwardian periods there was a considerable religious revival throughout the country. The large crowds at this opening bear witness to the popularity of religion in the district at that time. A long procession of clergymen, local dignitaries and village organisations, like the Church Lads Brigade and the Boy Scouts from the Elms school, were co-ordinated to follow the band up the hill. They were surrounded and followed by their families and friends, all prepared to enjoy the once in a lifetime occasion.

The smartly dressed boys of Colwall Church Lads Brigade march up the hill in the procession to the Wyche for the grand opening.

John Tilley produced a series of over 50 postcards of this event by stationing cameras at strategic sites up the hill, so that he and his assistants could photograph as many people and groups as possible on their parade to the church, and so increase his sales potential.

Pastimes

Glasses of beer beside them, these cyclists relax outside the British Camp Hotel on a hot Whitsun weekend in 1909, their bicycles leaning on the fence on the right. Strategically placed on the main road from Ledbury to Malvern, the hotel has always been a popular halt for walkers and cyclists. In 1975 it had a name change to the Malvern Hills Hotel. Changes have occurred; the patch of grass where Alex MacIver and his friends were enjoying their drink is now part of the coach parking area, and the tree in front of the hotel's entrance has been replaced by a car park. This was an

amateur photograph printed on postcard size photographic paper, privately used and never intended for sale, thus providing a unique view of a group of friends enjoying their holiday break in the country.

The Elms at Colwall Green was a boy's boarding school, run by the Rev. Charles Black M.A., for many years. This air rifle target practice session in the school grounds was evidently more absorbing for the marksmen than for their supervising master and their colleagues, who preferred to watch John Tilley at work photographing them. The boys' hobby was probably good training for the future; in 10 years' time the Great War would sweep these young men into the armed services and disrupt or destroy their lives for ever.

Spring, Autumn, Neptune, Little Bo-Peep, Father Christmas, a Japanese girl and other girls in national costumes are among the 14 children lined up in the summer sunshine. This colourful fancy dress competition was at the Church Bazaar and Fête on 14 July 1910 at Redlands, John Stallard's house in Colwall, whose large gardens were very suitable for such events.

Colwall & Bosbury

William Ploughman was listed in the 1909 Kelly's directory as sub-postmaster at the Post Office at Colwall Stone, where he also ran a bakery and grocery shop. This was, and indeed still is, a common combination of businesses under one roof. As an illustration of the speed and efficiency of the post in Edwardian times, letters were received here three times a day from Malvern head post office—at 6.45 am, 12.30 pm and 4.15 pm—and delivered round the village immediately. Similarly, letters were dispatched to Malvern for sorting at 10.10 am, 2.10 pm, 6.30 pm and 7.45 pm. It was no wonder that a letter written in the morning could be delivered the same day. 'Expect me for tea tonight' is not an uncommon message on postcards of the Edwardian period.

Packs of beagles were used for hunting hares. Expensive horses were not needed so it was a 'sport' that ordinary country people could enjoy, following the chase on foot. Here a small crowd watch the meet of the Ledbury Beagles in the winter sunshine outside the Crown Inn at Bosbury. As the numbers of hares have dwindled in the countryside, so packs of beagles have declined also. Like many another village pub, the Crown slowly suffered from lack of trade and it has now become a private house.

William Homes poses in the garden of Gold Hill farm, Bosbury with one of his prize winning Ryeland rams. For years he operated a mixed farm growing fruit, hops and stock, typical of many Herefordshire farming enterprises in the first half of the 20th century.

Worcestershire Imperial Yeomanry at Eastnor

Volunteers of the Worcestershire Imperial Yeomanry water their horses at a temporary trough after a day's training during their 1905 annual camp at Eastnor Park. Apart from the mud when it was wet weather, the 500 acre park provided a good military campsite for training the Territorial Army. Training was not too arduous and the social life was enjoyed by all involved.

So sure was John Tilley of the sales of his postcards at the annual Worcestershire Imperial Yeomanry camp at Eastnor Park that he printed a set of four in anticipation of the 1905 camp fortnight. Based on photographs of previous camps, they have different inset vignettes of the castle and the 1905 camp date. These were on sale at ½d. each to the soldiers and their friends and relations who visited them there.

The Worcestershire Imperial Yeomanry held their annual camp in June 1912 at Eastnor Park as usual, and seemed to enjoy it despite the wet weather. The bell tents usually accommodated eight men, with their horses picketed nearby. The large tents were used for eating, lectures and recreation. No one could foresee that these peacetime training manoeuvres in Eastnor Park would bear no relation to the actual wartime conditions in France and Flanders which, two years later, would engulf the entire army. Conditions in the Middle East, where they were sent in 1916, suited the Yeomanry better and they acquitted themselves well. The 19th-century Eastnor Castle still dominates the park, which these days accommodates holiday caravans and a herd of red deer.

Eastnor

Like many other benevolent 19th-century landowners, Lady Somers responded to the increasing demand for better education and built a village school for 134 pupils in 1845. This provided at least basic schooling for local children. In 1908 it had a staff of three teachers and was nearly full with about 100 pupils attending. The headmaster, Richard Robinson, poses here outside the school for an end of term photo with his senior children, most of whom were destined to find work on the estate.

Twenty-eight members of the Eastnor Church Choir pose beside their parish church with the Rector, Rev. Holmes, for their 1908 photograph.

John Tilley had built himself a reputation in the Ledbury area for good photography since joining his father's firm in 1903. The postcards on this page are all by Tilley. One of his advertisements in 1910 reads:-

Lord Somers held a lavish party at Eastnor Castle for his family and friends to celebrate his coming-of-age in May 1908. He also took over the village school for his estate workers' party. Pictured here is the group of male estate workers and tenant farmers, all in their Sunday best clothes, outside the flag bedecked school before their celebratory meal. Evidently wives were not invited.

Hope End & Stretton Grandison

Edmund Moulton-Barratt bought this Queen Anne house at Hope End in 1800 with profits from his Jamaican estates, and transformed it with eastern motifs and cupolas to this fanciful extravaganza. His daughter, Elizabeth Barratt-Browning spent an idyllic childhood here until a riding accident made her an invalid. Soon after the accident the family moved to London. The house was demolished and a new Victorian Gothic mansion erected in the grounds. This burnt down in 1910 and was never rebuilt. Elizabeth refers to this area in several of her poems. John Tilley produced this postcard from an early print of the house.

A small herd of beef shorthorn cattle, grazing in the park at the back of Stretton Grandison church, inquisitively face John Tilley's camera. Once common and widespread this breed is now virtually extinct, confined to rare breed farms. This pleasant little stone church, dedicated to St. Laurence, was built in the Decorated style with an octagonal spire and stands just off the road by the entrance to Homend Park.

Fromes Hill

A self-explanatory advertisement postcard, printed in eye-catching red, illustrates perfectly the speed by which John Tilley was able to produce real photographic postcards to order. By working long into the night he could process his camera plates into such postcards ready for sale on the next day. This was long before the days of newspaper photographs, cinema and radio and was the only medium to show the public pictures of the events in the news. They rapidly became collectors' items.

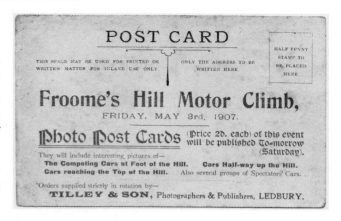

Tilley seems also to have made a point of including as many people as possible in his pictures to increase the sale potential of his postcards. This policy of quick sales and small returns must have been economic as he continued producing this type of card for more than 15 years. How many different cards he actually made is not known, but from the numbers surviving it must have been into the thousands. As many of these photographic cards were produced to order and not for general sale the numbers of each one produced would have been very low, and for many examples less than 10, hence their scarcity now.

FROOMES HILL MOTOR CLIMB, 1907, No. 9.   "BIGGEST OF 'EM ALL."

Since 1904, in the early days of motoring, Hereford Automobile Club organised annual hill climbs on Fromes Hill, which was renowned (or notorious, depending on your point of view) for its length and varying steepness, averaging 1 in 11. In the 1907 event there were 112 cars divided into 5 classes according to engine size. To demonstrate its reliability if not its speed, this petrol-electric Siddeley double-decker 'bus was an unusual entry in this event. It is seen here on the starting line, surrounded by curious spectators, many of whom had come considerable distances to see the fun. It was reported in the *Motor* for May 1907 that it was the first starter in its class as it was expected to take 11 minutes to complete the steep course. Its actual time was 9 minutes 54 seconds, although it was down to 2 m.p.h. on the steepest gradients. This was reckoned to be a very good time and 'the value of the wind behind thus being shown'. The two fastest cars were both Daimlers, which gave the Coventry firm a big publicity boost.

Canon Frome & Much Marcle

A group of workmen pause on the old canal bridge to watch John Tilley photograph them and the beautiful Italian-style gateway to Canon Frome Court that they had just erected.

In 1912 the Hereford and Gloucester canal in the foreground had been derelict for some 30 years. The canal construction started in Gloucester in 1792 and reached Ledbury in 1798. Work to extend it to Hereford started in 1830 and was completed in 1845.

THE ITALIAN GATES, CANON FFROME COURT, NR. LEDBURY.

The section at Canon Frome (above) is part of the long summit level which was supplied with water from the river Frome through a service tunnel to a point near this bridge. Successful for only a few years, the canal was closed in 1881 for the Great Western Railway to construct the Gloucester to Ledbury line on much of its course.

Oxford University saw the start of organised athletics in the 1850s and soon there were inter-university races. The idea of running races spread from there under the guidance of the Amateur Athletics Association. Distance running was regarded as character building as well as healthy exercise. The major event in Much Marcle's Flower Show and Sports Day, on 19 August 1909, was a 6 mile race for 14 runners, from Ledbury Market House to Much Marcle.

How styles of dress have changed! None of these children riding in the Gymkhana events at Much Marcle in 1910 were wearing hard hats for protection. The girls wore smart dresses and sun hats, while the boys sport collars and ties. A comparison with a present day gymkhana would show everyone wearing jodphurs, riding jackets and protective hats. These were probably local farmers' children who hacked a mile or two to the show.

Cider & Farming at Much Marcle

Henry Weston understood the value of publicity to promote the various ciders produced by his firm under the banner 'The Wine of the West'. This very eye-catching tableau of four rustics enjoying a pint or two of Weston's 'Bounds' cider deservedly won awards at the shows it visited in 1925. The solid-tyred lorry was usually employed travelling the roads of Gloucestershire and Herefordshire delivering loads of cider from their works at the Bounds, Much Marcle.

Hop growing has been an important part of Herefordshire's farming economy for many years as shown by the now redundant hop kilns throughout the county. Before the days of mechanisation harvesting was done by local labour. School holidays were often timed to coincide with seasonal farm work, preventing truancy and helping local families' incomes. It was the large farms that had to import pickers from the industrial towns to cope with the extensive acreage involved. This was a hop-picking scene at Hall End Farm, Much Marcle about 1905 where hops were still grown up the poles. Overhead wires are a more modern cultural method.

A traditional harvest scene, believed to be at Lyne Down. Tea and sandwiches refresh the harvesters in the middle of a hot day. The crop was oats and appears to be cut with a grass mower. The cut oats then had to be gathered and tied into sheaves with 'wisps' of stems instead of string. This was cheap on materials but very labour intensive, which was a minor point when farm workers wages were very low. Traditionally oats stood in the fields in stooks for three weeks before carting to the stack-yard to be thrashed later in the year when field work was impossible.

Ross-on-Wye

John Kyrle—the Man of Ross—was born at Dymock just over the county boundary on 22 May 1637. After his education at Gloucester and Balliol College, Oxford, he lived most of his life at Ross. There he is remembered as a philanthropist, giving much of his money to deserving causes, doweries for brides and public works. The Prospect is his lasting memorial, a picturesque walk overlooking the Wye. He died on 7 November 1724, at the good age of 88, and this chair, which belonged to him, went to Homme House, Much Marcle.

Many young men who had been trained as pilots in the 1914–18 war found themselves unemployed in the following decade. A few got together, pooled their resources, and set up an aerial photography firm based at Hendon, just outside London. As a result of their work there is a legacy of very good aerial views of towns, cities and larger villages across the country before the development transformations of the last 50 years. Unlike some places, the centre of Ross-on-Wye has changed little since this aerial view of 1924. Taken from the east, the Market House, Broad Street, High Street and New Street are all clearly visible. The Merton Hotel faces New Street and all the roads are noticeably empty of traffic. The mediaeval town layout with long narrow gardens behind each house can also be clearly seen.

Chair and Portrait of John Kyrle, "The Man of Ross".
Born at Dymock. 1637; Educated at the Grammar School, Gloucester; Died, 1724; Interred in Ross Churchyard. The Chair is now in the possession of the Money-Kyrle Family, at Homme House, Much Marcle.

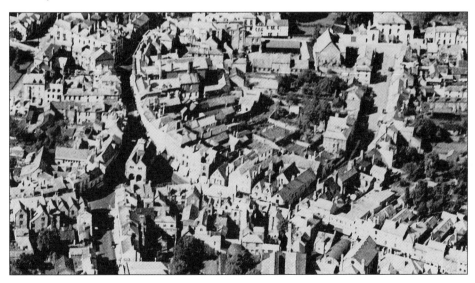

Ross-on-Wye

King's Acre was the rather odd name of this mill pool which originally provided motive power through a waterwheel for the mill on the far side of Brookend. Steam power replaced water power there in the 1890s. Edwardian postcards advertised that Bussell and Pike were corn merchants and millers (steam) at the Town Flower Mills. This building and the Railway Inn in the centre of the photograph have now become Byelaw's furniture showrooms. No one parking their car in the present Five Ways car park would imagine that 100 years ago this was a quiet mill pond where children came to feed the ducks. In the 1930s it degenerated into such a smelly refuse dump that the council filled it in. Now the name Mill Pond Street is the only reminder of the centuries of use of water power here.

Generations of Ross people have seen the river Wye flood like this Christmas Eve 1909 scene. Today's view up the river from the Prospect is now altered by the A40 bridge built in the 1960s and the number of trees that have grown on the river bank during the last century. The old tree on the left and the Rowing Club boathouse on the right are still recognisable landmarks in the flood.

Ross-on-Wye

Because of the losses of troops, especially on the Western Front, more and more men were needed to refill the ranks of the Army and Navy. 1916 saw conscription introduced for men between the ages of 18 and 41, which resulted in a severe shortage of labour on the land. These three sisters from Ross typify the effects that the manpower shortage had on women's attitude to performing men's work. All three girls volunteered for war work. May, the eldest, was a nurse in the Red Cross, both in this country and in France. Doris joined the Womens Land Army to help produce more food. The youngest was one of the first to join the WRNS (Womens Royal Naval Service) and worked as a decoder at the Admiralty. This response, by women of all classes to take over men's work in time of need, resulted in them finally receiving the vote in February 1918.

The 4th Battalion, Staffordshire Territorials march along Gloucester Road past the Cantilupe Road junction towards their camp at Hildersley, watched by interested groups of townspeople. Military parades of all sorts were commonplace while the camp was in use, and must have stimulated patriotic and militaristic feelings considerably in the run up to the Great War. The posters on the temporary fence opposite advertise 'Dekin's Genuine Antique Furniture at Broad Street and Croft House Ross'. Next door was William Woolf's furniture removals office. These training camps also provided an estimated £10,000 extra income for local businesses and were therefore warmly welcomed by the town.

Ross-on-Wye

This lovely photograph of Broad Street on a summer's day in 1907 is a fine illustration of pedestrianisation long before the word was even invented. It really does portray a slower and more tranquil age. Apart from the Maltings Arcade, the shop buildings have hardly changed in the past century apart from ownership and usage. It seems a pity that the bollards on the corners of Station Street have not been retained to protect pedestrians as they did in 1907.

A similarly excellent photograph of the top of Broad Street and part of the Market Place in 1909. On the left at No. 6 Market Place was William Watkin's grocery shop. Next door Arthur Keddles ran a tailor's and outfitting shop. The building with the pony and trap outside is the Crown and Sceptre where Richard Fowler sold Salt's ales. On the right is W.H. Smith's stationers and book shop. Next door, at No. 55, was George Eltome's hosier and clothes shop, whilst at No. 54 Innell & Wharton ran an ironmongers shop.

Ross Corn Exchange was built in 1862 at a cost of £4,000 and was first used by local farmers as a butter and poultry market as well as a corn exchange. The large hall was available at other times for lectures, public meetings, concerts and the like as there was seating for 750 people. Festooned with streamers and bunting and with patriotic flags covering the walls, it made a cheerful venue for these Ross inhabitants to enjoy a Christmas party some time during the First World War.

Ross-on-Wye

Like many other local teams at the beginning of the century there was little spare money for a complete set of team shirts. Players wore what they had available, even for a team photograph. Ross Hockey Club was no different and sported shirts from at least five different teams! Shin guards for self-protection were, however, worn by all. Their hockey sticks were longer and have a longer curve than the modern style favoured today.

This unidentified girls' hockey team in Ross *c.*1920 did not possess a team uniform either. How on earth could they play a fast energetic game like hockey wearing high buttoned blouses with long sleeves and ties? Their hockey sticks are shorter, Indian style, more like those used today with stops to prevent the ball flying up dangerously. This team was photographed beside the sports field off Wilton Road, where both men and women have played hockey for most of the past century.

Ross-on-Wye

Merton House, the present Merton Hotel, still looks down New Street as it did in Edwardian times when it was home to Arthur Cutfield, surgeon at Ross Cottage Hospital.

The smallest house with the tall chimney on the right was demolished during the 1930s. The site is now the entry to the smart 1960s houses in Morley Square where two rows of uninhabitable cottages were removed in a slum clearance scheme of 1935.

A tranquil view of the Smallbrook Road and Cantilupe Road junction on a 1906 postcard. Smallbrook Gardens old people's bungalows now fill the meadow in the centre of the picture, and the Wallace Hall monument and drinking fountain has been moved a short way along the road to make space for the busy roundabout in front of Safeways' entrance. The houses in the centre of the photograph stand on Gloucester Road.

A school photo 1912 style. The 45 boys of class 1, all dressed in their Sunday best, pose for the photographer in a sunny corner of Ross Council School playground. Their school was built in 1873 at a cost of £6,000 as a result of the 1870 Education Act to give children a better education. A few years later it was enlarged to cater for 700 children! At the time of this photograph William Edwards was headmaster.

18

Pencraig & Upton Bishop

For centuries Pencraig had been a quiet hamlet between Monmouth and Ross, but the opening of the M50 and the new A40 dual-carriageway to South Wales in the early 1960s changed the area completely. There is just a small pull-in on the north bound carriageway now, but most lorries and cars speed past. In 1913 a lady in a pony and trap could stop in the road outside the Post Office for a photograph in perfect safety, while Joseph Heath the Postmaster quietly watched.

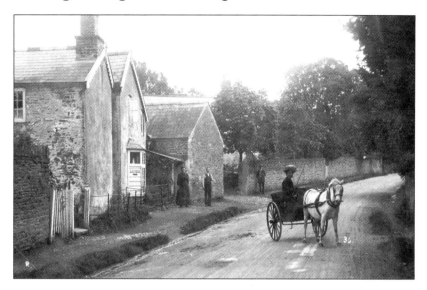

The Manor House at Upton Bishop was the comfortable home of Captain Evans Mynde Allen J.P. He used this postcard of his house and gardens sweltering in the hot summer sunshine as a Christmas card in 1911.

10 April 1909 was Arbor Day at Upton Bishop. Here 17 men are planting and tending young trees on the slope of Lyndor Wood overlooking what is now the M50 motorway. Fashion seemed to dictate that working men only removed their jackets, retaining their waistcoats and caps even on the hottest of days.

Bromsash

A small corrugated iron mission hall was all the sparse congregation of Bromsash could afford to build when religious fervour swept the countryside in late Victorian and Edwardian years. This little mission hall is similar to many in rural parts of the country which firms like Alexander & Duncan of Leominster advertised as 'cheap to buy and easy to erect'.

A spectacular night-time scene as a Dutch barn full of hay and straw burns out of control at Eccleswall Court on 9 August 1911. The heat distorted the roof trusses causing the roof to collapse. A very similar fire occurred at the same farm in 1982.

Backney and Weston-under-Penyard

Just 15 years after the opening in June 1855 of the Hereford, Ross and Gloucester Railway, a letter was published in the *Ross Gazette* requesting the Great Western Railway Co. to build a station at Weston-under-Penyard for the use of local inhabitants. It was, however, more than 60 years before their wish was granted. Faced with decreasing profits due to competition from bus and coach companies and, to a lesser extent, private cars, the G.W.R. built a number of halts at suitable sites, like Walford and Backney Bridge, to encourage country people to travel by train to nearby towns for their shopping. Weston-under-Penyard was typical of these halts and is pictured here a few years prior to its closure. Lack of capital is evident in the use of old sleepers and an old freight truck, all clearly shown in this photograph which was taken from the rear window of a mixed passenger and goods train.

Backney Bridge, photographed from the west bank of the river Wye in 1907. Originally it was built of timber trusses, but these were replaced in 1870 with iron girders. It was approached from the south on a long embankment to keep the line above the flood plain. In 1935 a halt was built at the north end (to the left of this photo), but much of this area has now been levelled to its original height and laid out as a picnic site by the council. An unusual feature of Backney Bridge is that it was built on a slight curve; now only the pillars remain. Trees have grown along the disused railway embankments and the banks of the river where fishermen still seek the increasingly illusive salmon.

On the reverse of the card 'Ted' wrote the following message on 1 November 1907: 'My one big meadow near this bridge (22 acres) is almost covered; I have never seen any flood in it before. Backney Common [is] also practically covered. Webbs' judges just weighed my mangolds — 64 tons per acre'.

Walford

When Mrs. Stratford Collins addressed a few words to the crowd at the opening of a garden party on the lawns of Wythall, her fine Tudor home, George William Young the local photographer was present to record the scene. This imposing timbered house was built about 1500 on the sheltering slopes of Bulls Hill, just visible from the road through Walford. Later Young used this postcard as a receipt for 3s. 6d. for some photos.

George William Young was a talented photographer and artist who lived and worked in the area for 30 years. He moved his photographer's business from no. 8 High Street, Abergavenny, to Walford in 1906. For a time he lived at Belle View on Bulls Hill, but in 1907 he moved to Howle Hill Post Office where he set up 'The Floral Studio' shown on this card.

At an unknown date he moved to Clytha House, New Street, Ross and for a while lived at Archenfield. Finally, for many years he had a photographer's studio in Cantilupe Road. He died in 1938, aged 65. He has left us a fine legacy of superb local postcards and photographs of the highest quality as well as paintings and cartoons which demonstrate his artistic versatility.

Kerne Bridge

Nowadays we take for granted the bridges over the river Wye as we speed across in our cars. Two hundred years ago there was only a ford below Goodrich Castle, not always passable, or a long detour on foot or horse and cart. To improve the communications to the furnaces at Bishopswood a toll bridge was planned at the 'Quern', as the area was originally known. The foundation stone was laid on 16 August 1826 and the bridge finished two years later.

This unusual view of Kerne Bridge from the north bank of the Wye looking towards Coppett Hill shows the old toll collector's house on the south side. It was demolished in the 1950s when the bridge was freed of tolls. Just visible in the shadows of the trees are the abutments of the bridge over the Ross-Monmouth railway constructed in 1870.

If only Dr. Beeching could have foreseen the present tourist boom, this lovely railway line from Ross to Chepstow might have survived the 1960s closures. The line followed the scenically splendid Wye Valley through two tunnels, over four bridges, stopping at several riverside stations adjacent to pleasant walks, rivalling any preserved line in the country now. In this 1908 view by R.E. Davies the midday train of five carriages and one flat truck pulls out of Kerne Bridge station towards Monmouth via the tunnel under Coppett Hill. The following wind drifts the smoke away from the well kept and well used little station.

Goodrich

Road bridges over other roads are common enough nowadays, but are very scarce before the appearance of the motor car. The dry arch carrying the road to Coppett Hill and Welsh Bicknor from Goodrich was built in 1828, at the same time as the new road cutting from Kerne Bridge, as part of the toll road scheme. It eliminated a very steep incline and was not subject to tolls. However, traffic using the new road through the cutting was subject to tolls, and the toll collector, William Holmes, would collect money for any animals using this road — even extra draught horses to pull laden wagons up the hill to Goodrich from Kerne Bridge.

The Stores at Goodrich, where the owners Mr. and Mrs. Cove and their customers take their time to pose for Mr. Davies' camera one hot summer afternoon in 1909. Mrs. Ellen Cove was also postmistress and the shop, along with the church and the pub, served as one of the social centres of the village. It was a good place to chat while waiting to be served.

Goodrich Court is now only a memory for the older generation of villagers. It was erected in 1829 in the Neo-Gothic style by Sir Samuel Rush Meyrick as a castellated mansion partly to house his immense collection of armour. Set in 60 acres of parkland, the imposing red sandstone towers and turrets gave extensive views over the picturesque Wye valley. Dismantled in the 1950s, now only the gatehouse on the A40 main road survives as a reminder of past wealth and splendid ostentation.

Symond's Yat

The 1947 floods were probably the worst and most vivid of all the inundations of the Wye in living memory. After a long, cold winter with heavy falls of snow, the resultant thaw released hugh amounts of water from the catchment area into the river. On 22 March the Wye roared down the valley flooding riverside properties severely, the Saracen's Head at Symond's Yat amongst them. People were forced to move upstairs as the smoking chimney on the left shows. Floods have always occurred as part of the natural weather cycle, but the world's inability to halt global warming means that such scenes will unfortunately and inevitably recur more often.

After a day trip to the area in 1912, Ernest T. Bush, a well known Cardiff photographer, produced a series of four postcards of Symond's Yat, including this one of 'Ye Olde Ferrie Inne'. At that time Tom Davis was the owner of the pub and the ferry; a group of passengers await his next crossing. The ferry still operates and makes a very pleasant interlude in a walk around the area. Because of the strength of the current the ferry boat is attached to a ring on an overhead cable and pulled across hand-over-hand.

A train to Monmouth emerges from the tunnel under Symond's Yat Rock into the sunlit splendour of the gorge close to the station. The details of the track layout, signals and platelayers' hut are a delight to railway enthusiasts. The tunnel is now closed for safety reasons, but it could have made an interesting short cut on the Wye Valley Walk. The path from the station up the hill to the woods and the Rock is still there, although the rails and the station have been swept away to become a car park.

Symond's Yat

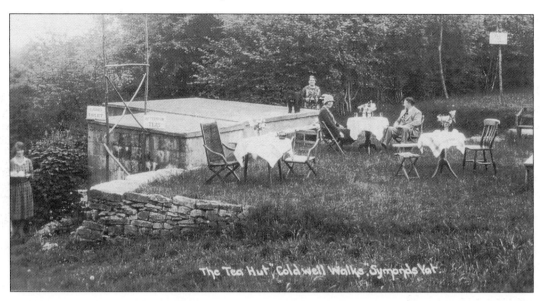

The Tea Hut, Coldwell Walks, Symonds Yat.

What could be more pleasant than a relaxing cup of tea while enjoying the wide views over the Wye Valley after the steep walk up to the Rock from Symond's Yat station? The owners of the 'Tea Hut' made the most of their position and provided waitress service, crisp table linen and vases of flowers to attract more customers as demonstrated on this 1925 postcard.

Bungalow Pavilion, Symonds Yat.

The Bungalow Pavilion stood on the banks of the river Wye below the Wye Rapids Hotel. It was built around 1924 to help attract more visitors to the area and George Young soon published this postcard of it.

Whitchurch & Welsh Newton

Most of these houses still stand in the centre of Whitchurch, but the view has been altered almost out of recognition by the building of the A40 dual-carriageway past the village. When this photograph was taken in 1909, Thomas James owned the Crown Hotel and Joseph Banchini kept the Post Office and grocer's shop.

In the shadow of the small Norman church of Welsh Newton, lies the grave of Saint John Kemble, a Roman Catholic martyr. Executed for his faith in Hereford in 1678 for conducting illegal services, his grave became a pilgrimage site for the pious as society became more tolerant in the intervening years. This pilgrimage took place in 1923.

Pembridge Castle is named after its first owner and is not related to the village in the north of the county. Standing in Welsh Newton village, close to the Monmouthshire border, it is in private hands and not open to the public. Built about 1200, it has had a chequered history, suffering damage in the Civil War and neglect from a succession of owners. About 1900 it was extensively rebuilt and, with a moat and drawbridged entrance, it is now a real gem. This photographic postcard shows work in progress on the entrance gateway. Pembridge Castle was the home of Saint John Kemble (see above). The message on the reverse reads: 'A gentle reminder of the restoring of Pembridge Castle'. For the 11 men hauling the stones into position by manpower alone, the work was anything but gentle.

Sports; Hole-in-the-Wall

Eight greyhounds with their handlers line up at the start of one of the regular hare coursing matches held at Fawley about 1916. A cross-section of society is represented here, men and women, rich and poor, all interested in a blood sport that is found abhorrent today. For a variety of reasons, mainly due to changes in farming, hares have now become scarce in south Herefordshire so a day's 'sport' like this would be impossible to arrange.

The Perrystone Cricket Team in 1935, when they played on the Oxpasture at Perrystone Farm.

Front row: Ted Lerigo, Jack Griffiths.

Middle row: Walter Moss, Charlie Clark, George Francis, Jack Loveridge, Albert Davies.

Back row: Percy Brown, Bill Alsop, Fred Sollers, Tom Gibbons, Reg Turner, Harry Davies & Chris Powell.

These cottages at Hole-in-the-Wall are now part of P.G.L.'s leisure complex for youngsters' adventure holidays. Hopefully the children appreciate their quiet and beautiful surroundings, where buzzards soar overhead and stoats hunt rabbits in the small water meadows beside the Wye. The road here is part of the Wye Valley Walk and just beyond these houses is a delightful stretch beside the river. Just visible in the cottage wall is a letter box, long since removed. For many years this cottage served as a diminutive village shop for the scattered farming community.

Brockhampton

Wye Valley Walkers miss this picturesque part of the river in Brockhampton as it lies a mile off the designated path. This is part of a very pleasant three mile circular walk from the picnic site above. In this photograph the river is at a low summer level so the fisherman can ply his rod comfortably in midstream. Now hidden by the trees is the old quarry reputedly the source of the stone used to build Hereford Cathedral. Above the trees on the right stands Capler Camp, a prehistoric hilltop fort well worth visiting for the views over south Herefordshire.

Instead of rebuilding or refurbishing the old parish church like so many other Victorian benefactors, Mrs. Foster of Brockhampton Court fortunately decided to build a new church in memory of her parents. All Saints Church, designed by the architect Wetherby and built in the Arts and Crafts style, is the pleasing result. Its medieval appearance hides the fact that it was constructed by local craftsmen using local materials as much as possible, even using thatch on the lych gate and church roofs. During her life Mrs. Foster was a generous benefactress, donating much of her income to local charities including large amounts to the ever needy Ross Cottage Hospital.

Brockhampton

Although the caption on this postcard reads Court Farm, this farm at Brockhampton is actually called Lady Ridge Farm. Modern buildings now obscure this view of the stables and house from the road, but they are still there, hardly changed, just as the cowman posing with his favourite cow on a hot summer afternoon in 1910 would remember them.

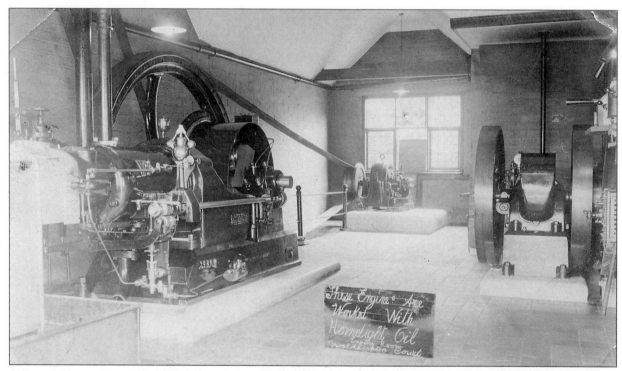

This publicity photograph is of the engine room interior at Brockhampton Court near Ross and shows the two large stationary engines used for pumping water and generating electricity. Mr. Bessent, the estate engineer, used this publicity card in 1908 to thank the Homelight Oil Co. of Queen Street, Cardiff for the promptness of their oil delivery. 'These engines are worked with Homelight Oil. Engine Room. Brockhampton Court', reads the board. We are now so accustomed to electricity that it is difficult to imagine the thrill our great-grandparents enjoyed when they could switch on bright electric lights and discard the dim, smelly and dangerous candles and oil lamps for ever, although it was many years before everyone enjoyed its benefits.

Fownhope

A quiet 1907 scene in the middle of the attractive village of Fownhope, with the ever popular pub — The Green Man — on the left. This is still a recognisable view although the cottages by the roadside have been replaced by the Fownhope Garage forecourt, rather altering the character of the village centre. Further down the quiet village street the thatched black and white cottage on the cross roads has been replaced by a more recent row of brick cottages.

This close-up photograph of the old thatched cottages in 1902 shows how dilapidated they had become although still inhabited. Though picturesque to our eyes most of these cottages were dark and insanitary and many were rightly demolished to make way for better housing between 1920 and 1960. Note the haystack in the yard behind. Donkey carts seldom feature in photographs of this period except at the seaside. Most light delivery carts were pulled by a pony. The gateway is now the entrance to Fownhope Garage forecourt.

Mrs. Hetty Brown stands outside the door to her Post Office and stationery shop in Ferry Road about 1908. A delivery boy stands ready with his bicycle to take a telegram. This was a vital and well used service in the days when telephones were too expensive to be in every house. The corrugated iron porch was the entrance to Halford's grocery shop, advertising Peak Frean Biscuits in the window. Now known as Ferry Lane, the further house has been demolished, there is an engineering works on the right and the Post Office has moved to the main street.

31

Mordiford

Half way between Mordiford and Fownhope and near the Holme Lacy Bridge over the river Wye stood the Lucksall Inn. Without enough local trade it was forced to close and is now a private house. On this 1905 photograph it advertised Herbert Mew's beer, whose brewery in Brookend Street, Ross, closed in 1930. The pub name is now used by the nearby caravan site. The shed in the centre of the picture has been demolished and the area is now a coal depot.

The house just visible in the centre was the toll collector's cottage on the old bridge. Tolls were abolished in 1936 and the toll house was demolished when the present bridge was built in 1973.

Some of the 140 children that regularly attended Mordiford Public Elementary School watch as Herbert Unwin, of 24 Commercial Road, Hereford, took a photograph of their school in the summer of 1908.

The school, which was built in 1873 for 150 children, was later enlarged to accommodate 200. The Schoolmaster, Alfred Meek, and his wife, Emily, lived in the adjacent schoolhouse.

Situated on the corner of the Woolhope road, The Moon at Mordiford has always been a popular pub. At the time of this postcard in 1933 A.S. Dare was landlord here. The baker's van outside belonged to Burtons of 13 West Street, Hereford. Despite the presence of village shops, vans like this delivering all sorts of necessities were a common and vital part of rural life before the almost universal present day use of the motor car.

Holme Lacy

This is the busy scene that Charles Brookes, the Holme Lacy stationmaster, could have witnessed from the road bridge above his station. Passengers from the Hereford to Ross train slowly leave the platform on their way home. The down goods train waits by the signal box for the passenger train to leave before rejoining the single track line. Two wagon loads of hop poles await unloading in the goods yard. On the right behind the station was the Phoenix Coal Company's small office. For a hundred years little country stations such as this provided cheap and efficient transport to the rest of the country until modern road transport took over. The Hereford to Ross line finally closed in 1964 and the whole site is now derelict and overgrown.

A small family watches Herbert Unwin, a Hereford photographer, as he records an idyllic summer scene in the centre of Holme Lacy about 1908. Those were the days when you could set up your camera in the middle of the road in complete safety. The house on the left stands beside the entrance to the former railway station, while the pretty black and white cottage has been extensively enlarged.

Clehonger & Allensmore

Cider has been a traditional Herefordshire drink for centuries, maybe even since pre-Roman times, and has certainly been an important part of the local economy since the Middle Ages. Kelly's 1909 directory lists 28 cider makers, 10 cider merchants and 7 cider retailers in the county. There were of course many more farmers making it for their own and their workers' consumption. For many years Richard Ridler farmed at Clehonger Manor and produced Gold Medal quality cider and perry. Here he surveys a good part of his 1909 crop picked by women wearing traditional headdress.

The tied cottage system for housing farm workers was a hangover from feudal times designed to keep the worker quite literally in his place. Any transgression of the rules, or a major illness could mean that the worker would lose the roof over his head — a not unusual occurrence. This poor man was evicted on 6 September 1910 at Allensmore. There is no mention of it in any records; maybe it happened so often that it was not worth mentioning in local papers. Only an anonymous postcard records this poor man's troubles.

Harewood End, Kingsthorne & Peterstow

As this 1935 postcard shows, the Harewood End Inn has provided all sorts of services for travellers for many years, as any good pub should. The sign offers accommodation for tourists and a garage for their cars. There is a hand operated Shell petrol pump behind the car and a Midland Red 'bus timetable on the sliding door to the garage. Add to this their usual hospitality and what more could a weary traveller wish?

Just off the A49 on the old Ross to Hereford road is the long straggling hamlet of Kingsthorne in the parish of Much Birch. In 1910 Thomas Williams ran a small bakery and grocery shop as well as the Post Office. With minor alterations it still serves the locality as village shop despite the competition from the supermarkets in the nearby towns.

This 1906 photograph of 46 children grouped on the corner of Peterstow's village green illustrates the change in road use in the last hundred years. Those were the days when Hack, a Ross photographer, could naturally set up his camera in the middle of the road to take their picture. Centrally, but obscured by trees, was Peterstow school. It closed in 1965 and is now a private house.

The shed behind the girls was the blacksmith's workshop. The surface of the road is loose stones as tarmac was not then in use on country roads. This quiet road has now become the A49, busy with cars and lorries on their way to and from south Wales and the Midlands. Such is the price of progress!

Wormelow

Decorated with all the signs, there was no mistaking the shop and post office opposite the junction of the Ross road at Wormelow Tump. The postmaster, William Littler, and his daughter stand outside watching the photographer capture this tranquil scene about 1930. This old post office is now a two-storey house aptly named the Post House. The present Londis Stores, just off the left of the picture, now houses the post office.

The ancient Welsh name *Bryngwyn* meaning 'holy or blessed well' has survived as a place name for the last 2,000 years. Sir James Rankin even retained the name when he built this enormous mansion in 1868. A local benefactor and M.P. for Leominster for many years, he would probably be horrified to see his old home turned into flats. Uneconomic to maintain, many of these huge country mansions have, in recent times, been demolished or been obliged to adapt to modern economic realities.

Two of the many gardeners at Bryngwyn pause outside the vine house on a hot summer's day in 1908. Despite the work and the weather they wear waistcoats and collars and ties. An important part of their job was to provide unusual, exotic and out-of-season fruit and vegetables for the mansion's kitchen in the days before extensive imports from around the world. T. Harden wears the straw hat to shade his eyes and was justly proud of the beautiful gardens in his care.

Much Dewchurch & Kilpeck

A view of part of the poultry farm at the Mynde, Much Dewchurch, in 1904, where large numbers of chickens, ducks and turkeys were reared extensively. Evidently it was widely known, and demand for their Christmas turkeys was keen as the message on the reverse addressed to Banbury Road, Oxford, on 18 December 1904 reads: 'Sorry all the big turkeys have gone. We can supply two at about 10lbs if that would suit'.

Tram Inn originated as an inn beside the Hereford to Abergavenny tramway built in 1829 and operated for 24 years. Horses pulled wagon loads of coal to Hereford and returned with agricultural produce. The drivers evidently found this a good place to stop for refreshment. The tramway closed in 1853 to allow the railway line to be built over much of its length. When the station was built it was unique in not having its platforms opposite each other. This was the view looking north towards Hereford. Dismantled during the 1960s closures, only the signal box remains to supervise the automatic barriers on the level crossing.

Tram Inn is a hamlet in the parish of Much Dewchurch. Because of the improved transport facilities several small industries were established there, including two coal companies and a chemical factory. Inevitably the young men of the area who worked in these local industries and nearby farms formed a football club proudly named 'Tram Inn United Football Club'. Here they pose with a 1910 trophy outside the pub.

A hundred years ago the whole family was expected to help on the farm at busy times. William James, the farmer at Lower Ridway, Kilpeck, had the help of all his family, young and old, to cart home his crop of peas in 1909. The little girl was about eight and was quite capable of raking up pea haulm for her father to pitch onto the wagon, whilst the horses wait patiently for the order to move forward.

Pontrilas

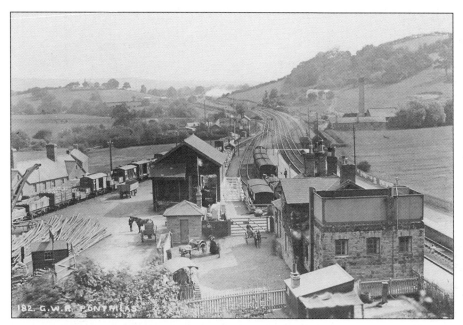

A view of Pontrilas station about 1910 when William Ferriday was stationmaster. It presents a picture of a typical Great Western Railway junction serving a thriving rural community. The station was the hub of commercial activity when virtually all commodities were carried by the railway system. Three pony carts await passengers or parcels. The Golden Valley train stands in the bay ready for its trip to Hay-on-Wye with its three passenger carriages and three goodswagons that would be dropped off *en route*. A long rake of goods wagons stands in the siding to be unloaded as a crane swings off a load of hop poles. Note the whitewashed cattle pens in the centre of the picture, and on the roof of the nearest building the huge water tank to replenish railway engines' water tanks quickly.

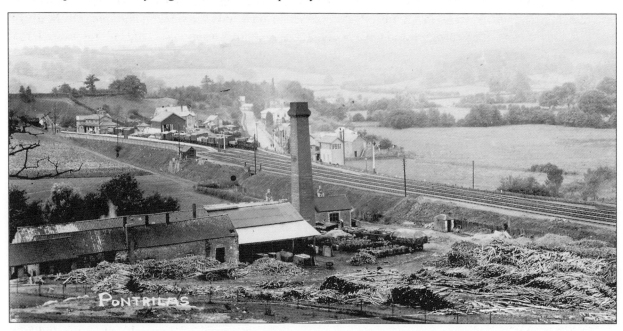

A view of the Wrekin Chemical Works, situated to the south of the Golden Valley railway junction, with Pontrilas in the background. Piles of timber are stacked ready for processing, while a rake of goods wagons in the siding below the chimney stack is loaded with drums of chemicals. Now only the office building survives.

Ewyas Harold

Upkeep of the roads had become the County Council's responsibility in 1888 and slowly much needed improvements were made. Although stones, dust, dirt, pot holes and mud were recognised as natural hazards by country people, even if they were only tolerated, the affluent car owners and cyclists who suffered punctures and breakdowns because of the bad roads complained vociferously. Road conditions improved from about 1907 with the introduction of tar to bind loose stones together and create a firm surface. Here a gang of 10 roadmen and their Aveling Porter road roller resurface the road in Ewyas Harold in front of the Temple Bar Inn. It is not clear if they are using tar or just building up the road where it periodically flooded.

This photographic postcard of the Red Lion demonstrates why postcards can be so important to local historians. The Red Lion stood on the west side of the road from Pontrilas to Ewyas Harold opposite the present garage. At some time after this 1909 photograph was taken the brickwork was plastered and painted white. About 1980 the building was demolished and soon afterwards a housing estate was built on the site, changing the scene completely and unrecognisably.

Michaelchurch Escley & Peterchurch

BRIDGE INN. MICHAELCHURCH.

A warm friendly welcome awaits anyone finding this old pub at Michaelchurch Escley, in one of the quietest corners of the county. The Bridge Inn has changed little in general appearance over the years, but is now served by two bridges, one for pedestrians, and the other to carry cars over the ford in the photograph. The road bridge was built in 1976 to give better access to the pub's picnic and camp site. On a quiet summer's evening there are few things better to do than watching the trout jump for flies in the pool in the Escley Brook in front of the pub.

Even in less affluent times, the village of Peterchurch was in the centre of a large enough area of population to sustain more than one grocery shop. Despite the competition from Lanes' Stores, which sold everything from farm machinery to baby clothes, Latimer Crosse carried on a successful grocery business in this smart shop. His Imperial Supply Stores window was packed full of all sorts of groceries in an impressive display to

The Imperial Supply Stores, Peterchurch.

attract custom. Prominent by the door are some large bags of dog food. The job of delivery boy in the Golden Valley must have been very pleasant in fine weather in the summer, but quite different in the cold winter rain. The area served covered a 3–4 mile radius and there was no protection from the elements on a delivery cart.

The county of Herefordshire has a long tradition of choral singing. The Three Choirs Festival is the oldest and best known, but other, smaller events took place — some competitive and others purely for enjoyment. In October 1909 an Eisteddfod was organised at Peterchurch. Much to their delight this Peterchurch choir won a prize and here they pose for a photographic memento of their success.

Preston-on-Wye & Madley

Just a few metal studs in the road mark the original site of this medieval preaching cross on Madley crossroads. In 1995 it was moved to a safer spot on the other side of the road after being hit too many times by speeding traffic, but where it is nowhere near as convenient for a youthful gathering like this. Benjamin Howe and his wife survey the view from the tiny front garden of their Post Office and grocery store. This has now become a private house and a pavement has replaced the tiny gardens to make the corner safer for pedestrians.

John Lewis owned the Post Office as well as the village bakery and grocery shop in Preston-on-Wye in 1909. Although Preston's population was only about 200 he could afford this smart delivery van to serve his customers in the scattered communities between the Wye and Blakestone Hill.

Dorstone & Cusop

The neat little village of Dorstone, picturesquely grouped around its village green, complete with seats, a well and an ancient cross, is still as charming as ever. The motor van on the left, outside the Pandy Inn, belonged to W. Morris, a Peterchurch butcher. Hands in pockets the butcher's boy watches the cameraman after completing his errand. Photographed about 1930.

William Bayliss was miller here a hundred years ago when this photograph of Cusop Mill was taken. The water impounded above the mill drove the machinery via a waterwheel in the lean-to on the left. Sacks of corn were lifted up the tall narrow hoist to the upper floor and fed by gravity to the millstones below. The scene is now very quiet. A lawn covers the area where there was once water, whilst the small feeder stream bubbles down beside the path from the hill. Recent restoration has left this gem little changed since the 1904 photograph.

Whitney & Winforton

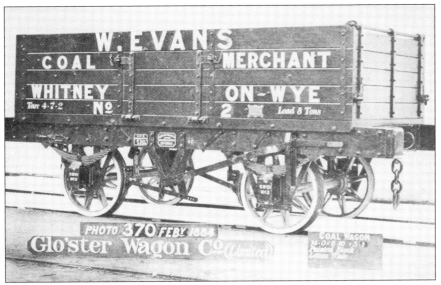

The Gloucester Wagon Company made thousands of trucks like this both for the numerous railway companies and for private firms who found it cheaper than hiring wagons. William Evans was a coal merchant with premises at Whitney-on-Wye station for about 30 years around the turn of the century. He bought at least two of these 8 ton trucks in 1884 to carry loads from south Wales collieries to his yard. Of very simple design, they had manually operated brakes and solid buffers. As well as the side doors, one end could swing open to make unloading a little easier.

This Wolseley Post Car drove between Hereford and Hay on Sundays from 1904 to 1906 to collect the mail as there was no Sunday service on the railway. There appears to be very little mail in his bag as the driver prepares to start on his journey from Winforton. The wicker basket on the roof was designed to carry the post bags and there were seats inside for passengers. This was really the predecessor of the Post 'buses introduced in the 1970s in remote parts of Great Britain to provide a similar service. In 1909 Miss Susan Perry was postmistress at Winforton, but cannot have been kept very busy by the needs of the population of 107! The photograph shows the corner of the yard in front of the Sun Inn, where the wall has since been demolished to make way for an enlarged car park.

Eardisley

A quiet afternoon in Eardisley in the summer of 1934. The photo is taken looking north towards Kington. Charles Meredith had no customers at his garage for his selection of different petrols — Shell, Shell-Mex, Ethyl and National Benzol. There is now no sign of the garage, as the pumps have been removed and the forecourt has become gardens once again, bordering the entrance to the village hall.

In various ways churches, both Church of England and Noncomformist, provided alternative attractions to the numerous pubs which seemed to be everywhere in Victorian Britain. With their attendant organisations they gave ordinary working people's families somewhere to socialise. From 1850 Sunday Schools became popular, not just for their Bible readings, but also for giving people basic literacy and recreational activities, like theatricals, trips, parades, fêtes and tea parties.

The ladies of the Methodist Chapel at Great Oak, Eardisley, where the chapel dates from 1848, prepare tea for their children's Sunday School anniversary. In fine weather this could be held under the branches of the nearby Great Oak.

Cider

HEALTH FRUIT DRINK

For the Hot Weather.

New SEASON'S Pure Apple CIDER.

IN CASKS.

Put vent peg here

Keep it tight except when drawing

Half Soda.

Half Cider.

Makes a delightful cooling draught.

A surprise, just like champagne, without its heating qualities.

Stillage on

Use a wood tap like this.

KEY

6d. and 8d. each at all Ironmongers.

PUT IN COOL LARDER OR CELLAR.

Have it in at once, and for a small sum you will have a delicious, invigorating, digestive health beverage to hand the whole summer.

For Testimonials, see other side.   Detach here.

ORDER FORM.

BANKERS: NATIONAL PROVINCIAL BANK, HEREFORD.

J BOULTON & SONS.LTD.   ESTABLISHED 1840.

CIDER & PERRY MERCHANTS.

TRADE MARK

BARR'S · COURT · CIDER · WORKS

TELEGRAPHIC ADDRESS
"BOULTON".
HEREFORD

Cider has been a local drink for centuries and was made in small quantities on most farms in the autumn after harvest. The best cider is made from the many varieties of traditional cider apples. One of the many small firms in the cider industry was Boulton and Sons, who started cider making at their Barrs Court Works in Rockfield Road in 1840 and continued there for over 100 years. In 1887 Henry Bulmer started making cider on a commercial scale in Hereford and his firm has now become the largest cider producer in the world. The card shown here was used as a receipt for returned empties in 1911.

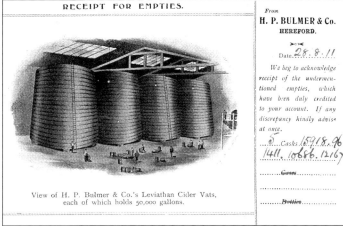

RECEIPT FOR EMPTIES.

From
H. P. BULMER & Co.
HEREFORD.

Date 28.8.11

We beg to acknowledge receipt of the undermentioned empties, which have been duly credited to your account. If any discrepancy kindly advise at once.

View of H. P. Bulmer & Co.'s Leviathan Cider Vats, each of which holds 50,000 gallons.

Such was the importance of the cider crop to Herefordshire's rural economy that there was an annual Cider Orchard competition organised by the local branch of the Cider Makers' Association and with prize money of £80 in 1935. The standard price for cider apples in the 1930s was about £4 per ton delivered. Spring frosts in 1935 reduced the crop so much that £5 15s. was offered that autumn for cider apples. Daily deliveries lasted from September to December as different varieties of apples ripened. As there were quite a number of smaller cider manufacturers competing for the cider apple harvest, merchants buying and selling apples appeared. One of these was Will Smith from Handsworth in Birmingham who bought and sold apple crops, employing casual workers to harvest them after hop picking had finished. Daily deliveries lasted from September to December as different varieties of apples ripened. Huge heaps of apples like these shown above demonstrate how labour intensive the process was. Before the days of bulk handling all these heaps of apples had to be shovelled into sacks for transport to the cider works. Mechanised picking has taken over, but the roads of Herefordshire are still thronged with tractors and trailers piled high with apples throughout the late autumn.

Hereford

John Jordan, the owner of Jordan's boats at the Wye Bridge, had a worrying time during the 1910 floods when the water level was 16 feet above normal and his boats were in danger of breaking loose. 'Please keep an eye out for one of my boats that has gone adrift in the flood', was his plaintive message on the back of this card to a boatyard in Monmouth!

The third arch of the bridge from the left is lower than the others because during the siege of Hereford in 1645 the Royalists, defending the City, breached the Wye bridge at this point as part of their defences. Cromwell eventually had the arch rebuilt to a stronger design during his years in power.

In an attempt to improve road travel in the early 19th century, a series of toll roads were established radiating out of the city. The money collected was supposed to be used for the upkeep of the roads, but as trade and travel increased the system was regarded as oppressive and inefficient. The turnpike trusts administering these roads were dissolved between 1860 and '70. Later the new county councils took control and responsibility for road maintenance.

This is a photograph of the Widemarsh Street toll gate about 1860, not long before its removal. High on the wall is the table of charges. Gas lamps light the area at night to prevent people dodging payment. This is one of a series of postcards of Hereford's toll gates produced about 1905 from early photographs and sold as souvenirs of Victorian Hereford.

Hereford

Hereford's right to hold a fair was granted in 1121 and the townspeople have enjoyed it ever since, though its form has, of course, changed over the years and there is now no hiring and bargaining. In this photo the May Fair of 1907 has taken over High Town and is in full swing. The driver of the Burrell showman's engine polishes the lamps while the crowds enjoy the show.

George Wright and Sons ran the Herefordshire Fruit Co. Ltd. from the Mansion House in Widemarh Street. They sold fruit and vegetables as well as other food throughout the county. Their lorries were pressed into service to transport employees on their ever popular staff outings as this superb photograph of a pre-First World War trip vividly portrays.

In 1912, the *Daily Mail* organised a series of air tours around the country to promote this new way of travel. Henri Salmet, a French pilot, took a leisurely flight to Cardiff and then up the Wye Valley to Hereford, where he arrived on 20 July 1912. He piloted his 50 h.p. Bleriot aeroplane to land at the racecourse in front of an enthusiastic crowd. The message on this postcard records the event: 'These are postcards of the *Daily Mail* aeroplane which came here on Saturday and stopped until Monday'. It was posted to King's Lynn at 7.15pm on 22 July, the evening the plane left Hereford, and demonstrates how quickly Francis Preece could produce postcards of the first aeroplane on the racecourse while the flight was still fresh in people's memory.

Hereford Railways

In Victorian times the railways created the first fast and efficient means of moving both people and goods around the country. The Post Office was quick to realise this and established a large number of main line and cross-country routes for its travelling post offices (T.P.O.s). A T.P.O., set up between Hereford and Tamworth, was opened in 1902, and ran until 1914; another ran to Aberystwyth. The London and North-western Railway Company provided the carriages in which the Post Office staff sorted the mail on the move. Special apparatus could pick up and drop bags of mail without stopping the train. Here five Hereford Post Office staff wait to board sorting Carriage No. 12 at Barr's Court station, just visible on the right, for their night's work. The notice on the letter box by the door reads: 'Letters posted here must bear an extra halfpenny stamp'. This late fee charge accounts for the occasional Edwardian postcard bearing a 1d. or two by ¹/₂d. stamps, denoting an extra charge for late posting and quick delivery had been paid.

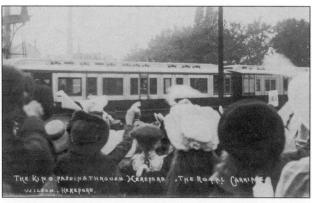

On Wednesday 8 August 1908 the Royal Train carrying King Edward VII and Queen Alexandria stopped for five minutes at Barr's Court station for the Mayor to present a loyal address. *En route* for more important places there was no time for a longer stop. This was the view of the crowds assembled for their monarch — other peoples' heads and a few carriages of the Royal Train.

Originally, the different railway companies that connected Hereford to Shrewsbury, Worcester, Brecon, Newport and Gloucester ringed the city with their lines and provided three separate stations for their passengers. Moorfields and Barton were forced by economics to move their traffic to Barr's Court. This is a view of Barton Station on the Midland Railway which closed for passengers in 1893 although remaining open for goods and freight for another 80 years. This area has now changed out of all recognition since the building of Sainsbury's superstore.

Herefordshire at War

The Herefordshire Regiment was a Territorial Army unit established when Haldane was Secretary for War in the then Liberal Government. He carried out extensive reforms of the army following the defects shown up in the Boer War. These new Regimental colours were presented to the 1st Battalion of the Herefordshire Regiment by King Edward VII on 19 June 1909. Lt. Col. Scobie was then Commanding Officer. Their barracks were in Harold Street, with drill halls in the other towns of the county. The 1st. Battalion saw service in Gallipoli, Egypt and Palestine in 1916–18 and later in France and Belgium. Until May 1919 it was part of the Army of Occupation in Germany.

A pause in the procession promoting women's work during War Weapons Week in Hereford in 1917. The Womens Forestry Corps banner reads: 'Many more Women required to work in the country converting timber to make aeroplanes. Healthy Open Air Work near home is possible'. The Womens Land Army banner behind reads 'We all feed you in the Land Army'. So many men had joined the army and the navy that there was an acute shortage of agricultural workers. The W.L.A. helped the war effort enormously in both World Wars to avert the threat of

food shortages. An often forgotten effect of the war was the sudden increase in the number of farm tractors and stationary engines to replace the thousands of horses commandeered for the Army's transport needs in France.

During the first decade of the 20th century the British Army was overhauled and modernised. By 1910 the Expeditionary Force numbered 160,000 with 14 divisions of the T.A. Small by European standards, the British Army was a well equipped and efficient force well prepared to face the looming European war. Annual training camps were an important part of this system to train the large numbers of volunteer units backing up the regular army.

Here a company of 32 Herefordshire Regiment Volunteer Cyclists arrive at Windmill Hill Camp on the edge of Salisbury Plain in Wiltshire. Herbert Unwin, a photographer of 42 Commercial Road, Hereford, had an eye for business and accompanied them on their 1906 exercises to photograph their exploits.

Herefordshire at War

27 June 1909 witnessed this church parade of units of the Territorial Army marching down Broad Street towards the cathedral. Hundreds of friends and families watched their menfolk parade smartly by. The building on the right was an apartment house belonging to Walter Pritchard. Next door at No. 23 was Mrs. Stalman's art and needlework shop, then were the entrance to Cathedral Close, the Metropolitan Bank and further up the street the prominent portico of the Roman Catholic church. The hut in the centre of Broad Street was a shelter for cabbies waiting for fares from the nearby hotels. The first two houses on the right were demolished in 1937, following a serious fire, to give a better view of the cathedral's west front.

On the return of the Herefordshire Regiment from active service, a colour party with fixed bayonets forms a hollow square in High Town with officers on the left and other ranks opposite. This was a ceremony to celebrate the safe return of their colours to the city in the summer of 1919, but the return of their menfolk meant much more to the watching crowds. Children sit on the canopy of Woollards Ironmongers and in the windows of Cash and Co. the Bootmakers and Gurneys the Grocers.

Herefordshire at War

The Herefordshire Royal Army Medical Corps was photographed here on manoeuvres at Tregaron in June 1911. The horse-drawn ambulances are behind the parade and the trumpeter is standing by. Part of the message on this card reads: 'Just come from manoeuvres 2 days 24 hours in the saddle following the P.I.Y. (Pembrokeshire Imperial Yeomanry) going like the devil'. The Herefordshire R.A.M.C. was based in Harold Street and was part of the South Wales Mounted Brigade.

These 16 young soldiers of the Herefordshire Regiment were conscripted to make good the losses suffered in the trenches of France and Belgium in the first two years of the war. Valentine, the local Oswestry photographer, pictured them in 1917 during a break in their training. Brussels sprouts can be seen growing around their barracks. As the increasing German submarine attacks on shipping threatened food supplies there was a vigorous campaign to grow more food and vacant land in all sorts of unlikely places was pressed into use.

The large numbers of wounded soldiers repatriated from the Western Front to convalesce soon severely overloaded hospital services and alternative accommodation was urgently needed. Many public spirited people let their large houses be used as military hospitals for the duration of the war. At 'Beechwood,' in Venn's Lane, 35 convalescent soldiers, among them some Australians, pose with their 12 nurses in the November sunshine of 1917.

Withington, Shucknall & Stoke Edith

Withington station photographed in 1910 in its heyday when George Jakeman was stationmaster. It served a large village with a population of 757 in the 1901 census. Agriculture, fruit, hops and the tile works provided work both for the villagers and for the Great Western Railway. The station only had a life of 100 years, being built in 1863 when the Worcester to Hereford line was opened. The Beeching cuts of the early 1960s saw its closure and rapid removal about 1965. In 1987 the line was single tracked to cut down on maintenance expenses but it was a retrograde step as it also reduced capacity.

Before the arrival of piped water this was a common scene in many rural areas. Everyone was glad to see the end of this chore when mains water finally reached the whole county during the 1960s. Water still runs from this spout at Shucknall beside the Worcester road and goes to waste in the drain below. The man has a wooden yoke on his shoulders to help carry his two buckets of water up the hill. They were suspended on chains so the weight was carried by his back and legs. Just visible up the hill behind spout is the Post Office and shop owned, at about the time of this postcard in 1937, by John Williams. For many years on market days he also acted as carrier to Hereford for local people.

'The Hamlet' is part of Stoke Edith, half-a-mile above the church on the slopes of the hill. It is such a quiet, remote spot that one wonders why Frederick Savory, a Hereford photographer of 29 Commercial Road, would bother to journey up here to take photographs for postcards. It can hardly have been for commercial reasons, as postcard sales of such a small place would have been uneconomic. The Hamlet remains quiet and remote and scarcely changed since he took this photograph in 1910.

52

Credenhill & Brinsop

An idyllic 1910 view of Credenhill Post Office, with roses planted around the door, when Mrs. Hall was postmistress there. With a total population according to the 1901 census of 203, business can never have been brisk although the hours were long. The post arrived from Hereford at 7.10am and the last letters left here at 6.45pm six days a week.

Brinsop Court is a fine example of a 14th-century moated manor house. Inside there is a very impressive timbered banqueting hall dating from 1340. The poet, William Wordsworth, visited his brother-in-law here several times in the 1820s. This view of the central courtyard is one of a series of 12 postcards by William Call of Monmouth, who specialised in ecclesiastical and architectural photography in the 1920s and 30s. Brinsop Court, still surrounded by its moat and large trees, is a real delight.

Tillington & Wellington

In 1909, the Bell Inn at Tillington was owned by George Rampling, a nearby farmer. This is a photograph of the old black-and-white building during alterations at about that time. Showing these old postcards around always creates discussion although people's memories do not stretch back to when the card was actually produced. The eyes of an old boy in the corner of the bar in the Bell lit up when he saw this photograph. 'My father told me this used to be black-and-white, but I never saw it myself', he said. Evidently the timber framing is now enclosed by a brick outer skin. Enlarged again recently, the inn is recognisable from this postcard only with difficulty.

A group of Wellington schoolchildren pose prettily for the cameraman at the old ford across the Wellington Brook in Bridge Lane. The black-and-white cottages are still recognisable, but slates have replaced the thatch on the cottage on the right. Now bridged, this scene by the ford captured by a *Leominster News* photographer in 1907 is unrepeatable. With views like this only a memory of the older generation, postcards are being recognised as important historical documents. Very often they are the only record of the social history of the first part of the 20th century.

The road into Wellington in 1908 appears more like a river than a road. The path on the left was raised for pedestrians to avoid the flood. The big barn on the right has disappeared in the last 90 years and the barns at Bridge Farm have minor additions and alterations. Gone too is the wall on the left.

Marden, Bodenham & Dinmore

The 'Volunteer' at Marden in the summer of 1904 when Ernest Lummas was landlord. Local horse sales were well advertised on the pub wall. As might be expected, horse transport was all there was to see in the inn yard. There is little evidence of external change apart from the new entrance; the stable door is still there, but without an equine occupant.

Although incongruous to modern eyes, everyone is dressed up in their Sunday best for a day out in William Jones' farm wagon. Before the days of motor transport this was the only way for a group to travel to a nearby town or to a local beauty spot for a picnic. In this case it was probably from Bodenham to Dinmore Hill.

Hope-under-Dinmore was an unusual railway station on the Shrewsbury-Hereford main line just south of the Dinmore Hill tunnel. Dug in 1853 the first tunnel was only single track and soon proved inadequate for the rise in rail traffic. To avoid delays, another 1,300 yard long tunnel was excavated in 1894 beside and slightly higher than the first. These differing heights resulted in platforms at different levels as this photograph by Savory demonstrates. The tunnel entrances are just visible through the road bridge arches in the distance. The station is now closed.

The Church Army, Burley Gate & Pencombe

These evangelists of the Church Army drove their caravan around the county, and probably over the border into Wales, spreading the word of God during the religious revival at the beginning of the 20th century. This beautifully made caravan was presented by the Bishop of Hereford especially for this work. Unhitched from the horse it provided both comfortable living quarters for the missionary and a suitable pulpit for preaching to villagers or factory workers from the driving platform.

A quiet view of Burley Gate Council School about 1910. It was erected, together with the schoolmaster's house, in 1895 to cater for 100 children. In 1909, when Walter and Florence Chapman were in charge, the usual attendance was 65. It has now become the village hall and a new school has been built beyond the schoolmaster's house.

The nearest house of this row at Burghope, Pencombe, has been enlarged and rebuilt, but the other three in the row are hardly changed on the outside since this 1908 photograph of this quiet cul-de-sac was taken. The thatched house in the background was, and still is, the village stores and Post Office. According to the 1909 *Kelly's* directory Charles Bishop owned the shop and his wife looked after the Post Office side of the business.

Bulmer's Cider

The following 12 postcards form a promotional set issued by Bulmer's about 1925. The captions are taken from the rear of the original cards and were correct for the mid-1920s, although some of the wording such as 'champagne' cannot be used these days to describe cider for legal reasons. The set provides scenes of buildings and production methods that have changed dramatically in the last 80 years.

Bulmer's Cider Works at Hereford

It was on this site forty years ago that H.P. Bulmer set up a small wooden hut and started making cider. This view, taken from the air, is of the present works — the largest cider works in the world.

Bulmer's Cider Apple Orchards

An Aeroplane view of one block of cider orcharding near Hereford showing about 70 acres, planted and owner by Bulmer's, producing vintage apples for Bulmer's Cider.

Gathering Bulmer's Cider Apples

Before being transferred to the works, apples are piled in shallow heaps in the orchards for sorting and maturing.
As many as 10,000 tons are handled in a season
at Bulmer's.

Bulmer's Cider

Apples arriving at Bulmer's Cider Works

The huge inspection platforms hold 250 tons each. Streams of fresh water at the rate of 100,000 gallons per day run along the bottom. The apples are thoroughly washed whilst being floated down to the Press House.

Bulmer's Cider Press House

An endless chain of perforated buckets elevates the apples to discharge down a shoot into the Press House. As many as 10,000 tons of apples are handled here, during the few short weeks of the crushing season.

Vats at Bulmer's Cider Works

The total capacity of these vats exceeds 2,000,000 gallons — easily the largest cider vats in the world. They give a uniformity to Bulmer's draught cider that cannot be attained by any other method.

Bulmer's Cider

Champagne Cider Cellars at Bulmer's

More than 3,000,000 bottles lie in these cellars in all stages of maturity. Every bottle of Bulmer's Champagne Cider is matured for years.

Champagne Cider 'Pupitres' at Bulmer's

To remove the sediment the bottles in these racks are undergoing the champagne process, and must be turned by hand every day for three months. 200,000 bottles are thus handled daily at Bulmer's.

Dégorgement of Champagne Cider at Bulmer's

A delicate process in the making of champagne cider during which the bottle is uncorked and the sediment removed. This is precisely the machinery used by the French champagne makers.

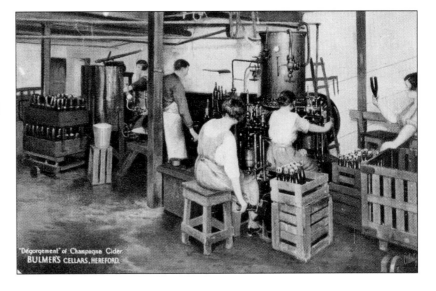

Bulmer's Cider

Bulmer's Pomagne

Acknowledged the best champagne
cider in the world. A delicious
beverage rivalling the
choicest sparkling wines
in delicacy, elegance
and flavour.

Bulmer's Draught Cider

Filling casks by means of a pipe
line from the vats. In Winter the
casks are then passed to the
Conditioning Room to ensure
life and sparkle to the
cider when drawn.

The last process at Bulmer's Cider Works

Foiling and labelling of the
champagne varieties
preparatory to
packing in cases for
Home and Export.

Bromyard

The building of the Worcester to Bromyard railway in 1878 brought many benefits to the town, among them cheap coal that could fuel a gas works. This was built beside the station in 1893 at a cost of £5,000. The Bromyard Gas Light and Power Co. supplied both electricity and gas and had offices beside the Stourport Road. The whole area has now been redeveloped as part of a new industrial site, but is still dominated by the Church of St. Peter.

Bromyard's Market Place at midday on a quiet day in 1906 with only a few well dressed children watching the unknown photographer at work. On the right is Benjamin Palmer's watch, clock and jeweller's shop, with a fine display in an unprotected glass window. Next door was the Post Office and stationers, run by Mrs. Margaret Bennett for many years. The gas lamp was supplied from the Gas Works by the railway station.

Bunting and flags to celebrate King George VI's Coronation criss-cross Bromyard's High Street on a hot summer afternoon in 1937. Only the shop fronts have changed to keep up with the times. The Falcon Hotel in the centre has had its render removed to once again expose the timber framing. The only car in sight is a shining new Ford Eight which cost £140 — a lot of money in the depressed 1930s.

Leominster Canal, Steen's Bridge & Ford Bridge

The Leominster to Stourport canal was begun in 1796, but it was never completed to the planned link with the river Severn and the rest of the country's canal system. Nevertheless, for a time it survived with local trade until the railways' arrival took its business. It crossed the river Teme on this high aqueduct, which was reputedly used as a training target for bombers in the Second World War, resulting in the ruins seen here.

Mrs. Elizabeth Davies' shop and Post Office at Steen's Bridge still stands beside the Bromyard road. The population in 1921 was 195, so business can never have been very great, but it was enough to provide a living until improved travel facilities led people to shop in nearby towns. The enamel sign for Biggs Tobacco is fixed to the fence. The house remains little altered, nestling beside a new housing development on the site of the old railway station.

Just three miles south of Leominster, on the Shrewsbury to Hereford line, the tiny hamlet of Ford Bridge was served by this little station. Frederick Bridgens, the stationmaster, and two of his staff pose with three builders for the anonymous photographer. Despite the small community it served (population 13 in 1901) the station was enlarged with a new waiting room in 1908. The builders had to literally watch their step as there were no safety rails on the scaffolding.

Leominster

Leominster railway station opened in December 1853, giving the town good communications to Hereford and south Wales as well as to Shrewsbury and the industrial north. Subsequently the town became an important junction when the Leominster and Kington railway opened in August 1858, and more so when the line to Bromyard and Worcester was completed in 1897. This included a branch line to Eardisley where it joined the Hereford, Hay and Brecon line, providing an outlet for agricultural produce

and a market for coal and industrial products. Leominster's large signal box was a later addition to cope with the junction's expansion and, unusually, is sited above the central platform. William Watson, the stationmaster, had plenty to keep him busy!

NEWMAN & Co.,
Wholesale & Retail Grocers,
14, Broad Street,
LEOMINSTER.

———

TRADING AT LLANDRINDOD WELLS AS NEWMAN & REYNOLDS.

Generations of the Newman family ran a grocery business from this Broad Street shop for nearly two hundred years. In 1905 they produced this advertising postcard to promote their shops — here in Leominster and also in Llandrindod Wells.

Children always love to copy their parents and elders, so it is little surprise to see these ten boys dressed up as soldiers holding a parade in the street like their fathers and uncles in the Territorial Army. With no passing traffic to worry them, friends and families watch with amusement. Fortunately none of them could have any idea that less than ten years later these same lads would experience the horrors of the First World War, quite unimaginable to their boyhood games.

Leominster

People throughout the country genuinely liked King Edward VII, despite his questionable private life, and regarded him as a peacemaker in European squabbles.

He died on 6 May 1910, and huge crowds lined the streets of London for his funeral on the 20th. In Leominster, the event was silently respected by the townspeople. Here local dignitaries head towards the church to honour his life.

Leominster's Cottage Hospital in South Street was completed in 1899 at a cost of £1,500 and served the community well. Before the National Health Service was set up in 1948 cottage hospitals like this were maintained by continual local fund raising efforts. These ten men and women seemed to have enjoyed the challenge to raise money by dressing up for this 1911 costume extravaganza.

Leominster

A postman hitches a lift on a delivery cart along Bridge Street to keep his feet dry during the floods of 1911. William Birch owned the baker's and confectionery shop at No. 5 on the left of the photograph and desperately used boards and bricks to keep the floodwaters out of his shop. His children watch the proceedings in the street from the safety of their barricaded doorway.

Mrs. Jones with May, Jackie and Kate Holloway stand in the doorway of their home in Bridge Street under the Constabulary Station plaque. Presumably this was a Police House as the County Police Station was at 15 Burgess Street, where a Superintendent, two sergeants and four constables upheld the law.

Leominster

Corn Square, Leominster, April 10th 1908.

Sir James Rankin, the local M.P., addresses an election meeting in Leominster's Corn Square during the 1908 campaign. His platform was an open-top horse-drawn carriage. The few women in the crowd look, not surprisingly, totally disinterested as he did not support the suffragette movement and their chance to vote would not come for another 10 years. Men in the alley-way continue to work unconcerned by the fuss, but Harold James' solicitors' clerk peers through his window to see the cause of the excitement.

The Leominster Town Band plays patriotic tunes to the assembled townspeople packed into Corn Square at the start of King George V's coronation festivities on 22 June 1911. The shops and houses in Corn Square have changed little since this photograph by Alfred De'Ath. Plenty of the children had flags to wave, but only Lloyds Bank was decorated for the occasion.

Leominster

For many years Alfred W. De'Ath ran a successful photographic business in Leominster, first at 22 Burgess Street and later at his new premises at 7 Broad Street. This 1908 photograph shows his windows full of examples of his work and promotional material. He advertised himself as 'a photographic artist and dealer in photographic materials, agent for Kodak and all leading makes of cameras, and picture frame maker'.

The engineering firm Alexander & Duncan overprinted this 1905 Hornsby Mower advertising card to promote their own business. Kelly's 1909 directory says, 'Messrs. Alexander & Duncan, of the Lion Works, have a large implement factory here, with a tram road running through the premises, which are completely fitted with the best modern machinery. In connection with these works is a large wholesale and retail ironmongery business'. They were also agricultural, hot water and sanitary engineers, and erectors of galvanised iron buildings. They later expanded their retail outlets to Hereford and Kington.

Orleton & Brimfield

The Maidenhead Inn stands on the crossroads leading to the village of Orleton. Like many other pubs in the 1920s they installed a Shell-Mex petrol pump to attract motorists' business. The pump has now gone to make way for the entrance to the car park and children's play area behind the pub. Externally very little has changed since Mrs. Pearce was landlady here in 1926.

Brimfield used to be on the main A49 Leominster to Ludlow road until it was bypassed in the 1980s. With the removal of the heavy, through traffic Brimfield became a real village again although it still suffers from noise pollution. William Elborn was landlord of the Roe Buck Hotel in the 1930s, when the white house on the left was the Post Office. This photograph dates from that time, when two little girls could safely sit on the verge enjoying the sunshine and the occasional passing car. Part of the message on the rear of the card reads, 'Come and have "one" at the Roe Buck. There is a bus that starts almost from our door onto Five Ways, but I don't know if one comes back from B'ham except this one on Thursday back again at 6 o'clock from town, but doesn't get here until 8.30'. That's a long journey for one drink.

Lucton & Wigmore

For many years, Mr. W.J. Rees farmed at Lucton, near Kingsland, and was rightly proud of his 1908 crop of mangolds. At 45 tons per acre there was plenty of stockfeed that winter for his cattle. George Hadfield, a fertilizer firm in Liverpool, used recommendations like this in their advertising campaigns across the country.

With slowly increasing prosperity, more people were able to afford motor cars and life in the villages started to change. Small garages and filling stations, like this one at Wigmore, sprang up in many places to cater for changing needs. Thomas Williams, pictured here in the boiler suit, proclaimed 'MODERN WORKS, Repairs Accessories and Cars for Hire' on the notice above his workshop. The hand-operated petrol pump stands right beside the road for drivers' convenience—pulling off the road was not even thought of!

Kingsland

Kingsland is a large scattered parish in the fertile Lugg valley with a population of 901 in the 1901 census. It required a large number of postmen to deliver the mail efficiently. This photograph was taken about Christmas time as two men with armbands pose beside the four regular uniformed postmen and their bicycles. Mrs. Thomas Dunn, the postmistress, and Albert Weaver, the village policeman, joined the group outside the whitewashed Post Office. Just visible on the left is Mrs. Dunn's boot and shoe shop. On the white post is one of the village's new oil lamps.

In 1909 the amalgamated Kingsland charities yielded £22 to buy food for poor villagers at Christmas. Mrs. Hamlen Williams, a local landowner, also gave food from her estate to the poor of the parish. In this photograph she poses in front of her cart, loaded with beef carcasses waiting for the butcher. A pair of magnificent Shire horses stand ready to pull the holly-decorated wagon to the village followed by a crowd of boys, with baskets, awaiting their share.

Kingsland

Kingsland's annual Flower Show was an excuse for everyone to dress up in their Sunday best and enjoy themselves. Stricklands' Fun Fair from Worcester set up their roundabout, gallopers, swings and various other sideshows in front of the marquee where the 1910 show took place. The striped tents, flags and smartly turned out carriages all added to the carnival atmosphere.

Sixteen of the staff of Kingsland Saw Mills line up beside the portable steam engine that powered their machinery. Mr. Wiltshire stands on the extreme left and his son is beside the flywheel on this photograph taken about 1920.

Pembridge

The Queen's Head no longer competes with the Red Lion for custom across Pembridge village street. In the 1920s they both installed petrol pumps to attract trade from the increasing number of passing motorists. On this 1930 postcard the Red Lion was advertising ROP petrol at 1s. 4d. per gallon. The pavements were still cobbled and girls could walk safely down the middle of the High Street. Gladys Gibbons owned the drapery and clothes shop on the corner of the Presteigne road.

The 14th-century church of St. Mary at Pembridge is one of only seven Herefordshire churches with a detached belfry. The unusual timber-framed octagonal design is most attractive. A striking clock was added in 1891 in memory of the rector, James Crouch.

Titley & Lyonshall

The message on this 1912 postcard of Lyonshall reads: 'This is a postcard of The Square at Lyonshall. When a photograph is taken here, as you see, half the village turns out to watch operations. Spot the lamp at the corner of Elsdon Road — it's never lit, only put up for ornament. Am sending a Jerusalem Cowslip for Dad's Garden. Tell him to look after it'. Note the good display of meat hanging outside William Clark's butchers' shop. How our ideas of hygiene have improved!

Although named Titley Junction, this station was in the parish of Lyonshall, some two miles from Titley village. It was an important link in north Herefordshire between the Leominster to Kington railway, and the Hay, Brecon and Hereford line at Eardisley, and was completed in 1874. The station master, Frederick Manatory, and three of his staff pose for the photographer, who is only now known by his initials, B.B.P. This view faces east towards Leominster with the junction line curving round to the right behind the buildings. The station closed in 1955 and is now a private house.

The kennels of the Radnorshire and West Hereford foxhounds have been at Titley since 1895. In 1907, when this postcard was used, there were 37 couples (74 hounds) that hunted Mondays and Fridays in the season under their M.F.H. Ralph Baskerville. Will this 'sport' last another 100 years?

Kington

Tuesday was Market day in Kington, which meant a busy time for the pubs. Church Street was lined with farmers' carts, traps and even a carrier's van. Horses could be stabled for the day at most of the hotels, ensuring some trade when their owners returned after selling their produce. Here farmers quench their thirst at the Royal Oak, the last inn in England, before heading back to Wales with their purchases. Kelly's 1909 directory lists nearly a hundred carriers who would carry out all sorts of errands for people in their area on market days. From Kington carriers travelled to Builth, Newbridge, Penybont, Radnor and Rhayader. Some developed into haulage or bus companies as road travel improved.

Thomas Stephens' grocery shop overlooks the corner of Kington's High Street in this 1922 scene. Only pedestrians can be seen and if cars were excluded now, it would present a very similar view with only the names above the shops being different.

Kington is in the centre of a prosperous rural area. There were regular markets for all sorts of farm produce. There were also special sales of breeding stock. The September highlights were the Sheep Sale on the 18th followed a day later by the nationally important Horse Show. This photograph gives some idea of the size of the ewe sale, when up to 1,500 were auctioned in a day. Buyers from central England attended these important sales because of the quality of the stock on offer and because animals could be easily transported from the nearby railway station. The Tavern, the house with the gable windows in the centre of the card, overlooked the auctioneers' field. Elizabeth Road now bisects the modern housing development on the site of these sheep pens.

Kington

The Old Radnor Trading Company were very proud of their new offices on the corner of Bridge Street and High Street and used this photographic card to advertise the quality of their products. 'It was built entirely in the Company's Gold Medal granite stonework'. Walter Chambers was manager at the time and their quarries at Dolyhir supplied limestone and roadstone for construction work anywhere in Herefordshire and the adjacent counties. The building is now the town's library.

Seven little boys form the crew of the proud ship *H.M.S. Queen Mary* in Kington's carnival to celebrate King George V and Queen Mary's Coronation on 22 June 1911. With such smart sailor boy uniforms how could they fail to win First Prize?

William Yates and his sons ran a very successful photographic business at 13 High Street from 1885 until at least 1937. During this period they produced many fine photographs of local scenes and events. Among them was this great view of work in progress widening the bridge over the river Arrow. The message on the reverse of this postcard sent on 16 January 1935 reads: 'Dear All, This is a photo of Kington Bridge now under reconstruction

and will be a great improvement to meet the ever increasing traffic and will be very much wider than the old one and will be completed by the end of March for the opening ceremony'.

Kington

Following the 1832 Reform Act there was an increasing demand for universal suffrage — votes for every adult in the country including women. As the century wore on more and more men gained the vote, but women were repeatedly refused. In 1903 Mrs. Emmeline Pankhurst formed the Womens Social and Political Union to campaign for the vote. The movement spread to the large cities and soon percolated to the smaller country towns. Kington was no exception as these 22 suffragettes in fancy dress show. Photographed in 1908, their banners proclaim 'Votes for Women' and 'We Intend to get Them'. Huge political demonstrations, militant acts of sabotage, the imprisonment of a thousand women campaigners, hunger strikes, force feeding and even suicide had no effect on the government attitude. It was only after women proved themselves equal to men by their essential work during the First World War that women over 30 were granted the vote in 1918, and it was not until 1928 that all women over 21 were finally enfranchised.

Thirty-five men stop work for the anonymous photographer of this 1906 scene in Richard Morgan's builders' yard in Victoria Road. He advertised in Kelly's 1909 directory as 'Builder, contractor, undertaker, house decorator and building material dealer'. In the 1920s Ernest Deacon took over the business and added 'Coal Merchant' to his advert. The buildings and yard are still much the same, although the materials and transport have altered.

The imposing Elizabethan mansion, Knill Court, stood in the valley below the slopes of Rushock Hill and was owned by the de Knill family and their descendants since the 12th century. As Lords of the Manor they owned the whole village except 12 acres and the population of 43 was mostly employed on the estate. It was one of Herefordshire's country houses to reflect the changing economic fortunes in employment, costs, taxation and the economic depression of the 1920–30s, which were all contributory factors in the break up of many big estates. The Walden family left Knill Court about 1920 and the house then passed through several owners, becoming home to a girls' school that was evacuated from Kent in 1940 to avoid the blitz. A disastrous fire in August 1943 destroyed the whole building apart from the laundry block and the stone porch. A new house has been built on part of the site.

Almeley & Dilwyn

Such was the enormous death toll in the Great War that almost every parish in the country erected a memorial to commemorate their loss. William Storr-Barber, a local sculptor and monumental mason designed and erected several of these in the county. He was based in Etnam Street, Leominster, and later had premises in Hereford. Major-General Sir Eliott Wood unveiled Almeley's memorial to the 18 servicemen of the parish who died in the war, on 11 August 1919. At a time when foreign travel was beyond the means of most people to visit loved one's graves, this was a very tangible memorial for the families of men whose graves were overseas.

Dilwyn's Public Elementary School was built in 1845 to provide basic education for village children. A house for the schoolmaster was built at the same time. Twenty-eight years later the school was enlarged to cater for 220 pupils. Here eight pairs of boys and girls prepare to dance around the Maypole in the school yard in bright summer sunshine under the watchful eyes of their master, R. Hughes-Richards.

Weobley

A quiet view of Broad Street in the very attractive village of Weobley about 1910, when George Anderson ran the grocery shop nearest the camera on the left. Unfortunately the houses on the right were destroyed in 1943 when a fire in a bakery spread uncontrollably along the row of shops. The street is slightly wider now and pretty gardens cover the site where these very geometric black and white houses once stood.

On 17 April 1912 R. Corbett Wilson set off from London in his Bleriot monoplane to fly to Dublin via Chester. When he became lost and his engine started misfiring, he decided to land to carry out repairs. In doing so, he became, by chance, the first aviator to land an aeroplane in the county of Herefordshire. The news spread quickly and large crowds flocked to see this latest wonder of the age at Newchurch Farm, three miles west of Weobley, where he was delayed until his repairs were completed the following afternoon.

Black Mountain Sheep Farming

The Black Hill between Longtown and Hay is high hill land quite different in character to the rest of Herefordshire. Popularly Known as the Cats' Back it is good hill walking country. The hill pasture rises up to 2,000 feet and is used as common grazing for hardy flocks of sheep and small herds of Welsh ponies. Conditions dictate that traditional practices are still followed, as the slopes are too steep for Quad bikes, so the farmers still round up their animals on horseback, Wild West style, and sort out their ownership on winter pastures below the hill.

One of the shepherd's essential summer jobs was to dip the sheep in a chemical bath to prevent scab and fly attacks. This McDougall's portable steep dip was on hire from Ellwood & Sons, chemists of Drapers' Lane, Leominster for use on local farms. One man controlled the sheep in the bath with a wooden T-shaped pole while the next ewe waits its turn in the dip. The slight slope on the cart directed excess liquid back into the bath whilst the sheep dry off.

Sheep Farming — Bredwardine

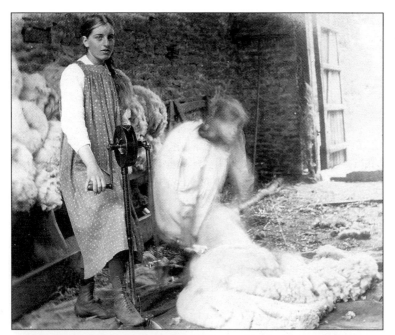

Girl power in 1904! One girl turns the handle to power the shears for her sister, keeping her foot on the legs of the machine to stop it moving about on the uneven floor. Her sister shears the fleece off the ewe on the floor beside her. The barn floor was covered by a canvas sheet to help keep the wool clean. Rolled fleeces line the wall behind. Shearing is hot, heavy work, not usually done by women even in these days of equality. Eventually small stationary petrol engines provided the power for several sets of shears. Now electric power has taken some of the hard work out of the job and this hand driven machine has become a museum piece.

Like all sheep farms, sheep shearing at Thomas Lewis's Town House Farm at Bredwardine was a busy time for everyone. One man turned the handle on the large wheel that powered the cutters his mate used to shear the wool off the sheep. There is a real knack in keeping the sheep under control while shearing and also a knack in rolling the cut fleece so it stayed in one piece for selling. Sheep seem to enjoy losing their winter coats, but these shearers preferred to keep their waistcoats on whatever the weather.

Herefordshire Postcard Publishers

Although there were and still are many national publishers of picture postcards there have also been a large number of local publishers in the 109 years since their introduction in October 1894. For the past five years I have been attempting to list and research all such people and firms who have published postcards relating to the county of Herefordshire up to the present day. The following is my current list which is still increasing. Any information any readers could give about these or other postcard publishers would be very gratefully received. On some I have very good information, on others I have only a name or initials and do not know where and when the publisher lived. Many worked part time, publishing cards as a small part of their business. I have not been able to give a location for some of these names. The ones in brackets are probable places, but I would like confirmation. There are also numerous anonymous cards with no publisher mentioned which need identification, but I fear this is now an impossible task.

A. (Leintwardine?)
A.E.J.T. (Weobley?)
A 7594.
Abacus Ltd., Cumbria.
A.B.C. Historic Publications, Dunstable.
P.B. Abery, Builth Wells.
Harry A. Adnitt, Hereford.
Aerofilms & Aeropictorial, Boreham Wood.
Aerofilms Ltd., London.
Airco Aerials Ltd., Hendon.
Geoffrey Alderson, Hereford.
Aldous (Ross?)
Alexander & Duncan, Leominster.
David Allen & Sons, London.
Frederick William Allen, Hereford.
Alton Court Guest House, Ross.
Amber Graphics, Ledbury.
Archenfield Veterinary Surgery, Ross.
Astor's Studios, Halifax.
Jeffery Cornelius Austen, Ludlow.
Avon-Anglia Publications & Services, Weston-super-Mare
The Axe and Cleaver Inn, Much Birch.

B.B.P. 228. (Titley?)
B.P.C. Co., London.
Charles Baker, Hereford.
J. Bamforth & Co., Holmfirth.
Barmak Ltd., Manchester.
Franklin Barnes, Hereford.
G. Barnes, Ledbury.
J. Barnwell & Son, Ross.
Frederick A. Barribal, Colwall.
J. Bartholomew & Co.
B.M.A. (Thornbury?)
Harvey Barton & Son, Bristol.
A.H. Bate, Malvern.

Baxter & Crabtree, Prestatyn.
E.Bayliss & Son, Worcester.
John Beagles & Co., London.
Alfred George Beeston, Ross.
Bell Photo.
Margaret Bennett & Sons, Bromyard.
T. Bennett & Sons, Worcester.
W. Bennett & Sons, Wilton, Ross.
Beric Tempest & Co. Ltd., St. Ives.
Bessent Series, Brockhampton, Ross.
Bevere Bevis, Worcester.
Alfred Bird, Ross.
Birn Bros. London.
A & C. Black Ltd., London.
Blacklock, Leominster.
Blake Bros, Ross.
Blum & Degen, London.
The Boat Inn, Whitney on Wye.
Booth Hall, Hereford.
Boots Cash Chemist Ltd., Nottingham.
Bosbury Press Ltd., Bosbury.
A.W. Bourne, Leicester.
H. Bowcott, Wellington.
Thomas Bowen, Hereford.
Bowen's Farmhouse, Fownhope.
Brietkoff & Hartel, Germany.
M. Brindley & Sons, Kingsland.
The Broad Oak, Garway.
Brockhampton Court Hotel, Brockhampton, Ross.
F. Bromhead, Bristol.
The Bromyard News & Record, Bromyard.
Bronsil Hotel, Eastnor.
Brooke, Gloucester.
Charles Edward Brumwell, Hereford.
P.A. Buchanan & Co. Ltd., Thornton Heath.
Buckenhill Manor Hotel, Bromyard.

H.P. Bulmer & Co., Hereford.
The Bunch of Carrots, Hampton Bishop.
Burns (Madley?)
Burrows Press Ltd., Cheltenham.
M.J. Burton. (Herefordshire?)
Burton House Hotel, Kington.
A.G. Bussell, Gloucester.
Henry Gee Bussell, Ross.
Bussell & Pike, Ross.
William Henry Bustin, Hereford.
The Button Museum, Ross.

C.F.P.N. (Titley?)
C.S. & Co. (Burrington?)
C.SY, Symonds Yat.
William A. Call, Monmouth.
Caradoc Fruit Plantation, Sellack.
H.L. Carter, Gloucester.
Cartes Ltd.
C.I. Casells. (Liverpool?)
The Castle House Hotel, Hereford.
Castle View Hotel, Kerne Bridge.
Chapman & Son, Dawlish.
Herbert James Charity, Hereford.
The Chasedale Hotel, Ross.
The Chic Studio, Llandudno.
H.C. Clark, Bosbury.
Stephen Clarke, Monmouth.
H. Clayton, Monmouth.
Clyde House School, Hereford.
John Coates & Son, Hereford.
John Edmunds Cole, Pontrilas.
William Edward Cole, Ross.
Colourpicture Publishers Ltd., Norwich.
A.& G. Colwell, Worcester.
Coney Beach Studio.
Conquest Publishing & Print Ltd.
D. Constantine Ltd., Littlehampton.
B. Cook, Brimfield.
Alexander Thomas Cooke, Hereford.
The Cooper Dip Livestock series.
Whitfield, Cosser, Southampton.
Cotswold Publishing Co. Ltd., Wooton under Edge.
Country Hostels Ltd., Reading.
Country Life Ltd., London.
E.S. Cove, Goodrich.
Crafts Shop, Weobley.
Cynicus Publishing Co. Ltd., Tayport, Fife.

Daimler Motor Co., Nottingham.
Frederick Arthur Dalley, Leominster.
Philip James Dallow, Hereford.
Davidson Bros., London.
Alice Louisa Davidson, Bromyard.
Edward George Davies, Madley.
Richard Edwin Davies, Ross.
Davis, Ye Olde Ferrie Hotel, Symonds Yat.

Dean and Chapter of Hereford Cathedral.
Dean Eng. Co.
Dean & Parker, Northiam.
Alfred W. De'Ath, Leominster.
Debenham, Knighton.
'Debenham Series', Eardisley.
Colman Debenham, Ross.
'Deerhurst series'.
Delittle, Fenwick & Co., York.
E.T.W. Dennis Ltd., Scarborough.
Department of the Environment, London.
D.J.D. Desmond, Hereford.
District View Publishing, Leicester.
J. Arthur Dixon, Isle of Wight.
Dodwell & Sons, Cheltenham.
The Doncaster Rorophoto Co. Ltd., Doncaster.
Doward Hotel, Whitchurch.
G.R. Dowding, Hereford.
Henry Dowell & Son, Ross.

E.H. London.
Eagle's Studio, Bromyard.
Augustus C. Edwards & Son. Hereford.
Edwards, Hereford.
Elliott & Fry, London.
Elliott Bros., Whitchurch.
George W.E. Ellis, Bodmin.
George Eltome, Ross.
English Life Publications, Derby.
Enlarging Co., Cheltenham.
Ensign Snapshot Service.
E.S. London
Derek Evans, Hereford.
William Edward Evans, Kington.
'Excel Series'.
'Excelsior Series', Swansea.
Eyre & Spottiswoode, London.

F.G.S. (Eardisley?)
F.S. HFD.
Mrs. Sara Fairbank, Leintwardine.
C.W. Faulkner & Co., London.
George Henry Finch, Ross.
Fitzwilliams, Ilford, Essex.
'Fleet Series', Newport, Monmouthshire.
Foster & Skeffington, Hereford.
James T. Foxhall, Bridenorth.
Derek Foxton Publications, Hereford.
Gordon Fraser.
Francis Frith, Reigate.
William Fuller, Tenbury Wells.

H. Gardiner, Symonds Yat.
John Gardiner, Symonds Yat.
Garrick Theatre, Hereford.
Geological Survey & Museum, London.
G.E. *visé*, Paris.

Gibson & Co., Gateshead on Tyne.
Gibson Art Co., Cincinnatti, U.S.A.
Gieson Bros. & Co., London.
Gillhouse Herd, Crediton.
Gloucester Railway Carriage & Wagon Co.
Gottshalk, Dreyfuss & Davis, London.
Mrs. Louisa Goulder, Whitchurch.
Barbara Graham, Hereford.
H.R. Grant, Hay.
J.H. Grant, Monmouth.
Great Western Railway Co., London.
Ll.B. Green. (Brampton Brian?)
The Green Dragon Hotel, Hereford.
The Green Man, Fownhope.
Harry & Clara Greening, Brockhampton, Ross.
'Grosvenor Series'.

H. (Leintwardine?)
H.B. Ltd., London.
H.T. (Hereford Times?)
Maurice H. Hack, Ross.
William Haddon,Tipton.
Hadfields, Liverpool.
W. Hagelberg, London.
Geoffrey Hammonds, Hereford.
A. Hampton, Hereford.
J.H. Hancox, Cradley.
T. Harding & Son Co., Bristol.
Harley House School, Hereford.
C.J. & R. Harley, Cheltenham.
Walter Ernest Harper, Ludlow.
Jones & Harper, Ludlow.
Elizabeth Harrel, Bromyard.
Kate & Elizabeth Harrel, Bromyard.
Harris, Monmouth.
W.W. Harris, Worcester.
John Harrison, Leominster.
Hartleys, The Chemists.
Frederick Hartman, London.
Hatfield Court Guest House, Nr. Leominster.
Hatton & Co., Hereford.
Mrs. Anne Hayes, Holme Lacy.
Mrs. Ann Heeks, Hereford.
E.H. Hemmings, Hereford.
'Heraldic Series of Postcards'.
The Hereford and Tredegar Brewery, Hereford.
Hereford Art Gallery.
Hereford Cathedral.
Hereford City Education Authority.
Hereford City Museum.
Hereford Corporation, Gas Department.
The Hereford Flour Mills.
Hereford Photo Series.
Hereford Map Centre.
Hereford Museum.
Hereford Town Council.
Herefordshire & Worcestershire County Council Record

Office.
Herefordshire Association of Women's Institutes.
Herefordshire Federation of Women's Institutes.
Herefordshire Gospel Car, Hereford.
Hereford Herd Book Society, Hereford.
A.J. Hewitt, Leominster.
A.J. Hewitt & Mary A. Hewitt, Leominster.
Heyworth, Knighton.
Hick, Hereford.
High Tree Guest House, Leintwardine.
Herbert Hill, Hereford.
S. Hildersheimer & Co., London.
L. John Corber Hillson, Symonds Yat.
John Hinde (Distributors) Ltd.
A.H. 'Homewood Series', Burgess Hill.
Holme Lacy House Hotel, Herefordshire.
'Home Words Series'.
Horrocks & Co.
G. Horsley, Golden Hop Inn, Kerne Bridge.
How Caple Grange Hotel, How Caple.
Hutson Bros., London.
C.V. Hyam, Monmouth.

Imperial Cafe Co., Hereford.
International Art Co., London.

J.W. & Co., London.
J.P. 117. (Wormelow?)
Jackson & Son Ltd., Grimsby.
Jakeman & Carver, Hereford.
Jakeman Ltd., Hereford.
Mrs. Emma James, Hereford.
Albert Sidney James, Orleton.
Jarrold & Sons, Norwich.
H.C. Jeffries, Ross.
Edwin James Jenkins, Peterchurch.
Jerome Ltd., London.
Bertie Porter Jessop, Hereford.
Johns & Sons, Ross.
Alex Johnston. (Clodock?)
Jones. (Eardisland?)
C. & J. Jones, Hereford.
Lewis Jones, Ledbury.
Lewis Jones & Miss Annie Jones, Ledbury.
E.F. & E. Jones, Bromyard.
Wallace Jones Studio, Builth Wells.
Ernest Joyce & Co. Ltd., Newport, Monmouthshire.
Judges, Hastings.

K. 607 (Marden?)
Kelly & Co., Monmouth.
A.W. Kerr, Coulsden, Surrey.
A.F. Kersting.
Thomas Alfred King, Hereford.
King's Head Hotel, Hereford.
King's Head Hotel, Ross.
Kingsley, Leicester.

King's Norton Press, Birmingham.
Kingswood. (Ross?)
Kinnersley Filling Station, Kinnersley.

Thomas Ladmore & Son, Hereford.
John Laing, Hereford.
Landscape View Publishers, Market Harborough.
Hyam Lang, Cardiff.
Charles Malcolm Langley, Linton.
Larkfield Printing Company Ltd., Brighouse.
Latvian Home, Almeley.
Lawrence & Fowler, Ross.
Ledbury Plant Centre, Ledbury.
Lemco.
Leominster News.
Leominster Printing Co. Ltd.
G. Lewin, Hereford.
James Lewis, Symonds Yat.
William Lewis, Symonds Yat.
W.B. Lilley, Much Marcle.
Lilywhite Ltd., Halifax.
Linton Library, Bromyard.
The Lion Hotel, Leintwardine.
Live Stock Journal, London.
Lofthouse, Crosbie & Co., London.
London County Council.
London Stereoscopic Company, London.
James Longford, Weston under Penyard.
W. Love, Tedstone Wafre.
F.M. Lowe. (Garway?)
M.M. Lowie. (Little Hereford?)
Luxia.

M.M.B. Ross.
Alex MacIven (Cheltenham?)
William Eric Mack, London.
Marcus Photos, Worcester.
Herbert T. Marfell, Ross.
W. Marsh, Monmouth.
Marshall, Keene & Co., Hove, Sussex.
B. Matthews, Bradford.
Norman May, Hereford.
Maylord Jakemans Ltd., Hereford.
William H. McKaig, New Radnor.
S. Meredith, Hereford.
Millar & Harris, Ross.
Millar & Lang, London.
Robert Milne. (Hereford?)
'Miniature Novels Series'.
Ministry of Works, London.
Ministry of Public Buildings & Works, London.
Miss Nellie Mitchell, Hereford.
William Henry Morton, Hereford.
Thomas Moxon, Hay.
Much Marcle Stores.
Much Marcle Vicar & Churchwardens.

W.H. Napper, Bromyard.
National Trust.
The New Inn, Pembridge.
Newman & Co., Leominster.
C. Nicholas, Hereford.
Thomas George Nicholas, Hereford.
J. Nock, London.
F. Norman, Cheltenham.
Norbury Studios. (Weobley?)
Nostalgia Ink.

O.I.A. London.
Oakley, Bromyard.
Offa's Dyke Association, Knighton.
H.M. Office of Works, London.
Ye Olde Cross Restaurant, Winforton.
Old House Committee, Hereford.
Old Radnor Trading Co., Kington.
Orphan's Printing Press Ltd., Leominster.
Overross Garage Ltd., Ross.
L. Owen, Tregaron.
Oxo.

P.E.W. Co.
P.G.L. Young Adventurer Ltd., Ross.
P.H.Q. London.
'Post Office Series', Peterchurch.
The Paddocks Hotel, Symonds Yat.
V. Palin, Peterchurch.
R.H. Palmer & Co., Hereford.
Henry Palmer, Ross.
The Pandy Inn, Dorstone.
Park, Newtown, Montgomeryshire.
Park & Barrett, London.
Beatrice Rosalee Parmee, Kington.
Percy Parsons, Worcester.
E.C. Parsons, Cradley.
Passey & Hall, Ross.
H. Pattinson. (Stoke Edith?)
Miss Alice Louisa Payne, Bromyard.
Edward John Paynter, Hereford.
Paynter & Jenson, Hereford.
'Peacock Series'.
Pearson Bark, Stoke Lacy.
Thomas Alfred Pedingham, Colwall.
Pencil Sketch Postcard. (Ross?)
Pengethley Hotel, Peterstow.
Pennington, Weobley.
Peterchurch Church.
A.E. Philips, Leominster.
Godfrey Phiillips Cigarettes, London.
Phoenix Co., Longhope.
The Photochrom Co. Ltd., London.
Photolitho Productions, Ilford.
Photo-Precision Ltd., St. Albans.
Photomatic Ltd., Hatfield, Herts.
Photo Tourist Association, London.

Pictorial Stationery Ltd., London.
Picture Post, London.
Pictures (UK) Ltd., Wadebridge.
Sidney A. Pitcher, Gloucester.
Plough Hotel, Ledbury.
J. Porter, Coleford.
Pluvex Dampcourse.
Thomas C. Pollard, Weobley.
The Portway Hotel, Staunton on Wye.
John Henry Portlock, Hereford.
Charles William Powell, Lower Breinton.
G.A. Powell, Cheltenham.
M. Powell, Moorhampton.
Francis Preece, Hereford.
Reg Preece, Leominster.
William Preece Junior, Ledbury.
William E. Preece, Ledbury.
Preston's Studios, Hunstanton.
A.G. Price, Hereford.
Prima Geolap, Ledbury.
'Princess Novels Series'.
P. Pritchard,
Walter Pritchard, Hereford.
Probert Bros., Ross.
Charles James Prosser, Staunton on Wye.
Pullen. (Wellington?)
Pump House, Dorstone.
J.H. Purcell, Cradley.
T.W. Purchas & Sons, Ross.
R.B.D.
R.M. & S. Ltd.,
Radermacher, Aldous & Co., London.
The Rapid Photo Printing Co., London.
Red Lion Hotel, Weobley.
Regal Art Publishing Co., London.
The Regent Publishing Co. Ltd., London.
Relfe Brothers Ltd., London.
'Rexatone Series'.
Stanley W. Rhodes, London.
Ridler & Sons, Clehonger.
M.J. Ridley, Bournemouth.
John Roberts Press, London.
A. Rogers (Ganarew?)
Aubrey Ross, Wigmore.
The Ross Gazette, Ross.
W.T. Rowe, Ross.
The Royal Hotel, Ross.
'Rudhall'.
The Ruberoid Co. Ltd., London.
Alfred C. Rumsey, Hereford.
Russell & Sons, London.
G.W. Russell & Co., Hereford.
John Howard Russell, Hereford.
J.A. Rymer, Chepstow.

John Salmon Ltd., Sevenoaks.
The Salvation Army.

Sanbride, Middlesborough.
The Sandiway Hotel, Weston-under-Penyard.
Saracen's Head Hotel, Symond's Yat.
Mrs. Elizabeth Savory, Hereford.
Frederick George Savory, Hereford.
J.A. Sayce, York.
E.A. Schwerdtfeger, London.
Saint Owen's Press, Hereford.
The Scientific Press Ltd., London.
W. Scott, Kington.
Walter Scott, Bradford.
J. Scott-Bowden, Colwall.
Senior & Co., Bristol.
The Sentinel Wagon Works (1920) Ltd., Shrewsbury.
I.S. Sherlock.
Seward.
Shobden Stores.
Shurey's Publications.
Madge & Arthur Shaw, Woolhope.
Simplacolour, Isle of Man.
Simpson & Son, Hereford.
Skyscan Balloon Photography.
Simpson & Son, Hereford.
Smartcards, Crawley.
Smith Bros., Ewyas Harold.
Smith Bros., Ledbury.
A.B. Smith, Hereford.
C.E. Smith, Hereford.
David Smith, Ledbury.
James C. Smith, Ledbury.
M. Chadney Smith, Bromyard.
Mrs. Rosa Smith, Hereford.
Samuel Giles Smith, Ledbury.
John Smith & Son, Leominster.
W.H. Smith & Son, Ross.
W.H.Smith & Son, London.
Will Smith, Handsworth, Birmingham.
Smith & Watson Ltd., Ross.
Smith's, Symonds Yat.
Smith's Library, Bromyard.
Mary C. Soulsby.
St. Albans series.
Southall & Son, Ross.
St. George's Church, Woolhope.
St. Vincent's Orphanage, Hereford.
Stengel & Co., London.
Lillian A. Stephens, Ledbury.
Mrs. Isabella Stephens, Kington.
Mrs. Isabella Stephens & T. Stephens, Kington.
Stevens, Malvern.
Stevenson, Kington.
Stewart & Woolfe, London.
Stoddart & Co., Halifax.
W.J. Stonyer, Withington.
Storr-Barber, Leominster.
Swan Hotel, Ross.
Symonds Pastimes.

T.C. Productions, Cheltenham.
Taber Bas Relief Co., London.
Frederick R. Tainton, Ledbury.
Talbot Hotel, Leominster.
A. & G. Taylor, London.
Temeside Private Hotel, Little Hereford.
Mrs. Beatrice Thompson, Kington.
B. & K. Thompson, Kington.
Thorley's Food for Cattle.
Thought Factory, Leicester.
'Through the Camera Series'.
Alfred W. Thursby, Bromyard.
Tilley & Son, Ledbury.
The Times, London.
J.A. Timothy. (Kingsland?)
Tippen. (Marden?)
Town Map Company, Ross.
The Trumpet Inn, Pixley.
Trust Houses Ltd., London.
Raphael Tuck & Sons Ltd., London.
I. Croot Tucker, Hereford.
George F. Turner, Hereford.

United Tobacco Co. (Greys Cigarettes).
Herbert J. Unwin, Hereford.

Valentine & Sons Ltd., Dundee.
Valley Hotel, Ross.
Vaughan & Bedford, Bromyard.
View Card Issuing Co. Ltd., Manchester.
Jesse Charles Vine, Ross.
Vivians Studio, Hereford.

W.C.
W.B.R.
F. J. Waite, Cheltenham.
Walker, Stratford on Avon.
John Walker & Co. Ltd., London.
Kate Wall, Upper Sapey.
Wallbrook Photography Ltd., Ross.
Arthur George Wallis, Hereford.
'Walturdaw Series'. (Kingsland?)
A.J. & S.H. Ward, Ross.
Charles B. Warner, Hereford.
Albert P. Warren, London.
Waterloo & Son Ltd., London.
Alfred G. Watkins, Hereford.

G. & H .Watson, Ludlow.
A.G. Watts, Hereford.
O.E. Watts, Ledbury.
Mr. & Mrs. Harry Webb, Holme Lacy.
West Midlands Press Ltd., Walsall.
Weston's Cider, Much Marcle.
D.W. White, Cradley.
Whitbread plc.
George E. White, Ludlow.
William Henry Whitefoot, Ross.
William Wigley, Hereford.
Wigmore Church.
Longworth Wilding, Shrewsbury.
Wildt & Kray, London.
Herbert Edward Wilkins, Ross.
Alfred Roger Wilks, Goodrich.
Williams & Williams, Dura Studios, Hereford.
E. Williams, Bromyard.
Mrs. Mary Elizabeth Williams, St. Weonards.
Harry William Willoughby, Ross.
A.J. Wilson, Hereford.
Donovan C. Wilson, Hereford.
Wilson & Phillips, Hereford.
T. Henry Winterbourne, Leominster.
Edwin C. Witherstone, Hereford.
Woodmansterne Publications Ltd.,Watford.
'Woodberry Series'. (Ross?)
'The Woodbury Series'.
The Woolstone-Barton Co. Ltd., London.
Charles Worcester & Co., Bristol.
Evelyn Wrench, London.
George E. Wright & Sons, Hereford.
Sidney A. Wright, Hereford.
Wye Rapids Hotel, Symonds Yat.
Wyman & Sons Ltd., Hereford.
Wymans Gravure series, London.
'The Wyndham Series'.

Percy B. Yates, Presteign.
William James Yates, Kington.
William James Yates & Sons, Kington.
Young & Co.
Y.M.C.A. for Wales & Borders, Hereford.
William George Young, Walford & Ross.
William George Young & Sons, Ross.
Youth Hostels Association, Birmingham.

Index

aerial photography 13
agriculture (see also cider, hops) 12, 37, 63, 65, 70, 75-6
agricultural shows 3, 30
Alexander & Duncan 63
Allen, Captain Evans Mynde 19
Allensmore 34
Almeley 73
Alsop, Bill 28
athletics 11

Backney Bridge 21
Barratt-Browning, Elizabeth 9
Bell Inn, Tillington 54
Black Hill, The 75
Bosbury 6
Boulton and sons 45
Bredwardine 76
Bridge Inn, Michaelchurch Escley 40
Brimfield 64
Brinsop Court 53
British camp Hotel 5
Brockhampton 29, 30
     Church 29
Bromsash 20
Bromyard 57
Brown, Mrs. Hetty 31
     Percy 28
Bryngwyn, Wormelow 36
Bulmer's Cider 45
Burghope, Pencombe 56
Burley Gate 56
Bush, Ernest T. 25

Call, William 53
Canon Frome 11
Church Army 56
cider making 12, 34, 45
Clarke, Charlie 28
Clehonger 34

Colwall 4, 5, 6
Cove, Mr. and Mrs. 24
Credenhill 53
cricket 28
Crown Inn, Bosbury 6
Cusop Mill 42

Davies, Albert 28
     Harry 28
De'Ath, Alfred 62, 63
Deacon, Ernest 72
Dilwyn 73
Dorstone 42
Dunn, Mrs. Thomas 66

Eardisley 44
Eastnor 8
     Park 7
Eccleswall Court 20
Edward VII, funeral of 60
education 18, 32, 56, 73
elections, county 3
     parliamentary 62
Elms, The, Colwall Green 5
Evans, William 43
Ewyas Harold 39

fairs 47, 67
farming 3
Fawley 28
fishing 29
flooding 14, 25, 46, 61
flying 47, 74
football 37
Ford Bridge 58
Foster, Mrs. 29
Fowler, Mr. 2
Fownhope 31
Francis, George 28
Frome's Hill Motor Climb 10

George V, coronation 62, 71
Gibbons, Tom 28
Goodrich 24
        Court 24
Great Oak, Eardisley 44
Green Man Inn, Fownhope 31
greyhounds 28
Griffiths, Jack 28
gymkhanas 11

Hack (a photographer from Ross) 35
Hamlet, The, Stoke Edith 52
Harden, Mr. T. 36
Harewood End Inn 35
Heath, Joseph 19
Hereford 46-8, 50, 51
Hereford & Gloucester Canal 11
hockey 17
Hole-in-the-Wall 28
Holme Lacy 33
Holmes, Rev. 8
        William 24
Homes, William 6
Hope End 9
Hope-under-Dinmore 55
hops 3, 12
Howe, Benjamin 41
hunting 6, 28, 69

Jordan's Boats 46

Kemble, St. John 27
Kerne Bridge 23
        Station 23
Kilpeck 37
Kingsland 66-67
        Saw Mills 67
Kingsthorne 35
Kington 70-72
Knill Court 72
Kyrle, John 13

Ledbury 1-3, 11
        Beagles 6
Leominster 59-63
        Canal 58
Lerrigo, Ted 28
Lewis, John 41
Littler, William 36
Licksall Inn, Nr. Mordiford 32
Loveridge, Jack 28
Lucton 65
Lyonshall 69

Madley 41
Maidenhead Inn, Orleton 64
Marden 55
Methodist Chapel, Great Oak, Eardisley 44
Michaelchurch Escley 40
Moon Inn, Mordiford 32
Mordiford 32
Morgan, Richard 72
Moss, Walter 28
Mounton-Barratt, Edmund 9
Much Dewchurch 37
Much Marcle 11, 12

Old Radnor Trading Co. 71
Orleton 64

Pencraig 19
Pembridge 68
        Church 68
Pembridge Castle, Welsh Newton 27
Pencombe 56
Perrystone Cricket Team 28
Peterchurch 40
Peterstow 35
Ploughman, William 6
Pontrilas 38
postal services 6, 43, 48, 53
Powell, Chris 28
Preece, Francis 47
Preston-on-Wye 41

Queen's Head, Pembridge 68

railways 21, 23, 25, 33, 37, 38, 43, 48, 52, 55, 58, 59
Railway Inn, Ross 14
Rankin, Sir James 36, 62
Red Lion, Ewyas Harold 39
Red Lion, Pembridge 68
Rees, Mr. W.J. 65
Ridler, Richard 34
road building 39, 46
Robinson, Richard 8
Roe Buck Hotel, Brimfield 64
Ross-on-Wye 13-18
    King's Acre Pool 14
Royal Oak, Kington 70

Samlet, Henri 47
Savory, Frederick 52
Scobie, Lt. Col. 49
shearing 76-76
Shucknall 52
Smith, Will 45
Sollers, Fred 28
Somers family of Eastnor 8
Steen's Bridge 58
Stephens, Charles 3
Stoke Edith 52
Storr-Barber, William 73
Stratford Collins, Mrs. 22
Stretton Grandison 9
Symond's Yat 25, 26
    Station 25

Temple Bar Inn, Ewyas Harold 39
Territorial Army 7, 15, 49, 50, 51
tied cottages 34
Tilley, John 1, 3, 4, 5, 7, 8, 9, 10, 11
Tillington 54
Titley Junction 69
Tram Inn, Much Dewchurch 37
Turner, reg 28
turnpike trusts 46

Unwin, Herbert 32, 33, 49
Upton Bishop 19

Valentine (photographer) 51
Vaughan, Thomas 1
Volunteer Inn,. marden 55

Walford 22
water supply 52
Weaver, Albert 66
Wellington 54
Welsh Newton 27
Weobley 74
Weston-under-Penyard 21
Westons Cider Co. 12
Whitchurch 27
Whitney 43
Wigmore 65
Williams, Mrs. Hamlen 66
    John 62
Wilson, R. Corbett 74
Wiltshire, Mr. & son 67
Withington 52
women, recruitment in First World war 15, 49
women's suffrage 72
Wood, Maj.-Gen. Sir Eliott 73
Worcestershire Imperial Yeomanry 7
Wormelow 36
Wrekin Chemical Works, Pontrilas 38
Wright, George & sons 47
Wyche, The, Colwall 4
Wythall, Walford 22

Yates, William 71
Ye Old Ferrie Inn, Symond's Yat 25
Young, George William 22, 26

A History of Theatres and Performers in Herefordshire
by Robin Haig   £7.95

Writing about a performance at the Hereford Theatre in 1824, the author of the *Hereford Weekly Reporter*, complained that he was 'near being wounded by a piece of the glass chandelier which fell a sacrifice to the sabre of Mr. Henderson, who seemed to commence an attack in a truly soldier-like manner'. This was bad enough, but he also had to contend with peas thrown by unruly elements in the gallery—or 'the gods'. He commented: 'We were glad to see the seats of the gods so well filled and their excellencies in such good humour. Bye the bye, as we sometimes take our seats in the pit, we beg to address our prayers to the divinities above alluded to, that they will not be so profuse in their blessings in the form of pease, which are all very well in the shape of a pudding – or (in their element of soup) in the pit of the stomach; but are really very hard of digestion in their crude state in the pit of a theatre'.

As the birthplace of David Garrick, Roger Kemble and (probably) Nell Gwyn, Hereford has a theatrical heritage to be proud of, indeed the city had a reputation for supporting theatre out of proportion to its population. This book tells the story of the multitude of performers who have given entertainment over the years to the people of Herefordshire—from mummers players, and tightrope walkers at the Hereford Theatre (built in 1786) to Professor Crocker's Educated Horses—involving no less than 30 horses and donkeys—who came to the Drill Hall in Hereford in 1899. Circuses were especially popular around the end of the 19th century, and when 'The Greatest Show on Earth' came to Hereford in 1899 it attracted a staggering 25,000 people over the course of the day, whilst the elephants of the Sanger Circus took part in a football match in Leominster in May 1900. Among the performers at the Kemble Theatre between the wars were a one-armed motorcyclist who coaxed his machine around a series of obstacles on stage; and a man in evening dress who coaxed a flight of reluctant cockatoos into firing miniature cannon. Strangest of all the visitors, perhaps, was the Chevalière D'Eon, a transvestite French aristocrat who came to Hereford to give a fencing display in 1795.

This book is full of stories and anecdotes about the history of the theatres and other places of entertainment—barns, inns, coffee houses, assembly rooms, music halls and drill halls—throughout Herefordshire, and concludes with a chapter about the many performing groups and amateur dramatic societies based in the county.

Herefordshire Folklore
by Roy Palmer   £12.95

Roy Palmer presents the folklore of the county as a series of themes that embrace landscape, buildings, beliefs, work, seasons and people. In so doing, ten chapters are crafted that can stand alone or be read as a whole, each full of snippets of insight into the county's past in a way that adds to anyone's enjoyment of Herefordshire. Having read the book, features of the landscape, for example, will appear as landmarks associated with certain folk beliefs adding to their interest and to one's own sense of 'belonging' to the county.

Much, but by no means all, of the information presented here first appeared in Roy Palmer's Folklore of Hereford and Worcester, published by Logaston Press in 1992, when Herefordshire was joined with Worcestershire. That book has been out of print for a few years, and it is surprising how much more folklore continues to come to light. More remedies that have been handed down within families are recorded; the occasional old ballad or song sheet is found hidden behind wallpaper or in the bottom of trunks; oral knowledge from somewhere in the county is committed to print—and new 'customs' are revived or even created.

Sir Samuel Meyrick & Goodrich Court

by Rosalind Lowe

320 pages with over 130 black and white and 30 colour illustrations   £17.50

Sir Samuel Rush Meyrick was the founding father of the systematic study of arms and armour. Although he died more than 150 years ago, his name is still revered by enthusiasts all over the world. His last days were spent in Herefordshire, where his magnificent collection of arms, armour and antiquities could be visited in his mock Gothic castle called Goodrich Court. The collection is now largely dispersed, but the British public can still see some of the choicest pieces at the Wallace Collection and at the British Museum.

Goodrich Court was not to the taste of William Wordsworth and other admirers of the Picturesque, particularly as it overpowered the ivy-clad towers of Goodrich Castle nearby. Those who made the tour of the building described in this book were rather more impressed. When the Meyrick family moved on, the Court enjoyed seventy years as a grand house until its idyll was brought to an end by the Second World War. After sheltering Felsted School during the war, it remained empty and forlorn until demolished in 1950. Its exotic gatehouse still remains alongside the A40 trunk road between Ross and Monmouth to intrigue the modern traveller.

Sir Samuel and the Meyrick collection played an important role in the early 19th century movement towards historical accuracy in the portrayal of correct costume in works of art and the theatre. Artists such as Bonington, Cooper, Corbould, Cottingham and Haydon sketched the armour: the architect William Burges bought items from the collection and was surely influenced by Sir Samuel's views on medieval decoration. Meyrick's lavishly illustrated works were an unparalleled source for later writers, and he published many historical articles. He is better known in Wales as the editor of the genealogical collections of the 16th century herald Lewys Dwnn.

Sir Samuel's story, and that of Goodrich Court and its treasures is no dry antiquarian tale, but full-blooded and sometimes humorous. His life was a roller-coaster of public acclaim and private tragedy, played out against the military and political movements of the pre-Victorian age. Although respected for his scholarship by the royal family and the public at large, he was no stranger to scandal and controversy. At the moment of his greatest triumph he sowed the seeds of his own painful death.

A History of the Castles of Herefordshire & their Lords

by the Rev. Charles J. Robinson   £16

This volume is a reprint of Rev. Robinson's book of the 1870s, but which includes a new and expanded index.

Camping on the Wye

sketchbook of 1892, full colour, £9.95

In 1892 a group of four undergraduates from University College, London, set off on a boating and camping trip on the Wye. Two of the four were medical students, one the future father of the actor Marius Goring, and the other from a Jamaican 'Plantocracy' family. The third member of the party was a 'dabbler in art', whilst knowledge of the fourth friend has faded with time. They hired a skiff from Jordan's in Hereford, took it by train to Whitney with all their stores and embarked—watched by a small crowd on the bank.

The journey was recorded in a sketchbook and diary, here brought together. With a dry sense of humour it tells of various campsites by the river, of visits to riverside inns and places of interest, of splendid sunny days, of sheltering from wet weather, of battles with bugs and insects, of nosey cows, of highs and lows of a river journey.

What is particularly intriguing is how little some things have changed, yet how others have altered markedly. The friends appear to adopt the kitchen sink mode of travel, whilst now such trips would be done with the minimum of clutter. The number of riverside inns and farms with their own 'cyder' are far fewer. Yet the immediately suspicious nature but innate warmth of country people remains the same, and the day to day concerns of people are what they have always been. It is also strangely gratifying to see that our forebears adopted the same tricks now used on current generations when visiting distant lands. When the travelling companions were camping at Goodrich Castle, one local tried to interest them in artwork supposedly undertaken by King Henry IV (and featured in this book), just as we're now offered ancient coins and artefacts outside tourist traps abroad!

The Pubs of Bromyard, Ledbury & East Herefordshire

by Ron Shoesmith & John Eisel £9.95

This book continues the series that details the history and social background of the hotels, taverns and inns that have existed in the county. All existing hostelries are included, along with many that have come and gone, including the Frenchman's Inn, which now appears just to be a pile of stones, and the insalubrious sounding The Swill—which perhaps deserved its fade into obscurity.

The information details not just the history of the buildings themselves, but also of the landlords—some upright characters and others just staying sufficiently within the law to retain their licences. many landlords had other jobs besides—as farmers, wheelwrights, carpenters, even running post offices, which puts into perspective the fact that some of the pubs covered are once again acting as the village post office. Few, however, would welcome the return of Inland Revenue offices to their local!

Pubs provide a wealth of social history, and this book contains some wonderful stories—of circus elephants kept at the back of one pub which ate not just the cakes from the local shops, but also people's clothes hanging on their washing lines! Of a piglet offered to one sullen landlord who told his customers that he couldn't supply a ham sandwich. Of landlords that banned all local organisations meeting on their premises, but of many more that encouraged them. Of glasses marked with the pub name on the bottom so that when hop-pickers left the area glasses they had 'borrowed' could find their way back to the right pub.

Various groups of people can be associated with moderate to heavy drinking—be they amateur sportsmen, those out on a pub crawl or Morris men. But whereas the latter failed to drink sufficient to keep one local going, less expected are the stories of the activities of bell ringers in a number of hostelries. One pub which made its own cider and perry offered a regular challenge to anyone to try and drink three pints and remain upright. If anyone felt they'd succeeded, they were requested to walk home—the fresh air on exiting the pub would often prove to be the last straw.